The World

David Waugh
Head of the Geography Department
Trinity School, Carlisle

Nelson

Thomas Nelson and Sons Ltd
Nelson House   Mayfield Road
Walton-on-Thames   Surrey
KT12 5PL   UK

51 York Place
Edinburgh
EH1 3JD   UK

Thomas Nelson (Hong Kong) Ltd
Toppan Building 10/F
22A Westlands Road
Quarry Bay   Hong Kong

Distributed in Australia by

Thomas Nelson Australia
480 La Trobe Street
Melbourne   Victoria 3000
and in Sydney, Brisbane, Adelaide and Perth

© David Waugh
First published by Thomas Nelson and Sons Ltd 1987
ISBN 0-17-434210-1
NPN 9 8 7 6
Printed and bound in Great Britain by The Eagle Press plc, Glasgow

The author extends his grateful thanks to Marian Green, John Patrick, Jonathan Waugh and Anne Whipp for their help in the production of this book.

The author and publishers are grateful to the following for permission to reproduce copyright material.

Photographs

Aerofilms, 8.16; Associated Press, 8.29, 17.12, 17.28; BBC Hulton
Picture Library, 17.24; Barnaby's Picture Library, 10.20; Penni Bickle,
15.31; Cameron Hall Development Limited, 6.4, 6.6; James Davis 10.6;
Embassy Luchtfoto Bart Hofmeester, 3.28; Rex Features, 16.9, 17.11,
17.23; Format Photographers (Maggie Murray), 13.11, 13.12; Sally &
Richard Greenhill, 13.18; Robert Harding Associates, 5.4, 11.6(b); John
Hillelson Agency, 7.6; Hutchison Library, 3.18; 3.20, 3.26, 4.10, 5.3, 5.9,
7.9, 8.17, 8.34, 10.14, 10.18, 10.22, 10.26, 10.30, 13.3, 16.15; Japanese
Information Centre, 3.14, 8.3, 10.12; London Docklands Development
Corporation, 9.3, 9.4; Frank W Lane, 17.1, 17.2, 17.7; Network
Photographers, 3.9(b); Peter Newark Western Americana, 16.12;
Novosti Press, 10.9, 10.34, 10.35; Picturepoint, 3.13, 7.18, 8.35, 10.1,
10.2(a), 10.5, 10.12, 10.21, 10.27, 15.21, 15.22, 15.23, 15.24, 15.32, 16.4,
16.5; The Photo Source, 3.15, 17.15; Paul Popper, 17.14; Port of
Felixstowe, 5.11, 5.12; J & S Professional Photography, 8.21; Sefton
Photo Library, 3.9(c), 10.2(b); John Topham Picture Library, 3.21, 10.7;
David and Jonathan Waugh, 3.9(a), 3.23, 3.24, 7.11, 7.13, 8.34, 8.35, 9.1,
9.7, 9.8, 10.24, 11.6(a), 13.10, 15.9, 15.13, 15.17, 15,20, 15.34, 17.20,
17.30, 17.31; Zefa Picture Library, 3.19, 10.8, 10.16, 17.8.

Title page photograph supplied by Science Photo Library and Daily Telegraph Colour Library

Diagrams, tables and maps

Collins-Longman, *Atlas Four*, 1.11; the *Guardian*, 1.12; the Controller of
Her Majesty's Stationery Office (Crown © reserved), 2.3, 3.27, 8.15,
9.10, 9.11; (from *Regional Trends, 1985*), 4.5, 5.15, 8.13; 8.25; (from *Census
of Population*), 4.12; 4.14; the *Geographical Magazine*, 3.25, 7.3, 7.10, 8.7;
the Lake District Special Planning Board, *National Park Plan, 1978*, 3.27;
the Northern Ireland Housing Executive, 4.15; London & East Anglian
Group for GCSE Examinations, 5.8; British Rail, 5.13, 5.14; GOAD Plans
6.3; Cameron Hall Development Ltd, Gateshead, 6.4, 6.6; the Watt
Committee on Energy, London, 7.4; BBC Enterprises Ltd, from *Japan –
the Overcrowded Islands*, 8.5, and, adapted from *Update USA*, 8.23;
Cwmbran Development Corporation, 8.22; Corby Industrial
Development Centre, 8.27; Times Newspapers Ltd, 9.2; Michael
Morrish, *Development in the Third World*, © Oxford University Press,
10.3; the Food and Agriculture Organisation of the United Nations,
10.38, 10.39 and 10.41; Christian Aid, 14.7; the Institute of Child Health,
14.8; K. Maclean and N.R. Thomson, *World Environmental Problems*,
Holmes McDougall, 14.11; J.B. Whittow, from *Disasters*, (Allen Lane),
16.2, Neville Grenyer, *Investigating Geography* © Oxford University
Press, 1985, 16.7; United States Department of Commerce, National
Oceanic and Atmospheric Administration, 17.16.

Extracts

Pan Books, *North–South: A Programme for Survival*, the Brandt Report.
BBC Enterprises Ltd, *Japan, The Overcrowded Islands*; Methuen & Co,
Modern Abyssinia; William Heinemann Ltd, *The Grapes of Wrath* by John
Steinbeck.

Illustrations supplied by Maltings Partnership,
Marlborough Design and Tom McArthur
Designed by Julia Denny

Contents

Distribution and density

△ **Figure 1.1** Dot map showing world population distribution

▷ **Figure 1.2** Factors affecting distribution and density of population

1 For any given example, there are usually *several* reasons for the sparse/ dense population distribution rather than only the one reason given here, e.g. how many of the reasons listed above contribute to make (i) the Amazon rainforests sparsely populated and (ii) the Netherlands densely populated?

2 Even within areas there are variations in population density, e.g. parts of Japan have exceptionally high population densities, yet only *one-fifth* of the country is inhabited; Manaus, in the Amazon rainforest, has a population of over one million.

3 A danger in providing a table such as this is the temptation to fill in *every* space to avoid gaps. Sometimes this can lead to questionable examples, e.g. is the Paris Basin a 'grasslands area' or is it all 'densely populated'?

Factor	Sparsely populated	Example
Physical (relief)	Rugged, high fold mountains, especially those with active volcanoes	Andes
	Ancient, worn-down Shield lands	Canadian Shield
Climate	Areas of very little rainfall throughout the year	Sahara Desert
	Areas of very low temperatures throughout the year	Greenland
	Areas of extremely high humidity	Amazon Rainforest
	Savanna areas with seasonal drought and unreliable rainfall	Sahel countries
Vegetation (natural)	Areas covered in dense forests such as the tropical rainforests and the coniferous (Boreal) forests	Amazonia Canadian Shield
Soils	Thin soils as found on high mountains	Scottish Highlands
	Soils which have been leached (nutrients washed out); acidic	Lake District
Water supply	Lack of supply resulting from drought, seasonal irregularities, lack of reservoirs and clean drinking water	Ethiopia
Disease and pests	Areas affected by mosquitoes, tse-tse fly, locusts	East Africa
Resources	Areas lacking in mineral wealth or local energy supplies	Sudan
Communications	Areas where vegetation, climate and topography act as barriers	Himalayas
Economies	Those which are poorly developed such as nomadic and shifting cultivation	Lappland
Political policies	Lack of investment in rural areas in comparison with urban centres	Scottish Highlands

The distribution of population over the world's surface is very uneven and there are great variations in density. Distribution means the way in which people are spread out across the world whereas density shows the average number of people living in a square kilometre.

- On a global scale, the pattern of distribution is affected by major environmental factors such as relief, climate, vegetation, resources and water supply.
- On a regional scale, the pattern is influenced by economic (employment and resource opportunities), political and social factors.

Figure 1.1 shows, by the use of dots, the distribution of people over the world (every dot represents 100 000 people). Figure 1.2 gives some of the reasons, with specific examples, for this uneven population distribution. Can you go through this list and add a different example to the one, or ones, shown?

Regional and local distributions and densities

The distribution and density shown in Figure 1.1 is very generalised, and tends to hide small scale differences.

▷ **Figure 1.3** Choropleth map showing population density in Brazil

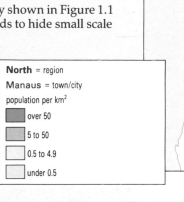

North = region
Manaus = town/city
population per km²
- over 50
- 5 to 50
- 0.5 to 4.9
- under 0.5

Densely populated	Example
Flat, extensive plains and low-lying undulating areas Foothills of active volcanoes	Ganges Valley (India) Mount Etna
Areas with a reliable, evenly distributed rainfall and with no extremes in temperature Areas with (i) high sunshine totals or (ii) heavy snowfalls encouraging tourism Monsoon with heavy seasonal rainfall allowing high-yielding crops to be grown	North West Europe (i) Mediterranean coastal areas (ii) Alps Bangladesh
Open grasslands, especially in temperate latitudes	Paris Basin
Alluvial soils deposited by rivers	Nile Valley
Areas with rainfall spread evenly throughout the year, with reservoirs to store water and the provision of clean drinking water	North West Europe
Areas without climatic extremes and with money for pest control and health facilities	Eastern USA
Areas with numerous, easily obtained mineral resources with plentiful energy resources	Great Britain
Areas with good road and rail links (originally water) Ports and route centres	West Germany Japan
Those with a high level of technological development Capital cities with their associated administration and service jobs	California London
Where governments have created new towns, are investing in rural areas, or are opening up new land	Around London Dutch Polders

1 Study Figure 1.3 which shows the distribution of population in Brazil. This is a choropleth map which shows, by different colours or shadings, the different densities in the distribution of an area. This information is divided into classes (see key). Using Figures 1.2 and 1.3:
   (a) describe the distribution and density of population in Brazil (i.e. the areas with the most and the least inhabitants, together with those areas falling between the two extremes).
   (b) give reasons for these differences (i.e. between the 'north' and the 'south east').

2 Uneven distributions can also be shown on a more local scale. Try to find a map of either:
   (a) the county or (b) the town or city in which you live or which is nearby. Is the population spread out evenly or not? Can you list reasons for any differences in distribution?

5

Population growth

The annual growth rate of the world's population rose slowly but steadily until the beginning of the 19th century. Since then it has grown at an increasing rate. Figure 1.4 is a bar graph showing the growth in population during the present century in each continent. As well as emphasising the uneven distribution in population mentioned on page 4, it shows that:

□ The continents with the greatest increase in population are the developing ones of Asia, Africa and Latin America. One estimate suggests that by the year 2000, 36% of the world's population will live in the two countries of China and India. Already in 1980 (Figure 1.5), the three developing continents were home to 76% of the world's inhabitants.

□ The continents with the slowest increase in population are the developed ones of Europe, North America and Oceania (Australasia) as well as the USSR. Estimates suggest that by the year 2000 several countries in North West Europe will have a zero population growth.

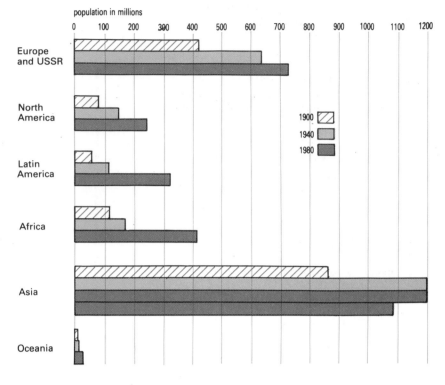

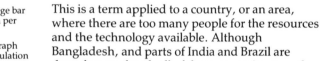

Future trends

Since the concern expressed during the 1960s and 1970s at the increased growth rate in world population, evidence has shown that fertility in the developing countries is now falling. The 1985 United Nations estimate claimed that the annual growth rate of the world's population of 2% in 1965 had fallen to 1.7%, and could fall to 1.5% by the year 2000. This would mean that the world's population would reach only 6100 million by AD 2000 (Figure 1.6) instead of the 7600 million it would have reached had the growth of the period 1950-1980 continued.

△ **Figure 1.4** Bar graph showing world population growth

▽ **Figure 1.5** Percentage bar graph of population per continent, 1980

▽ **Figure 1.6** Linear graph showing world population growth

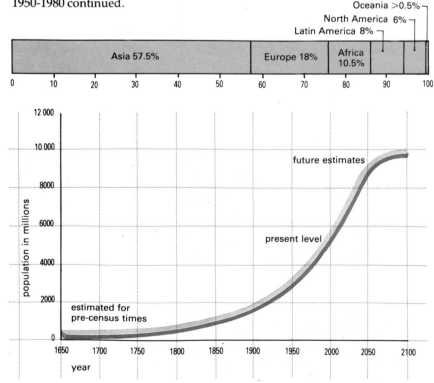

Overpopulation

This is a term applied to a country, or an area, where there are too many people for the resources and the technology available. Although Bangladesh, and parts of India and Brazil are densely populated, all of these countries, together with such African countries as Ethiopia and Sudan, are said to be overpopulated because they have insufficient food, minerals and energy resources, a situation made worse by famine, disease and poverty. The north east of Brazil is said to be overpopulated despite having an average of fewer than two inhabitants per square kilometre. In comparison, parts of California, Japan and the Netherlands are not thought of as overpopulated despite having over 500 people per square kilometre, because under normal conditions there are enough houses, jobs, food and energy supplies for the inhabitants.

Population change

This depends on birth rate, death rate and migration. The annual growth rate is the difference between the birth rate (the average number of births per 1000 people) and the death rate (the average number of deaths per 1000 people). Based on growth rates in the industrial areas of western Europe and North America, a model has been produced (Figure 1.7) which suggests that the population (or demographic) growth rate can be divided into four distinct stages. This model has also been applied to developing countries despite the fact that the model assumes that the falling death rate (Stage 2) is a response to increased industrialisation, a process not yet applicable to all developing countries.

Stage 1. Here both birth rates and death rates fluctuate at a high level (about 35 per 1000) giving a small population growth.

Birth rates are high because:

- ☐ No birth control or family planning.
- ☐ So many children die in infancy that parents tend to produce more in the hope that several will live.
- ☐ Many children are needed to work on the land.
- ☐ Children are regarded as a sign of virility.
- ☐ Religious beliefs (e.g. Roman Catholics, Moslems and Hindus) encourage large families.

High death rates, especially among children, are due to:

- ☐ Disease and plague (bubonic, cholera, kwashiorkor).
- ☐ Famine, uncertain food supplies, poor diet.
- ☐ Poor hygiene – no piped, clean water and no sewage disposal.
- ☐ Little medical science – few doctors, hospitals, drugs.

Stage 2. Birth rates remain high, but death rates fall rapidly to about 20 per 1000 people giving a rapid population growth.

The fall in death rate results from:

- ☐ Improved medical care – vaccinations, hospitals, doctors, new drugs and scientific inventions.
- ☐ Improved sanitation and water supply.
- ☐ Improvements in food production (both quality and quantity).
- ☐ Improved transport to move food, doctors, etc.
- ☐ A decrease in child mortality.

Stage 3. Birth rates now fall rapidly, to perhaps 20 per 1000 people, while death rates continue to fall slightly (15 per 1000 people) to give a slowly increasing population.

The fall in birth rate may be due to:

- ☐ Family planning – contraceptives, sterilisation, abortion and government incentives.
- ☐ A lower infant mortality rate meaning less need to have so many children.
- ☐ Increased industrialisation and mechanisation meaning fewer labourers are needed.
- ☐ Increased desire for material possessions (cars, holidays, bigger homes) and less for large families.
- ☐ Emancipation of women, enabling them to follow their own careers rather than being solely child bearers.

Stage 4. Both birth rates (16 per 1000) and death rates (12 per 1000) remain low, fluctuating slightly to give a steady population.

(Will there ever be a Stage 5 where birth rates fall below death rates to give a declining population? Some evidence suggests that this might occur in several western European countries.)

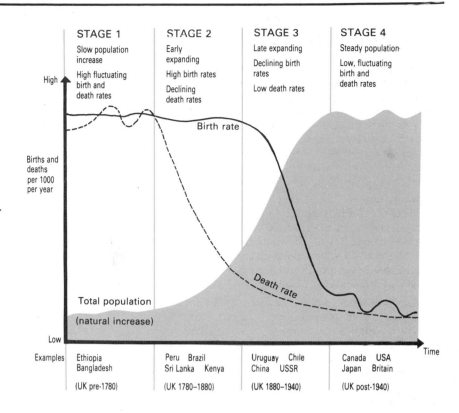

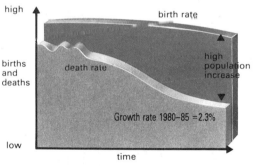

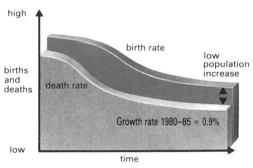

△ **Figure 1.7** Demographic transition model

◁ **Figure 1.8** Population growth in developing and developed countries

Population change in developing and developed countries. Many developing countries still fit into Stage 2, with a high birth rate and a falling death rate, whereas most developed countries have reached Stage 4 with low birth and death rates (see Figure 1.8).

Population structures

The rate of natural increase, birth rate, death rate and life expectancy (life expectancy is the number of years that the average person born in a particular country can expect to live) all affect the population structure of a country. The population structure of a country can be shown by a population pyramid or, as it is sometimes known, an age-sex pyramid. The population is divided into five-year age groups (e.g. 5–9 year olds, 10–14 year olds), and also into males and females. The population pyramid for the United Kingdom is shown in Figure 1.9. The graph shows:

☐ A narrow pyramid indicating approximately equal numbers in each age group

☐ A low birth rate and a low death rate indicating a steady, or even a static, population growth

☐ More females than males live over 70 years

☐ There are more boys under 4 years of age than girls

☐ A relatively large proportion of the population in the pre- and post-reproductive age groups, and a relatively small number in the 15–59 age group which is the one that produces children and most of the national wealth. This can be shown as the 'dependency ratio' which can be expressed as:

$$\frac{\text{non-economically active}}{\text{economically active}} \quad \text{i.e} \quad \frac{\text{children (0–14) and elderly (60 +)}}{\text{those of working age (15–59)}}$$

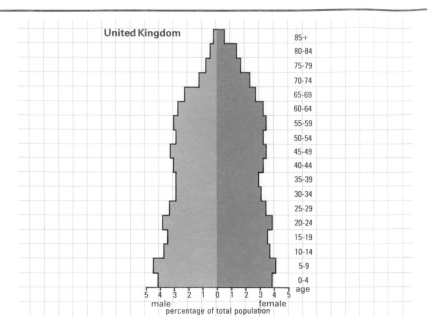

△ **Figure 1.9** Population (age-sex) pyramid for the UK, 1981

e.g. **UK 1971** (figures in millions)

$$\frac{13.387 + 10.512}{31.616} \times 100$$

= dependency ratio of 75.59

That means that for every 100 people of working age, there were 75.79 people dependent upon them.

UK 1981 (figures in millions)

$$\frac{11.455 + 11.023}{32.635} \times 100$$

= dependency ratio of 68.87

So, although the number of elderly had risen slightly, the greater drop in children meant that there were fewer people in the UK dependent upon those of working age (this does *not* take into account those of working age who are unemployed). Most developed countries have a dependency ratio of between 50 and 70, whereas in developing countries the ratio is often over 100 due to the large numbers of children. Population pyramids enable comparisons to be made between countries, and can help a country to plan for future service needs such as old people's homes if it has an ageing population or fewer schools if a declining, younger population. Unlike the demographic transition model (Figure 1.7), they include immigrants, but like that model they can produce four idealised types of graph representing different stages of development (Figure 1.10). How well do you consider that the four population pyramids shown in Figure 1.11 fit in with the models shown in Figure 1.10? What value do you consider Figure 1.10 to have in studying changing population structures?

Two points to help you with Figure 1.11:

1 The increase in the number of males between the ages of 24 and 39 in Egypt is due to migrants from surrounding countries coming to look for work.

2 The decrease in Italians in their 50s was a result of deaths during the Second World War.

▽ **Figure 1.10** Changing population structures

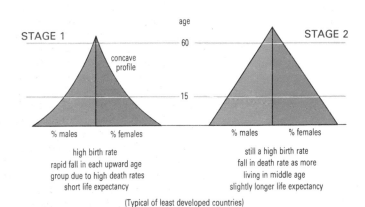

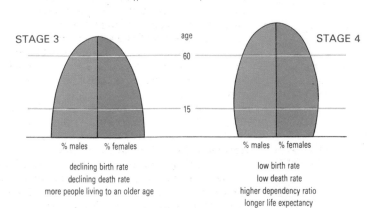

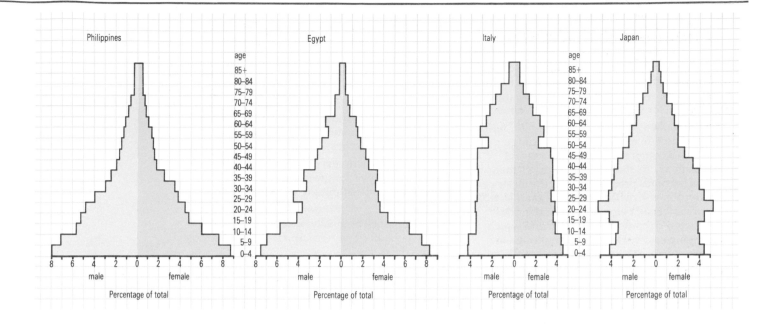

Philippines Egypt Italy Japan

age
85+
80–84
75–79
70–74
65–69
60–64
55–59
50–54
45–49
40–44
35–39
30–34
25–29
20–24
15–19
10–14
5–9
0–4

male   female
Percentage of total

male   female
Percentage of total

male   female
Percentage of total

male   female
Percentage of total

△ **Figure 1.11** Population pyramids for selected countries

▽ **Figure 1.12** Britain's changing population structure

Changing population structures

The world's ageing population

Due to improvements in medical facilities, hygiene and vaccines, life expectancy has increased considerably. This means, of course, that there are more elderly people to look after. In 1970 it was estimated that there were 291 million people over 60 years old (7.8% of the world's population), and 26 million over 80 years old (0.78%). It is predicted that these figures will rise to 600 million (9.8%) and 58 million (0.9%) respectively by the year 2000. This trend was shown in the United Kingdom in the 1981 census (see Figure 1.12).

Census charts the ageing British people

People are living longer into pensionable age and fewer children are being born, according to official census statistics published yesterday.

The figures, based on the 1981 census, show dramatically how Britain's population is ageing.

During the 1970s, nearly a million more people became pensioners and by 1981 nearly a quarter of all households consisted solely of elderly people.

This meant that there had been a 10 per cent increase in Britain's pensioners, with roughly one in six people qualified for retirement and a state pension. Twice as many women as men lived beyond their 75th birthday.

Despite the fact that 22.3 per cent of the total population was under 16 years old when the census was taken last April there was nevertheless a 12 per cent drop compared with 10 years earlier. This illustrated the declining birth-rate, the recession, and various other factors which dominated the 1970s.

Guardian, 30 June 1982

Attitudes towards having children

The developed and the developing world

Whereas the average family in the developed world has only two children, those in developing countries still average over five who live beyond infancy (remembering that many mothers will have given birth more than ten times). In 1985 Europe had 21% and North America 22% of their populations under 14, whereas in Latin America the figure was 38% and in Africa 45%.

Government incentives In Sri Lanka, males who are sterilised after two or three children receive a bonus child allowance. In Korea couples with two or fewer children are given priority in obtaining new homes. In Singapore the cost of having a child in hospital increases as the number of children in the family increases, but costs are waived if the mother is sterilised following childbirth. In the Philippines paid maternity leave is only granted for the first four confinements.

However, the greatest attempt by a government to discourage more births has been in China. Although by 1975 the average family size had fallen to three children, this was still regarded as too many. The government has tried to encourage a 'one child only' policy. Inducements to have only one child include free education, priority housing, pension and family benefits – inducements lost after a second or third child is born. In addition, the legal marriageable age is set at 22 for men and 20 for women, and couples must apply to the state for marriage and then again to have a child.

Inducements reduced the birth rate from about 37 per 1000 in the early 1950s to 18 per 1000 in 1979, and government legislation reduced this further to 15 per 1000 by 1985. However the results have not always been good. Reports from China suggest forced abortion (if one child per family is exceeded), forced sterilisation and even female infanticide, whereby if the first born is a girl she is killed in the hope of a later child being a boy.

Site and situation

Site describes the point at which the town (village, farm, industry) is located. It is concerned with the local relief, soils, water supply, etc. It is the initial determining factor in the growth of a settlement.

Situation describes where the settlement (or farm/factory) is located in relation to surrounding features such as other settlements, rivers and communications. As the settlement grows then its *situation* becomes predominant as the factor which determines growth. Paris, for example, had the site advantage of being on an island in the River Seine which could be defended and which made bridging easier. However it continued to grow because it was the centre of a major farming area where several routes (rivers) converged.

Early settlements These developed initially within a rural economy which aimed to be self sufficient, and they were influenced mainly by physical factors which included:

Wet-point sites, especially in relatively dry areas, e.g. springs at the foot of chalk escarpments. Water was needed frequently throughout the year, and was heavy to carry. In times of early settlement rivers were sufficiently clean to give a safe, permanent supply.

Dry-point sites which may have been 'islands' in an otherwise marshy area, e.g. Ely.

Building materials which had to be located nearby and which ideally included stone, wood and clay.

Defence against surrounding tribes. Such sites may have been protected on three sides by water

(e.g. Durham) or on a hill with steep sides and commanding views (e.g. Edinburgh).

Fuel supply which was essential for heating and cooking and which, in earlier days, was usually wood (still applicable today in developing countries).

Food supply from land which was suitable for animal grazing and, nearby, land which could be used for growing crops.

Nodal points where several valleys (natural routes) met to give a route centre; or which commanded routes through the hills (e.g. Guildford).

Bridging points, originally possibly a ford in the river, e.g. Bedford, where natural routes were able to cross rivers.

Shelter and aspect In Britain it was an advantage to be sheltered from winds blowing from the north, and to be facing south which meant more sunlight (e.g. Torquay).

Study Figure 2.1 which shows an area of land available for early settlement.

1 List the advantages and disadvantages of each of the five sites labelled A to E.

2 Is there an ideal site?

3 Bearing in mind that you (as one tribal leader) may feel that certain factors in choosing the site for a settlement are more important to you than to your neighbour (as leader of another tribe), rank the five possible sites in your order of preference.

4 If a new settlement were to be created in this area in the late 1980s, which of the nine factors listed above might still be important?

▽ **Figure 2.1** Which would be the best site for an early settlement?

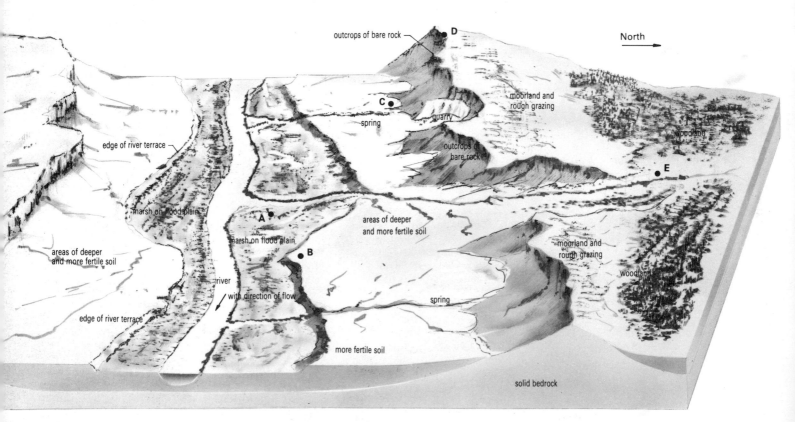

SETTLEMENTS
Functions

The function of a town relates to its economic and social development. In some cases the original function is no longer applicable, e.g. British towns no longer have a defensive function. Many attempts have been made to classify towns according to their main functions. Classifications are valuable if, for convenience, they can group together towns which have similar characteristic functions. Some classifications are too simple and general, e.g. dividing all towns into three groups based on primary, secondary and tertiary (service) industries (see page 60). Other classifications are far too detailed to be applied easily, and so are not convenient to use.

Market towns originally grew up as collection and distribution centres for the surrounding farming area. Today their functions will probably include the manufacturing and servicing of agricultural machinery and the processing of agricultural produce (e.g. Winnipeg, York).

Mining towns have grown due to the exploitation of a local fuel or mineral (e.g. coal at Treorky in the Rhondda Valley and iron ore at Schefferville in Labrador).

Manufacturing/industrial towns have grown where raw materials are processed into manufactured goods (e.g. Birmingham, Toronto).

Ports include those on coasts, rivers, and lakes (e.g. Southampton, Thunder Bay). These have grown at points where goods are moved from land to water, or vice versa.

Route centres are located at the junction of several natural routes or at nodal points resulting from economic development (e.g. Carlisle, Paris).

Service centres have grown to provide the needs of a local community. Such services may include shopping, recreation, education and health (e.g. Cambridge).

Cultural and religious settlements attract people from many parts of the world, even if only temporarily, to live and study (e.g. Oxford, Rome).

Administrative centres may vary from smaller regional centres (e.g. county towns such as Exeter) to capital cities (e.g. Ottawa).

Residential towns are those in which the majority of the inhabitants are either retired or work elsewhere. In the widest definition this could include commuter, overspill and new towns (e.g. Cumbernauld).

Tourist resorts (with the exception of spa towns, such as Bath) are modern in origin. Most are on coasts or in mountains (e.g. Blackpool, Banff).

Today, especially in the developed world, most towns tend to be multi-functional (i.e. they have several functions) though a particular function may be predominant. Also, many towns may have had a change in function from their original one, e.g. a Cornish fishing port may now be a tourist resort (e.g. Penzance), a mining village may have become a new town with some manufacturing industry (e.g. Washington, County Durham).

Figure 2.2 locates some of the major towns in Canada, and has an incomplete key (you may have to do some research to find out the answer to Question 3).

1 Re-draw this map.

2 Add a colour to the nine types of town given in the key.

3 Try to decide what is the main function (or functions) of each town, and colour it in accordingly. How will you show a town with more than one main function?

4 Describe any pattern of functions shown on your map.

▽ **Figure 2.2** The main functions of Canadian towns

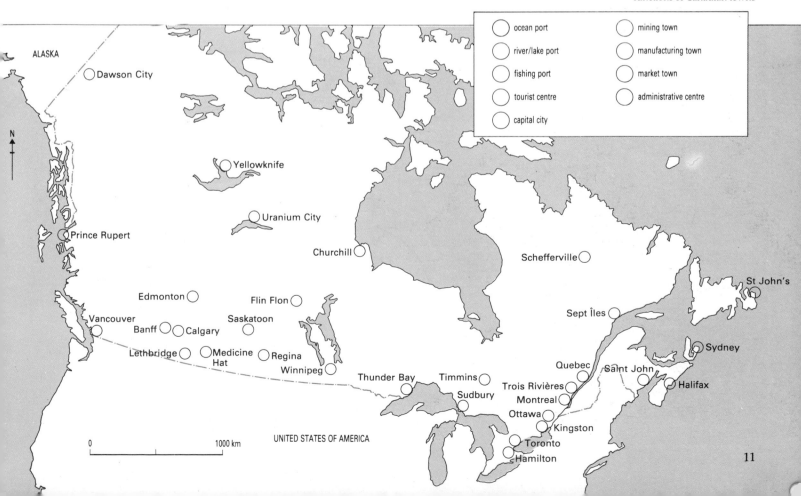

Patterns

Geographers have now become interested in the patterns or shapes of villages and towns as well as in their particular functions. Villages have certain characteristic shapes although these vary from place to place both within Britain and across the world. Although it is unusual to find all the main characteristic shapes within a small area, many can be seen in Figure 2.3 which is part of a 1:50 000 Ordnance Survey map. The village of Hedon, in grid square 1928, is about 3km east of the city boundary of Hull.

1 Isolated This is usually an individual farmhouse found either in areas of extreme adverse physical conditions as in the Highlands of Scotland, or in areas of pioneer settlement where land was actually divided into planned lots (e.g. the Canadian Prairies). Isolated or, more accurately in this case, individual farms can be seen in Figure 2.3 in grid squares 2426 and 2230.

2 Dispersed This consists of groups of two or three buildings, perhaps forming a hamlet, and separated from the next small group of buildings by two or three kilometres (e.g. Prospect Hill in 2530). Such settlements are common in northern Germany where the name *Urweiler* means literally 'primaeval hamlet'.

3 Nucleated or compact These were found every three or four kilometres in rural England, so that there was sufficient land around the village to make it self sufficient with its own crops and its own animals. The buildings were grouped together for defensive purposes as well as for social and economic ones. The village of Preston, in grid square 1830, illustrates the grouping of buildings at a crossroad. This pattern is typical in the Ganges Valley and the Indian Deccan.

4 Loose knit These are similar to the nucleated type in that they are found at crossroads and junctions, but here the buildings are more spread out as in Burstwick (grid square 2227).

5 Linear or street Here the buildings are strung out along the main road as in Thorngumbald (grid squares 2026 and 2126) or, in the case of the Netherlands, along a dyke or canal.

6 Planned villages These include suburbanised villages which are near enough to large cities to house their workforce, as in square 1828 at Hedon. They tend to contain small crescent-shaped estates with individual buildings. These are also seen on the Dutch Polders.

Naturally some villages show characteristics of more than one pattern, e.g. Keyingham (2425) and Ryhill (2225).

▽ **Figure 2.3** Ordnance Survey extract

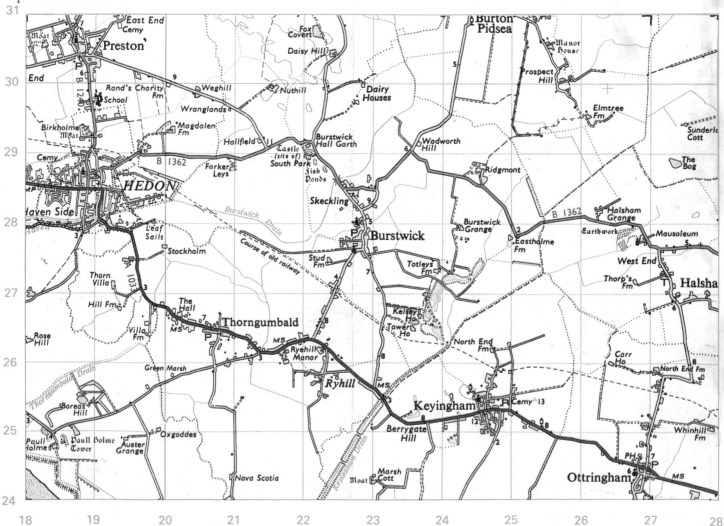

Hierarchy

This term refers to the arrangement of settlements within a country in 'an order of importance' – usually from many small hamlets and villages at the base of the hierarchy, to one major city, usually the capital, at the top. Three different methods to determine this order of importance have been based on:

1 The area and population of the settlement, i.e. its size.

2 The range and number of functions and/or services within each settlement.

3 The relative sphere of influence of each settlement.

Size Early attempts to determine a hierarchy were based on size. However, no-one has been able to produce a commonly accepted division between, for example, a hamlet and a village, and a village and a town. Indeed, many villages in China and India are as big as many British towns. Figure 2.4 lists a fairly conventional hierarchy in terms of type of settlement, and a debatable 'division' based on actual numbers (more applicable to Britain than elsewhere).

Range and number of functions or services These, like the size of the settlements, must also be based upon arbitrary criteria. The table in Figure 2.5 is a starting point which you could test for yourself in the field if you live in or near a rural area.

An ordnance survey map may also give some guidance. Look again at Figure 2.3 and find the same settlements as on page 12 (Hedon, Preston, Thorngumbald, Ryhill, Keyingham, Ottringham, Burstwick, Halsam and Prospect Hill and in square 2124). If a settlement is on a main road, give it two points, if it is on a 'B' class road, award one point. Give one point for every public house, church, school, post office and telephone box that each place has. For example, Keyingham is on the main road (two points) and has two churches and a post office (three more points) giving a total of five points. Obviously not all services or functions are shown on the OS map, but you could produce a rank order and see if this appears to agree with the differing sizes of the settlements.

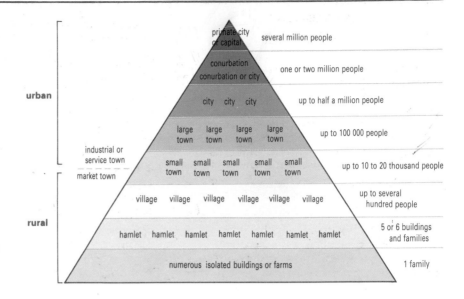

urban		several million people
	private city or capital	one or two million people
	conurbation conurbation or city	up to half a million people
	city city city	up to 100 000 people
industrial or service town	large town / large town / large town / large town	up to 10 to 20 thousand people
market town	small town / small town / small town / small town / small town	up to several hundred people
rural	village village village village village village	5 or 6 buildings and families
	hamlet hamlet hamlet hamlet hamlet hamlet hamlet	1 family
	numerous isolated buildings or farms	

hamlet	perhaps none
village	church, post office, public house, shop for daily goods, small junior school
town	several shops, churches and senior school, bus station, supermarket, doctor, dentist, banks, small hospital and football team
city	large railway station, large shopping complex, cathedral, opticians and jewellers, large hospital and football team, museum
capital	cathedrals, government buildings, banking HQ, railway termini, museums and art galleries, main theatre and shopping centre

△ **Figure 2.4** Hierarchy of settlements according to size

△ **Figure 2.5** Hierarchy of settlements according to services

▽ **Figure 2.6** Spheres of influence of shops in and around Sheffield

Sphere of influence This may be defined as the area served by a particular settlement. The size of this sphere of influence depends on the size and functions of a town and its surrounding settlements, the transport facilities available and the level of competition from a rival settlement. Two main ideas should be noted:

1 A **threshold population** is the minimum number of people needed to ensure that demand is great enough for a special service to be offered to the people living in that area. For example, estimates suggest 350 people are needed to make a grocer's shop successful, 2500 for a single doctor to be available, and 10 000 for a secondary school. Boots the Chemist prefers a threshold of 10 000 people in its catchment areas, Marks & Spencer 50 000 and Sainsburys 60 000.

2 **Range** is the maximum distance that people are prepared to travel to obtain a service. Figure 2.6 shows that people are not prepared to travel far to a corner shop, but will travel much further for a hypermarket – presumably because of the range and volume of stock and competitive prices.

Changes in time Few settlements remain constant in size. Most villages have increased, e.g. suburbanised villages, or have become towns, while towns have become cities and cities have merged into conurbations. A few settlements have decreased in size – notably villages in isolated areas and, more recently, conurbations.

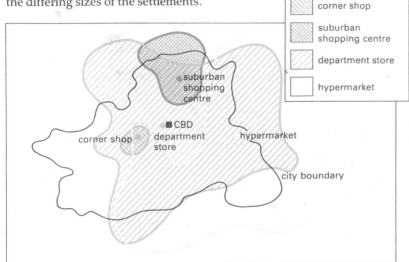

	corner shop
	suburban shopping centre
	department store
	hypermarket

Population and settlement

1 (Pages 4-5)

a) How is population density calculated? (1)

b) A, B, C and D are four types of hostile environment where relatively few people live.
(i) Against each of these four letters write down the correct type of hostile environment from the following list: mountains; tropical rainforest; arctic; hot deserts. (4)
(ii) For any *two* of these hostile environments, give four reasons why each has a low population density. (2 × 4)

c) Areas E and F have high population densities.
(i) Name a country in which E is found, and the country in which F is found. (2)
(ii) For *either* E *or* F, give three reasons for high population density. (3)

d) Areas G and H also have high population densities. For either area give three reasons for this. (3)

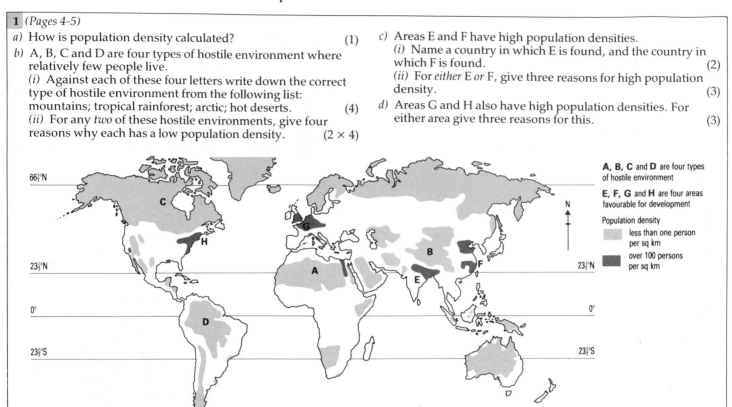

A, B, C and **D** are four types of hostile environment

E, F, G and **H** are four areas favourable for development

Population density
- less than one person per sq km
- over 100 persons per sq km

2 (Figures 1.4 and 1.5, page 6)

a) What was Asia's population in 1900? (1)

b) Which continent had the second largest population in 1940? (1)

c) Which two continents more than doubled their population between 1940 and 1980? (2)

d) (i) By how many millions did North America's population increase between 1940 and 1980?
(ii) Express this increase as a percentage. (2)

e) In 1980 what percentage of the world's population lived in:
(i) The three developing continents?
(ii) The three developed continents? (2)

3 (Page 7)

a) What is meant by the following terms?
(i) Birth rate. (ii) Death rate. (iii) Natural increase. (3)

b) Using the demographic transition graph for Brazil opposite:
(i) Give the birth rate and the death rate for the present day. (2)
(ii) Give the figure 'per 1000' by which the population is increasing at the present day. (1)
(iii) Say which of the following periods was the one during which the population of Brazil grew most rapidly: 1900-1910; 1920-1930; 1940-1950; 1960-1970. (1)

c) Give three reasons for a high birth rate in Brazil. (3)

d) Give three reasons why Brazil's death rate has fallen rapidly since 1940. (3)

e) Using the graph:
(i) Complete the total population for Brazil for the years 1920 to the present day. (1)
(ii) Predict what the birth rate and death rate for Brazil might be in the year 2000. (1)
(iii) Give reasons for your prediction. (2)

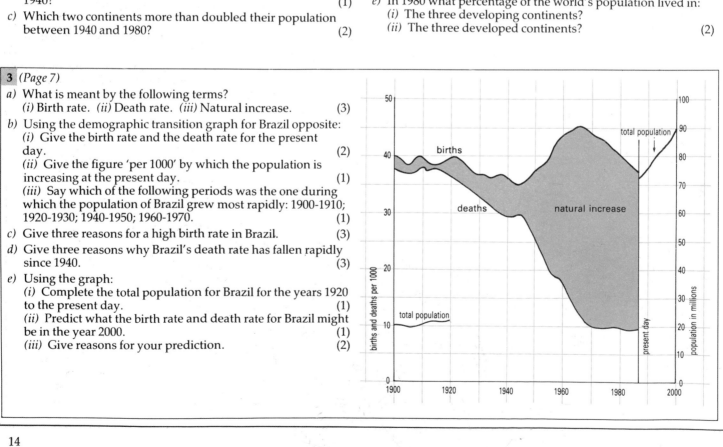

4 *(Pages 8-9)*

The two graphs, (a) and (b), show population pyramids for two countries in different parts of the world.

a) (i) Describe any three differences between the two
graphs. (3)
(ii) State which graph is more typical of a developing country
and which more typical of a developed country. (1)
(iii) In graph (a), what percentage of the female population is
aged between 40-44 years? (1)
(iv) What percentage of the total population in graph (b) is:
over 60 years of age; under 15 years of age? (2)

b) Which country, (a) or (b), has:
(i) The higher birth rate?
(ii) The higher death rate?
(iii) The more rapid population growth?
Give reasons for your answers. (6)

c) (i) What is meant by the term 'dependency ratio'? (1)
(ii) Compare the size of the dependent population for
country (b) with that of country (a). (2)
(iii) What are the consequences for countries with a rising
dependent population? (2)

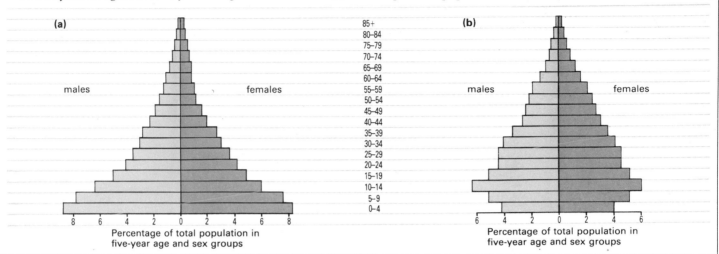

(a) males ... females
Percentage of total population in five-year age and sex groups

85+ 80–84 75–79 70–74 65–69 60–64 55–59 50–54 45–49 40–44 35–39 30–34 25–29 20–24 15–19 10–14 5–9 0–4

(b) males ... females
Percentage of total population in five-year age and sex groups

---

5 *(Figure 2.1, page 10)*

a) (i) How many sites were close to a permanent water supply?
(ii) How many sites had a nearby supply of wood for fuel
and building?
(iii) How many sites had good soil?
(iv) Which site was most likely to flood?
(v) Which site was most exposed to wind and rain?

b) Which factors favourable to early settlement might still apply
to the siting of a present-day new town?

6 *(Page 13)*

Study Table 1, which gives the population figures for five
settlements in the United Kingdom.

Table 1

Name of settlement	Population
Bristol	399 600
Hayton	360
Corby	52 100
Hornsby	24
London	6 765 100

Using Table 2, complete the remaining two columns:
(i) By ranking the settlements according to size, with the largest
in first place. (2½)
(ii) By placing, in the correct order, the following types of
settlement: village, conurbation, town, hamlet, city. (2½)

Table 2

Rank	Name of settlement	Type of settlement
1		
2		
3		
4		
5		

---

7 *Spheres of influence (thresholds) (page 13)*

a) (i) What does the term 'sphere of influence' mean?
(ii) Which service has the smallest threshold?
(iii) Which service has the largest threshold?
(iv) How far is it between the village and the town? (4)

b) Give a reason why the sphere of influence of the theatre is
larger than that of the chemist. (1)

c) If a main road were built linking the village to the town, how
might this affect the spheres of influence of the theatre,
chemist and supermarket? (3)

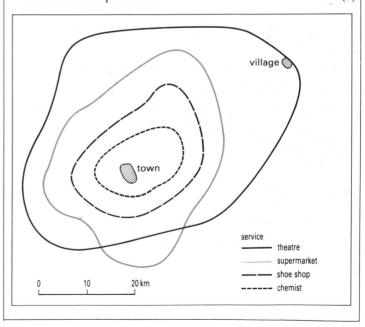

village

town

service
—— theatre
——— supermarket
– – – shoe shop
------ chemist

0   10   20 km

15

URBANISATION
Growth of cities

'Urbanisation' means an increase in the proportion of people living in towns and cities. Even in the early civilisations of Mesopotamia, the Nile Valley, the Indus Valley and the Hwang-Ho (North China), towns were important. However, it was not until the growth of industry in the 19th century that large-scale urbanisation occurred. In Great Britain, where the industrial revolution began, only 10% of the population was living in towns in England and Wales in 1801, compared with over 80% by the mid 1980s.

The percentage of people living in urban areas in 1980 is shown in Figure 3.1. In parts of the developed world, North America, North West Europe and Oceania over 75% live in cities.

However, recently the most rapid growth has been in the developing world where the 5% of 1920 had grown to 30% by 1985.

In 1960 one third of the world's population lived in urban areas. By AD 2000, when this population will have doubled, half will be living in large cities. Two additional factors are the growth of large cities which now exceed one million inhabitants (Figures 3.2 and 3.3), and the changing distribution of these cities.

☐ Prior to 1940, the majority of 'million' cities were found in the developed countries, in the temperate latitudes of the northern hemisphere.

☐ Since 1940 there has been a dramatic increase of 'million' cities in the developing countries, the majority of which are found within the tropics.

▽ **Figure 3.1** World urban population as a percentage of the total, 1980

▽ **Figure 3.2** World cities with populations of over one million, 1980

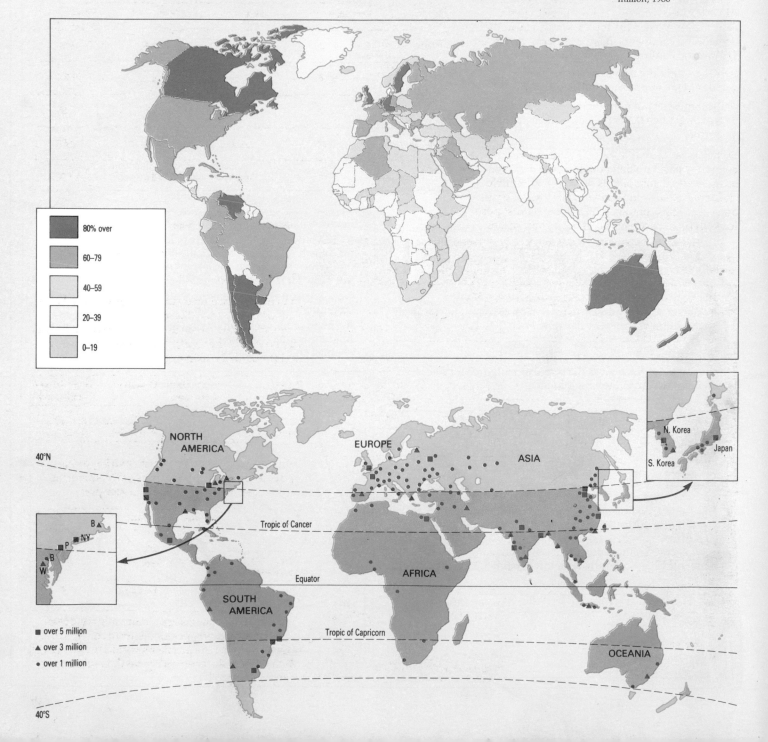

80% over

60–79

40–59

20–39

0–19

40°N

NORTH AMERICA

EUROPE

ASIA

N. Korea

Japan

S. Korea

Tropic of Cancer

B

P NY

B

W

Equator

AFRICA

SOUTH AMERICA

OCEANIA

Tropic of Capricorn

■ over 5 million

▲ over 3 million

● over 1 million

40°S

1 How many 'million' cities were there in
 (a) 1920 and (b) 1980?

2 Approximately what proportion of these were found:
 (a) north of 40°N and (b) within the tropics, in 1920 and in 1980?

3 (a) Has the average size of 'million' cities increased during this period?
 (b) Has the percentage of people living within these cities also increased?

4 (a) Name the 21 cities which had populations of over five million in 1980 (Figure 3.2).
 (b) Name the 20 cities which had populations of between three and five million.

Figure 3.4 shows the rank order of the world's twelve largest cities over a period of years. In 1970 half of these were still in the industrialised, developed continents of North America and Europe. By 1985 no city in Europe was expected to be in the top twelve, and estimates suggest that by AD 2000 the two largest cities will be in Latin America, and ten of the top eleven will be in the developing continents of Latin America and Asia. This would confirm the present trend of:

□ cities within the tropics growing faster than cities in the temperate latitudes, and

□ the largest city in most developing countries growing much faster than any other city in that country.

Both São Paulo and Mexico City are growing by an estimated half a million people a year. Can you imagine all the inhabitants of Leeds or Sheffield suddenly arriving in São Paulo or Mexico City in one year? Think of the problems that it must pose for both the newcomers and the city authorities.

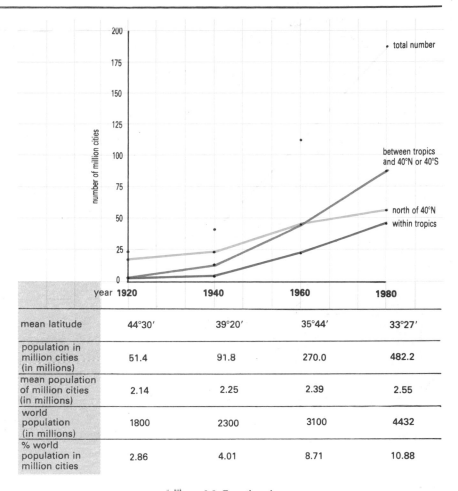

	1920	1940	1960	1980
mean latitude	44°30'	39°20'	35°44'	33°27'
population in million cities (in millions)	51.4	91.8	270.0	482.2
mean population of million cities (in millions)	2.14	2.25	2.39	2.55
world population (in millions)	1800	2300	3100	4432
% world population in million cities	2.86	4.01	8.71	10.88

△ **Figure 3.3** Growth and distribution of 'million' cities

◁ **Figure 3.4** The world's largest cities

Primate cities

In many developing countries, especially in Latin America and Africa, there is a tendency for one large or primate city to dominate the country. This city is usually the capital, the commercial centre and the area of maximum economic growth.

Town	Population (millions)	Country	Population (millions)
Santiago	4	Chile	11½
Buenos Aires	10	Argentina	28

In several cases there may be two large cities, one of which will be the capital and commercial centre, and the other often the major port.

Towns	Joint population (millions)	Country	Total population (millions)
Cairo – Giza Alexandria	8½	Egypt	44½
Quito Guayaguil	2	Ecuador	9

Primate cities tend to attract more migrants from rural areas than other settlements in the country, which increases the problems within the city (page 24) and limits the economic growth in other parts of the country.

rank order	1970	1978	estimate 1985	estimate 2000
1	New York 16.5	New York 16.4	Tokyo 23.0	Mexico City 31.0
2	Tokyo 13.4	Tokyo 14.7	New York 18.0	Sao Paulo 26.0
3	London 10.5	Mexico City 14.0	Mexico City 17.9	Tokyo 24.0
4	Shanghai 10.0	Shanghai 10.9	Sao Paulo 16.8	Shanghai 23.0
5	Mexico City 8.6	Los Angeles 10.6	Shanghai 14.3	New York 22.0
6	Los Angeles 8.4	Paris 9.9	Los Angeles 13.7	Peking 19.0
7	Buenos Aires 8.4	Buenos Aires 8.4	Calcutta 12.1	Rio de Janeiro 18.0
8	Paris 8.4	Moscow 8.0	Bombay 12.1	Bombay 17.0
9	Sao Paulo 7.1	Chicago 7.7	Peking 12.0	Calcutta 16.0
10	Moscow 7.1	Peking 7.6	Buenos Aires 11.7	Jakarta 15.0
11	Peking 7.0	Sao Paulo 7.6	Rio de Janeiro 11.4	Seoul 15.0
12	Chicago 6.9	London 7.2	Seoul 11.2	Los Angeles 15.0

Figures in millions

Latin America	Europe	North America	Asia

Urban growth

In developed countries

This occurred mainly in the 19th century, and was a direct response to the development of industry and the need for a large labour force to work in labour-intensive factories. Although many cities grew at a rate of 10% every decade, virtually all the newcomers were able to gain jobs and houses. In the 20th century, people continued to move to urban areas for a variety of reasons: more, and better paid jobs, many of which were cleaner and needed more skill than those in rural areas; nearness to their place of work; better housing, services and shopping facilities and more entertainment.

▽ **Figure 3.5** Extract from 'North-South', *Brandt Report*

▽ **Figure 3.6** Rural 'push' and urban 'pull'

> The rush to the towns has created the same kind of misery as existed in the nineteenth-century cities of Europe and America. But industrialization in those days was labour-intensive, so that the cities grew as the jobs expanded . . . The migration in today's developing world is often due to the lack of opportunity in the countryside – it is 'rural push' as much as 'urban pull'. The consequences of high birth rates and rapid migration are all too visible in many cities of the Third World, with abysmal living conditions and very high unemployment or underemployment. The strains on families, whose members are often separated, are very heavy. In São Paulo in Brazil, the population was growing at around 6–7 per cent annually in the late sixties and early seventies, in such appalling conditions that infant mortality was actually increasing. The fact that people still migrate to these cities only underlines the desperate situation which they have left behind.

In developing countries

This movement began in the 20th century, but it has now accelerated so that many cities are expanding at the rate of 20% every decade. Figure 3.5 is a quotation from the Brandt Report. It suggests that in developing countries, movement to the city is partly due to 'rural push' and partly due to 'urban pull' (see Figure 3.6).

'Push' factors (why people leave the countryside):

☐ Pressure on the land, e.g. division of land among sons – each has too little to live on.

☐ Many families do not own any land.

☐ Overpopulation, resulting from high birth rates.

☐ Starvation, resulting from either too little output for the people of the area, or crop failure. Often, it may also be caused by a change in agriculture – from producing crops for local/family consumption to a system that produces cash/plantation crops for consumption in the developed world.

☐ Limited food production due to overgrazing, or to misuse of the land resulting in soil erosion or exhaustion.

☐ Mechanisation has caused a reduction in jobs available on the land together with, in many areas, reduced yields.

☐ Farming is hard work with long hours and little pay. In developing countries a lack of money means a lack of machinery, pesticides and fertilisers.

☐ Natural disasters such as drought (Sahel countries), hurricanes (West Indies), floods (Bangladesh) and volcanic eruptions (Colombia) destroy villages and crops.

☐ Extreme physical conditions such as aridity, rugged mountains, cold, heat and dense vegetation.

☐ Local communities (Amazon Amerindians) forced to move.

☐ Lack of services (schools, hospitals).

☐ Lack of investment as money available to the government will be spent on urban areas.

'Pull' factors (why people move to the city):

☐ They are looking for better paid jobs. Factory workers get about three times the wages of farm workers.

☐ They expect to be housed more comfortably and to have a higher quality of life.

☐ They have a better chance of services such as schools, medical treatment and entertainment.

☐ They are attracted to the 'bright lights'.

☐ More reliable sources of food.

☐ Religious and political activities can be carried on more safely in larger cities.

Figure 3.6 refers to the family's 'perceptions of the city'. This is what they think, expect or were led to believe the city is like. The reality is very different.

push factors

small, fragmented farms

deforested hills leading to soil erosion

crops dying due to drought or to being eaten by pests

overgrazing by many but poor quality animals

river – seasonal flooding or dries up polluted water supply

pull factors

WORLD PLASTICS

LEISURE PARK

HEALTH CARE

SCHOOL

EMPLOYMENT VACANCIES

FLATS FOR SALE OR RE

FOOD HALL

family's perception of large city

large families

Urban models in a developed country

A model is a theoretical framework which may not actually exist, but which helps to explain the reality. It has been suggested that towns do not grow in a haphazard way, but that they show certain generalised characteristics. The two simplest models to show this possible growth are shown in Figure 3.7.

1 **Burgess,** initially using Chicago as his basis, suggested that most towns grew outwards in a concentric pattern, meaning that buildings become more recent the closer one gets to the edge of the city. It is possible that five rings may develop.

2 **Hoyt,** in contrast, proposed the idea that towns grew as sectors, or in wedge shapes. That means that if, for example, industry grew up in one part of the town in the 19th century, later industries would also develop in that sector.

Since then further models have been suggested, but it should be understood that most urban areas are complex and probably show the characteristics of more than one model, and that each city is unique.

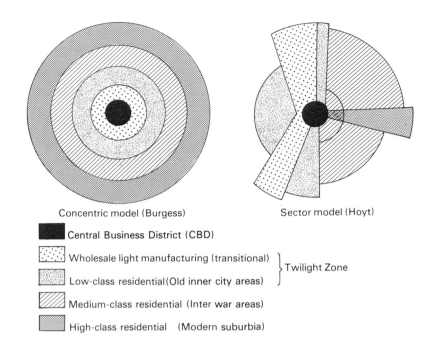

Concentric model (Burgess)   Sector model (Hoyt)

■ Central Business District (CBD)

▫ Wholesale light manufacturing (transitional) } Twilight Zone

▒ Low-class residential (Old inner city areas) }

▨ Medium-class residential (Inter war areas)

▦ High-class residential (Modern suburbia)

Land use and functional zones in a city

Each of the zones shown in Figure 3.7 has a function and shows a different type of land use. These differences may result from:

Land values Land is expensive in the CBD (Central Business District), where competition is greatest. It gradually becomes cheaper towards the urban fringe.

Space There is very little available space near to the city centre, but this increases towards the outskirts, again partly due to declining land values.

Age Towns develop outwards so that the oldest buildings are near to the city centre, and the newest ones are on the outskirts.

Accessibility The CBD is where the main routes from the suburbs meet, and so the area is easier to reach from all parts of the city.

Wealth of the inhabitants The poorer members of the community tend to live in the cheaper houses near to the CBD (with its shops) and the inner city (where most jobs used to be found). These people are less likely to be able to afford transport (private or public) in order to get to work if they lived on the outskirts.

Planning policies These have helped to control the growth of the town (particularly since 1945), and have affected its redevelopment.

Both the land use and the functions of different parts of the town alter with time:

1 Industry in the 19th century grew up next to the CBD (inner city area) whereas today most new industries will be on the edge of town trading estates.

2 Terraced 19th century housing may have been replaced with high-rise flats or areas of open space.

△ **Figure 3.7** Urban models

▽ **Figure 3.8** Transect across a typical British city

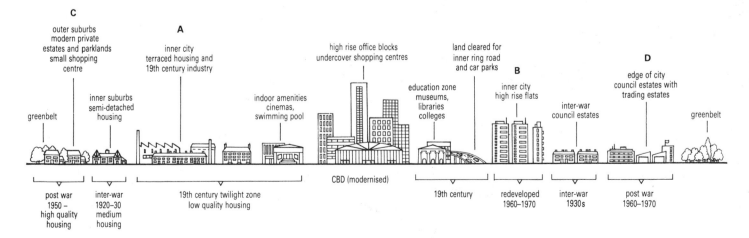

Residential environments

A Old inner city area

B Inner city redevelopment

▷ **Figure 3.9** Physical appearance

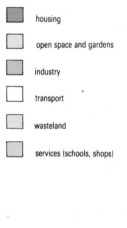

housing

open space and gardens

industry

transport

wasteland

services (schools, shops)

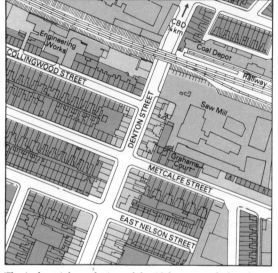

▷ **Figure 3.10** Land use

The industrial revolution of the 19th century led to the growth of towns. The rapid influx of workers into these towns meant a big and immediate demand for cheap housing, and so builders constructed as many houses as possible in a small area, resulting in high density housing with an overcrowded population. The houses were built in long, straight rows and in terraces. In those days of non-planning, few amenities were provided either in the house (e.g. no indoor wc, bathroom, sewerage, electricity) or around it (e.g. no open space and no gardens).

When in the 1950s and 1960s vast areas of inner cities were cleared by bulldozers many of the displaced inhabitants either moved to council estates near the city boundary, or were rehoused in huge high-rise tower blocks which were created on the sites of the old terraced houses. Although these high-rise buildings contained most modern amenities, they had to be reached by lifts which led to narrow, dark corridors. Also, despite the areas of greenery between the flats, there was still a very high housing density.

▷ **Figure 3.11** Description
▽ **Figure 3.12** Census data

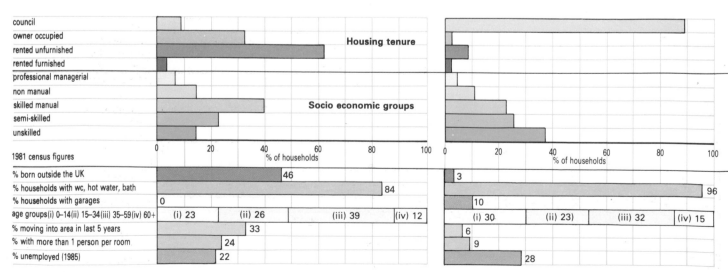

	Old inner city area	Inner city redevelopment
Housing tenure		
council	9	89
owner occupied	24	6
rented unfurnished	64	8
rented furnished	4	3
Socio economic groups		
professional managerial	5	7
non manual	15	10
skilled manual	41	27
semi-skilled	20	25
unskilled	14	38

1981 census figures   % of households

	Old inner city area	Inner city redevelopment
% born outside the UK	46	3
% households with wc, hot water, bath	84	96
% households with garages	0	10
age groups (i) 0–14 (ii) 15–34 (iii) 35–59 (iv) 60+	(i) 23 (ii) 26 (iii) 39 (iv) 12	(i) 30 (ii) 23 (iii) 32 (iv) 15
% moving into area in last 5 years	33	6
% with more than 1 person per room	24	9
% unemployed (1985)	22	28

C Suburbia

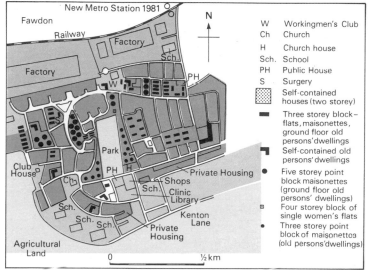

The rapid outward growth of cities began with the introduction of public transport and accelerated with the popularity of the private car. This outward growth (also known as urban sprawl) led to the construction of numerous private, 'car based' suburbs.

The houses built in the outer suburbs before the Second World War are characterised by their front and back gardens. Usually they have garages and are semi-detached with bay windows. The more recent estates have housing which differs in both style and type, but they remain well planned and spacious.

D Outer city council estate

As local councils cleared the worst of the slums from their inner city areas in the 1950s and 1960s many residents were rehoused on large council estates on the fringes of the city. Attempts were made to vary the type and size of accommodation:

☐ High-rise tower blocks, often of 10-12 storeys.

☐ Low-rise tower blocks, usually 3-5 storeys high. These were built nearer the city boundaries, where there was more open space.

☐ Single-storey terraces with some gardens and car parking space.

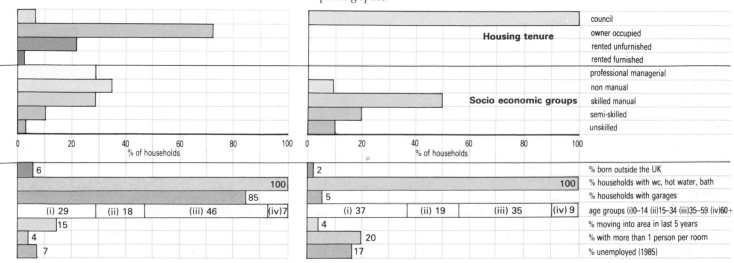

	C Suburbia	D Outer city council estate	
Housing tenure	council	council	
	owner occupied	owner occupied	
	rented unfurnished	rented unfurnished	
	rented furnished	rented furnished	
Socio economic groups	professional managerial	professional managerial	
	non manual	non manual	
	skilled manual	skilled manual	
	semi-skilled	semi-skilled	
	unskilled	unskilled	

% of households 0 20 40 60 80 100

C	D	
6	2	% born outside the UK
100	100	% households with wc, hot water, bath
85	5	% households with garages
(i) 29 (ii) 18 (iii) 46 (iv) 7	(i) 37 (ii) 19 (iii) 35 (iv) 9	age groups (i)0–14 (ii)15–34 (iii)35–59 (iv)60+
15	4	% moving into area in last 5 years
4	20	% with more than 1 person per room
7	17	% unemployed (1985)

URBANISATION
Problems in developed cities

The two largest metropolitan areas in the mid-1980s are Tokyo and New York (Figure 3.4). Together they illustrate problems facing large cities in the developed world.

Overcrowding in the CBD In the daytime congestion results from shoppers (Figure 3.13) and business people, while at night it fills with people seeking entertainment.

High cost of land in the CBD The demand for a prime site in this, the most accessible part of the city, has led to a skyscraper development. Recently, in New York, there has been a trend in which large companies have been forced to leave this area due to high costs and environmental problems.

Traffic congestion Both cities have developed an elaborate and expensive urban motorway system, yet they are so overcrowded that over 75% of commuters use public transport. In New York most commuters have to use the relatively few bridges and ferries or the underground to cross into the CBD on Manhattan Island. In Tokyo, where space is at a premium, railways run above main roads and even tunnel through buildings (Figure 3.14). 'Pushers' are used to cram more people onto Tokyo's suburban trains.

High population densities Areas near to city centres suffer from overcrowding both in terms of houses per kilometre and people per house. Estimates claim that parts of Tokyo house 30 000 people per square kilometre.

Urban decay The inner city housing of New York was built, as in Britain, in the late 1800s. These tenement blocks and flats have suffered from years of neglect. They have few modern amenities such as hot water, baths and garages, and they suffer from damp. Many are rented, but when rents rise some may become unoccupied and are soon vandalised (Figure 3.15). These ghettos are home to the poorest of families – often ethnic minorities, families with young children, the unskilled and the unemployed. Most of Tokyo's houses are post- 1945, but even here small dwellings are packed into the minimum of space.

◁ **Figure 3.13** The Ginza – Tokyo's main shopping area

▽ **Figure 3.14** Elevated motorways, Tokyo

▽ **Figure 3.15** Children play among the tenements of Harlem, New York

Unemployment and crime These are major problems in New York. The vast majority of the 1½ million unemployed (i.e. one in seven New Yorkers) live in the ghettos. As openings for unskilled workers get fewer, more people have to rely on 'relief' (public grants of food and money). Crime has increased rapidly, with street violence, subway muggings and drug addiction, and a murder, on average, every five hours. Racial tension is often high even though many ethnic minorities congregate into their own small communities.

Pollution Factories and traffic cause high levels of noise and air pollution. Tokyo's 80 000 factories and 3½ million cars add to the risk of smog, and the use of smog masks is common (Figure 3.16). Companies polluting the air are fined, but penalties are small in value to the large, rich, industrial corporations. Over half of the homes are not connected to the mains sewerage, and rubbish is dumped on offshore islands. Both cities suffer noise pollution from their international airports.

Lack of open space Land is too scarce to leave open for parks and trees, with Tokyo hemmed in by mountains, and Manhattan on an island (Central Park is an exception).

Increasing costs of services As the wealthy move away from the central areas, those remaining have less money to pay for public services and yet they are often the ones who need the extra services (e.g. hospitals). Many cities, like New York, are facing the threat of bankruptcy.

Lack of planning This has led to a maze of streets in inner city areas, and to an uncontrolled urban sprawl. New York has spread along Long Island, and Tokyo has had to build outwards into the sea.

Climate New York, a large city, becomes very hot in summer. Many well-off residents have second homes away from the city, but for those remaining the heat can be unbearable. New York also experiences blizzards in winter (adding to traffic congestion), while strong winds funnel down the 'canyons' between the skyscrapers. Tokyo, despite being in a sheltered bay, lies in the path of typhoons.

Earthquakes and tsunamis Japan is on a destructive plate margin where the Pacific plate dips underneath the Eurasian plate. Tokyo and its port of Yokohama were destroyed in 1923 with the loss of 150 000 lives. Today shops and office blocks have been built to withstand earthquakes, though houses have not. Coastal areas are vulnerable to large tsunamis, or tidal waves, triggered by submarine earthquakes (pp. 131 and 139).

Inequalities in a developed city

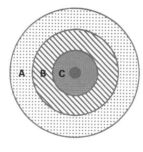

early 20th century

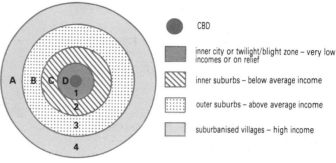

late 20th century

CBD

inner city or twilight/blight zone – very low incomes or on relief

inner suburbs – below average income

outer suburbs – above average income

suburbanised villages – high income

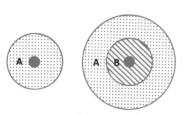

early 19th century   late 19th century

if applied to New York

A established inhabitants of NW European descent (British, German, French)

B immigrants and their descendants from poorer European countries (Irish, Italian, Eastern European)

C Blacks from the south east of the USA and immigrants from the Caribbean (Puerto Rico)

D recent immigrants, including refugees

1 Harlem (tenement blocks and flats)

2 Bronx and Brooklyn (apartment blocks and flats)

3 Queens, Yonkers, Western Long Island (detached)

4 Eastern Long Island and the states of New York, New Jersey and Connecticut (detached)

◁ **Figure 3.16** A woman in Tokyo wearing a smog mask as protection against pollution in the atmosphere

△ **Figure 3.17** Centrifugal movement in New York

▽ **Figure 3.18** Inner city flats

British inner cities

The outbreak of riots in autumn 1985 in Toxteth (Liverpool), Handsworth (Birmingham), Brixton and the Broadwater Farm Estate in Tottenham (both in London) have been attributed to many causes, but most of these were fundamentally social and economic – those of inequality, prejudice and a low quality of life (see p. 32). Many members of ethnic minorities have to live in the poorest quality housing, and this leads to racial tension. Unemployment often exceeds 70%, much of it long term. Lower education opportunities and, often, lower expectations, mean the inhabitants develop few skills. A lack of money on the part of the inhabitants and the various levels of government means inadequate services. While 'authority' points to the high rate of crime – violence, drugs and muggings – residents point to police harassment. The resultant lack of trust leads to further tension.

Following the Tottenham riot an architect claimed that *the stark grey blocks, built on stilts above marshy ground, provided a concrete 'underworld' for crime to thrive. Badly lit, these dark arches became a muggers' paradise, with tenants afraid to venture out after dark. Front doors were reinforced with steel plate to deter housebreakers. Water leaking through flat roofs short-circuited lighting. Poor sound insulation meant neighbours' conversations could be heard, plumbing was audible and the communal heating system transferred noise from one home to the next. Cockroaches, rubbish fires and nervous breakdowns were common. An increasingly large number of housing vacancies appeared.*

URBANISATION
Problems in developing cities

Problems in Calcutta

Calcutta is the most notorious example of the ways in which problems are created when cities grow too quickly. The city is built on flat, swampy land alongside the River Hooghly which is part of the Ganges delta. Covering 103 square kilometres, Calcutta's population is reputed to have grown from 7 million in 1970 to 9 million in 1980 and to an estimated 12 million by 1985.

Housing Estimates suggest that one-third of Calcutta's inhabitants live in bustees (Figure 3.19).

Sanitation and health Sanitation is almost non-existent in the bustees. Most drains and sewage pipes were built over a century ago, and many have cracked, spilling their contents onto the streets. Most areas do not have even this form of sanitation, and human effluent is allowed to run down the narrow lanes. Here one water tap and one latrine has to be shared by 25 to 30 people. Drinking water is often contaminated with sewage, giving rise to cholera, typhoid and dysentery (Figure 3.21). Rubbish is dumped in the streets and is rarely, if ever, collected, and this provides an ideal breeding ground for disease. Most children have worms and suffer from malnutrition because their diet lacks vegetables, proteins, calories and vitamins.

Services Not only is there a lack of guaranteed fresh water and collection of rubbish, but there is a lack of doctors, hospitals and schools, and there is no electricity. As more incomers arrive, the pressure on the limited services continues to increase.

Employment Those with jobs tend to use their home as their place of work. Often the front of the house can be 'opened up' to allow the occupants to sell wood, food and clothes. Although few people are totally unemployed, their jobs take up only a few hours a week and their income is extremely low. Recently the Calcutta Development Authority has employed 120 000 people in an attempt to improve living conditions, using manual labour rather than modern machines which they would find difficult to buy.

Crime and violence Both are a major problem as there is little money to try to prevent crime or catch criminals.

Transport In London there are 222 cars for every 1000 people. In Calcutta there are only 13 cars for the same number. This means people have either to walk, or use the overcrowded public transport system. Despite the addition of new buses, these are insufficient to carry everyone, and often travellers can be seen hanging to the outsides of vehicles. Rickshaws add to the congestion. A second bridge over the Hooghly should take some strain off the existing one and an underground was opened in the mid-1980s.

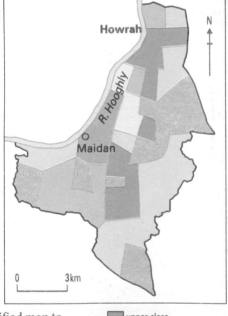

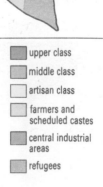

△ **Figure 3.20** Many families have no homes at all and live on the pavements. Over a quarter of a million people are reported to sleep in the open, covered only by bamboo, sacking, polythene or newspaper. Other dwellings, called bustees, are built from wattle, with tiled roofs and mud floors – materials which are not the best to combat the heavy rains associated with the monsoon climate. The houses, packed closely together, are separated by narrow alleys. Inside there is only one room, and that often no bigger than an average British bathroom. In this room the family, often up to eight in number, live, eat and sleep. Yet, despite this overcrowding, the insides of the dwellings are clean and tidy. The houses belong to landlords who rent them out to bustee dwellers who are evicted if they cannot pay the rent.

Segregation Figure 3.19 is a simplified map to show where people of different caste and occupation live. The original Bengali-speaking Hindus live apart from non-Bengalis, and from later Hindu refugees from Bangladesh.

The Calcutta Metropolitan Development Authority was set up in 1970. Since then it has attempted to make the bustees more habitable by paving the alleys, digging extra drains, providing more water taps and lavatory blocks. Pre-fabricated houses have been built, and a community spirit has been created, but despite help from many voluntary agencies, a lack of finance has meant a slow rate of progress in attacking the problems of bad housing, water, sewerage, transport and unemployment.

■ upper class
■ middle class
□ artisan class
□ farmers and scheduled castes
■ central industrial areas
■ refugees

△ **Figure 3.19** Housing areas in Calcutta

Housing inequalities in São Paulo

Just as in the developed world, there are marked differences between the residential areas of cities in the developing world. However, the gulf between the types of residential area in the developing world is greater. In São Paulo in Brazil there are:

☐ Very few rich people in comparison with the total population.

☐ A large number of poor inhabitants.

☐ An increasing number of migrants.

In São Paulo the gap between the highest and lowest incomes is widening. Between 1970 and 1976 the real income of the lowest-paid 10% of the population rose by 44%, while that of the top 10% grew by 160%. In a large manufacturing company the highest paid may earn 30 times more than the lowest paid (in Europe the difference is normally five or six times). As a result the contrast (see Figure 3.22) between the well-off areas and the poorest areas shows a great difference in housing density and quality, the quality of the environment and the provision of amenities.

Housing for the well off This group of people will live in expensive housing ranging from elegant apartment complexes, each with its own social and recreational facilities, to Californian-style detached houses with large gardens and individual swimming pools (Figure 3.23). The size of family will probably be limited to two children, with housemaids and security guards. These houses will be located near to the CBD where most of its

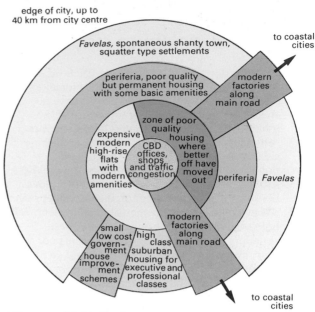

△ **Figure 3.22** Model of land use structures and residential areas in a developing city (based on Brazil)

△ **Figure 3.23** Californian-type housing for the rich in São Paulo

▷ **Figure 3.24** Favelas. Housing for the poor in São Paulo

◁ **Figure 3.21** Drinking water in Calcutta is often contaminated by sewage

inhabitants will work – presumably in commercial premises. The children, who will be healthy and well educated, will eventually go into well-paid jobs. Such homes will also be near to the shops and amenities in the CBD.

Housing for the poor (favelas) The poor of São Paulo, and the new migrants who amount to half a million people a year, live in temporary accommodation built sometimes on vacant space next to modern factories, sometimes alongside main roads leading to the city centre, but usually on the outskirts of the existing urban areas. These people are 'squatters' and have no legal right to the land they occupy. The rapid growth of these spontaneous settlements, or *favelas* as they are called in Brazil, is common to cities in the developing world (Figure 3.24). Houses will be built from any available material – wood, corrugated iron, cardboard and thatch. Some may have two rooms, one for living and cooking in, the other for sleeping. There will probably be at least six children and *no* running water, sewerage, gas, electricity, local jobs, public transport, shops, schools or hospitals. Disease, especially typhoid and dysentery, is easily spread, and life expectancy is relatively short. The percentage of people living in favelas is increasing rapidly in every Brazilian city, and accounts for a minimum of 40% of the total population.

Periferia housing Although governments try to rid the city of favelas, there is no alternative accommodation. As a result, the favelas become 'permanent' and upgraded by the local authority (see Figure 3.22). The homes may now be rebuilt with brick and concrete, and a clean water supply, electricity and a sewerage system will be added. The occupants will have work – although this will be badly-paid factory jobs often found a long way from their homes. Unfortunately, these improvements cannot compete with the growing demand for more homes.

Self-help schemes in developing cities

1987 was designated by the United Nations as the 'International Year of Shelter for the Homeless' (IYSH). One hundred million people have no shelter of any kind, and over one-third of the inhabitants of developing cities live in squatter settlements – sites only vacant because they are subject to flooding, landslips or industrial pollution. Many local authorities encourage these settlements as it is convenient for them to have a ready pool of cheap labour on their doorsteps even if they fail to take any responsibility for them. Self-help schemes seem the only hope for these squatters to improve their 'homes'. The poor's most immediate needs are often simple – a plot on which to build, a small loan to improve or extend the house, cheap building materials and basic services. There is no need for advanced technology or expensive building schemes.

Lusaka, Zambia

The growth of squatter settlements increased rapidly after the country's independence in 1964. Despite a government commitment to build homes for migrants to the city, the numbers of newcomers were too great for the authorities to keep pace.

Study Figure 3.25 and describe and give reasons for the location of:
(a) low density housing for the well off
(b) high density housing for the less wealthy
(c) squatter developments for the newcomers. (Are these linked to industrial areas, road and rail links, cheaper land?)

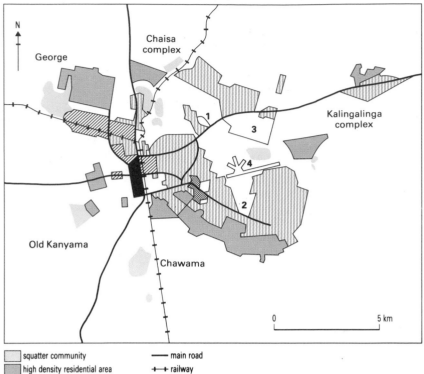

squatter community
high density residential area
low density residential area
industry
government offices
commercial centre

— main road
+++ railway
1 National Assembly
2 State House
3 University of Zambia
4 municipal airport

△ **Figure 3.25** Squatter settlements in Lusaka, Zambia

▽ **Figure 3.26** Self-help housing in Zambia

In Lusaka no official aid is given other than a small loan for the purchase of building materials and some technical advice. Individuals are encouraged to form groups of about 25 to be given a standpipe and eight hectares of land. The groups decide how the area should be planned, and are given help towards the cost and construction of their houses. The residents can do basic work such as digging ditches to take the water and sewage pipes. If they do this the money they save for the authorities can be put towards the provision of such amenities as a tarred road or electricity in their community centre.

Experience has shown a remarkable spirit of co-operation. It has also allowed the residents to live in the village-style environment to which they were accustomed. Each has some land for growing crops and keeping animals and so can adjust more slowly to urban life, while the houses are suited to the local climate and available materials (grass roofs and mud walls are replaced by corrugated iron, concrete and breeze-blocks) (Figure 3.26).

The advantages of such self-help schemes are that they can be done in stages, they can create a community spirit, and the buildings can be erected relatively cheaply, enabling the residents to repay the loan.

The disadvantages of some schemes in other parts of the world include: the lack of desire and ability of the residents to plan, to co-operate and to carry out the improvements; the provision of materials which are unsuited to the local climate; the provision of schemes too far removed from the rural background of the residents; and the charging of expensive rents.

Suburbanised villages in developed countries

In parts of the developed world there has been a reversal of the movement to large urban areas, and groups of people have moved out into surrounding villages. This has led to a change in the character of such settlements and to their being called suburbanised (because they adopt some of the characteristics of the nearby urban areas) or commuter-dormitory towns (because many residents who live and sleep there travel to the nearby towns and cities for work).

Who moves into these villages?

☐ The more wealthy urban residents and those with improved family status. These groups have the money to afford the larger and often expensive houses, and the cost of travel to work, shops and amenities.

☐ Those wishing to move into a more attractive environment with less pollution and more space.

☐ Elderly people who have retired and wish to live in a quieter environment.

☐ Those seeing a chance to work in or develop a service industry that has resulted from the rising resident population and influx of visitors from nearby urban areas.

Changes in the villages Braithwaite is a small village on the edge of the Lake District in Cumbria (Figure 3.27). The 1925 map shows the original form of the village which then consisted of tightly grouped farms, outbuildings and terraced cottages along narrow lanes. Most buildings originated during the 18th and 19th centuries and one was a listed building. The village green gave an open character to the western half.

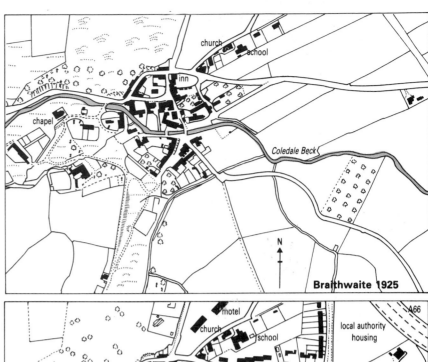

Braithwaite 1925

Braithwaite 1976

◁ **Figure 3.28** Suburbanisation north of Amsterdam. Along the canal (right) is the old core of the village of Schermerhorn; in the foreground is a new residential area; and in the background (looking west) is the rectangular landscape of a polder, a lake drained in the 17th century.

△ **Figure 3.27** A suburbanised village in the Lake District

By 1975 the character had changed due to increased mobility and accessibility. The village lies less than three miles from the tourist centre of Keswick, and next to the improved A66 which links West Cumbria and the M6.

Using the two maps (Figure 3.27) and your own knowledge, describe the likely changes in the village in terms of:
(a) The design and cost of houses
(b) The age and occupations (socio-economic groups) of the inhabitants
(c) Public and private transport
(d) Provision of services
(e) Quality of life of the original inhabitants
(f) The land use within and around the original village
(g) The demands made upon the area by nearby urban settlements.

What is migration?

Migration is a movement and in human terms usually means a change of home. However, as seen in Figure 4.1, it can be applied to temporary, seasonal and daily movements as well as to permanent changes both between countries and within a country.

Permanent migration (international) is the movement of people between countries. *Emigrants* are people who leave a country; *immigrants* are those who arrive in a country. The migration balance is the difference between the numbers of emigrants and immigrants. Countries with a net migration loss lose more through emigration than they gain by immigration and depending on the balance between their birth and death rates (page 7) they may have a declining population. Countries with a net migration gain receive more by immigration than they lose through emigration, and so will have an overall population increase (assuming birth and death rates are evenly balanced). International migration can be divided into two types – voluntary and forced:

Voluntary is the free movement where the migrants are looking for an improved quality of life and personal freedom, e.g.

- Employment — either to find a job, to earn higher salaries or to avoid paying tax
- Pioneers developing new areas
- Trade and economic expansion
- Territorial expansion
- Better climates, especially on retirement
- Social amenities such as hospitals, schools and entertainment
- To be with friends and relatives.

Permanent	External (international)		Between countries	
	i) voluntary		West Indians to Britain	
	ii) forced		Negro slaves to America	
	Internal		**Within a country**	
	i) rural depopulation		most developing countries	
	ii) urban depopulation		British conurbations	
	iii) regional		north west to south east of Britain	
Semi-Permanent	for several years		migrant workers in France & West Germany	
Seasonal	for several months		Mexican harvesters in California	
Daily	commuters		South East England	

△ **Figure 4.1** Types of migration

Forced is when the migrant has no personal choice but has to move due to natural disasters or to economic or social impositions, e.g.

- Religious and political persecution
- Wars, causing large numbers of refugees
- Forced labour as slaves or prisoners of war
- Racial discrimination
- Lack of food due to famine
- Natural disasters caused by floods, drought, earthquakes, volcanic eruptions or hurricanes
- Overpopulation when the number of people living in an area exceeds the resources available to them (page 6).

Figure 4.2 shows some major international migrations before 1900 AD, and Figure 4.3 some of the more recent changes. Using these maps, the list of reasons for migration given above, and your own knowledge, answer the following questions:

Voluntary migration List possible reasons for the following migrations:

Bantus into South Africa; British doctors to the USA; growth of the Roman Empire; development of British colonies; pop groups to America; elderly, wealthy Americans to Florida; West Indians to Britain; Europeans into the Prairies; and Mexicans into California.

Forced migration List possible reasons for the following migrations:

Negroes to the USA; Ethiopians into the Sudan; Jews from Nazi Germany; Joseph's brothers into ancient Egypt; Chinese into South East Asia; Pilgrim Fathers to New England; Ugandan Asians; Palestinian Arab refugees; Colombians from Armero; and tribesmen from Afghanistan.

▽ **Figure 4.2** Some of the major migrations before 1900 AD

indo-aryan
mongoloid
negroid
caucasoid
others

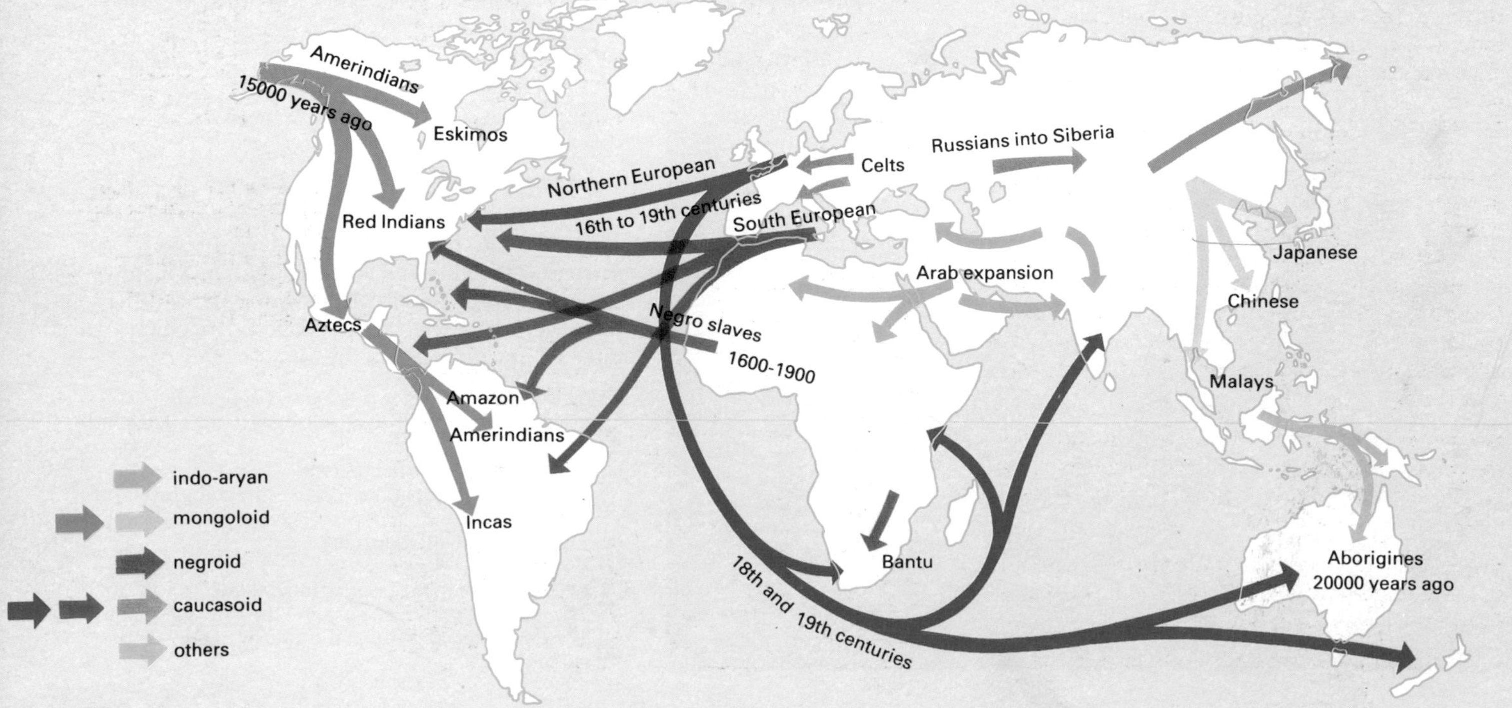

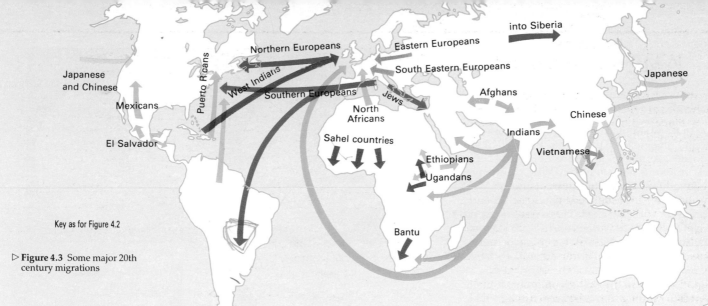

Key as for Figure 4.2

▷ **Figure 4.3** Some major 20th century migrations

Internal migration

Rural depopulation One of the major problems facing almost all the countries in the world, and especially those in the developing world, is that of rural depopulation, i.e. the drift (or in many cases the rush) from the countryside to the towns and cities. Most migrants travel only a short distance, and many from rural areas often migrate to a small town before moving to a larger city. The reasons for these movements are given on page 18.

It is claimed that between 1925 and 1950 10% of the world's rural population moved to urban areas, whereas between 1951 and 1975 this figure had accelerated to 24%. Zimbabwe is a typical example of a developing country experiencing rural depopulation. What does Figure 4.4 show about the age and sex structure of those migrants leaving rural areas and moving to the towns? What problems are created in the rural areas as a result of this population loss?

Urban depopulation Larger conurbations in the more developed countries are now showing a reversed trend with some of their inhabitants moving away into new towns, or into suburbanised villages (page 33). Greater London, for example, declined from 8.2 million people in 1951 to 6.7 million in 1981.

Regional movements These also reflect changes in areas of economic growth and decline in a country. In the USA there has been a steady westward movement in population, whereas in Brazil it has been towards the coast, and in the United Kingdom from the north and west to the south-east. Figure 4.5 shows how the distribution of population changed in the UK between 1921 and 1981.

Semi-permanent These migrations include the movement of 'guestworkers' from such areas as North Africa to France and from Turkey to West Germany (page 30).

Seasonal This type of migration includes nomads, transhumance farmers, Mexican harvesters in California (page 30) and tourists.

Daily Commuters are referred to on page 38.

Refugees

These are people who have fled from their homeland for fear of persecution for reasons of race, religion or nationality, or due to internal strife or environmental hardship, and have sought help and asylum from another country. In 1985 the United Nations (UN) suggested that there were 10 million refugees of whom 8 million lived in Africa (1 million in the Sudan). Half of the world's refugees are children, most adults are women, and four-fifths are in developing countries – those countries least able to help financially.

The recent refugee problem began nearly 50 years ago in war-torn Europe, although many refugees were later assimilated by their host country. It was the Palestinian Arab refugee camps which first showed that the problem had become permanent and seemingly insoluble. During the 1980s the major exoduses have been from Kampuchea, El Salvador, Afghanistan and Ethiopia (Figure 4.3). Among the receiving countries, in 1982, one immigrant in five in Jordan was a refugee, one in seven in Somalia and one in ten in Lebanon (in the UK it was only one in 384).

Refugees live in extreme poverty, lacking food, shelter, clothing, education and medical care. They have no citizenship, few, if any, rights, virtually no prospects and are unlikely to return to their homeland.

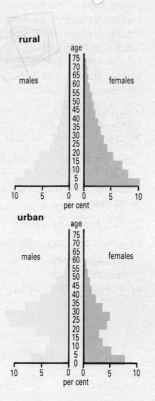

△ **Figure 4.4** Rural and urban population in Zimbabwe; age-sex structure

◁ **Figure 4.5** Distribution of population in the UK (percentages of total UK population)

Standard region	1921	1931	1951	1961	1971	1981
North	6.9	6.6	6.2	6.1	5.9	5.6
Yorks and Humberside	9.3	9.4	9.0	8.8	8.7	8.8
North West	13.6	13.4	12.8	12.4	12.1	11.5
East Midlands	5.3	5.5	5.8	5.9	6.1	6.8
West Midlands	8.0	8.1	8.8	9.0	9.2	9.2
East Anglia	2.8	2.7	2.8	2.8	3.0	3.2
South East	27.9	29.4	30.2	31.0	31.1	30.1
South West	6.2	6.1	6.5	6.5	6.8	7.7
Wales	6.0	5.6	5.1	5.0	4.9	5.0
Scotland	11.1	10.5	10.1	9.8	9.4	9.2
Northern Ireland	2.9	2.7	2.7	2.7	2.8	2.9

Migrant workers

Turkish migrants into West Germany

Due to a low standard of living and a shortage of jobs at home, many Turks have migrated to other countries. As shown in Figure 4.6(a), most of these migrants have moved to West Germany.

Like other western European countries, West Germany needed rebuilding when the Second World War ended in 1945. There were many more job vacancies than workers and so extra labour was needed. Later, as West Germany became increasingly affluent, it attracted workers from the poorer parts of Europe and the Middle East (Figure 4.6(b)). Many of these migrants initially went into farming, but they soon turned to the relatively better-paid jobs in factories and the construction industry. These jobs were not wanted by the Germans because they were dirty, unskilled, poorly paid and often demanded long and unsociable hours (in 1980, 5000 Turks were employed by Ford's car factory in Cologne). By 1983 West Germany had 4.6 million 'Gastarbeiter' or 'guest workers', accounting for 9.5% of the total workforce, and 29% of these migrants had come from Turkey. However, although the Turks had found full employment in the 1950s and 1960s, by 1983 nearly 17% were out of work. This was mainly because it was the manufacturing industry which was hardest hit by the recession, and in this situation it is the unskilled jobs which tend to be lost first.

Figure 4.7 shows the imbalance between males and females, and between age groups of migrant workers into West Germany (this is typical of other cities and countries receiving large numbers of migrant workers). Some of the advantages and disadvantages of this pattern are listed in Figure 4.8.

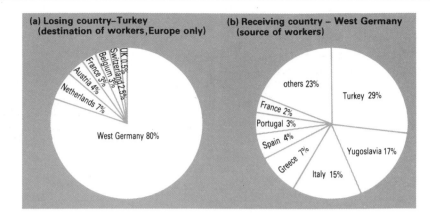

(a) Losing country–Turkey (destination of workers, Europe only)

(b) Receiving country – West Germany (source of workers)

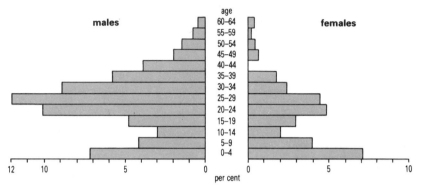

males   females

△ **Figure 4.6** Turks in West Germany, 1983

△ **Figure 4.7** Age-sex structure of Turkish immigrants into West Germany

▽ **Figure 4.8** Advantages and disadvantages of migration to the 'losing' and 'receiving' countries.

In common with other western European countries, West Germany imposed a ban on the recruitment of foreign workers after 1973, although Turks still arrived to make family reunions and to seek political asylum. In 1980 new laws reduced the right of asylum and grants were given to Turks wishing to return home. Very few have taken advantage of this offer though even fewer have taken out German citizenship. The Turks have their own 'centres' in West Berlin, Cologne, Frankfurt and Dusseldorf where they have their own dress, films, kebabs, coffee and music and where, without them, transport, hospital and electricity services would probably come to a halt.

Mexican workers in California

Since 1940 many Mexicans have migrated northwards into the USA on a temporary rather than a permanent basis. Mexican males move to the USA to work on large agricultural estates and in hotels and restaurants. Many do not possess documents and enter the USA illegally, leaving their families behind. The attraction is earning more during one to three months in the USA than during a full year in Mexico. Estimates suggest that the 3000km frontier between the USA and Mexico is crossed by over 4 million illegal migrants each year despite efforts made by patrol guards using horses, aeroplanes and other advanced detective equipment. Yet these migrants are essential to the American economy where they take the harder, dirtier, more monotonous, less skilled, less well-paid jobs in the construction industry and on farms at harvest times. Migrant labour provides half of California's workforce, yet at times of industrial recession, or at non-harvest times, they are 'returned home'.

	Advantages	Disadvantages
Losing country		
	Reduces pressure on jobs and resources (e.g. food)	Loses people in working age group
	Loses people of child-bearing age causing decline in birth rate	Loses people most lively to have some education and skills
		Mainly males leave causing a division in families
		Left with an elderly population and so a high death rate
Receiving country		
	Overcomes labour shortage	Pressure on jobs but most likely to be the first to be unemployed in a recession
	Prepared to do dirty, unskilled jobs	Low-quality, overcrowded housing lacking in basic amenities (bidonvilles in France, favelas, inner city slums)
	Prepared to work long hours for low salaries (London underground)	Ethnic groups tend not to integrate
	Cultural advantages and links (e.g. Notting Hill carnival)	Racial tension
	Some highly skilled migrants (e.g. Pakistani doctors)	Limited skilled/educated group
	In a developing country these migrants could increase the number of skilled workers	Lack of opportunities to practise their own religion, culture etc.
		Language difficulties
		Often less healthy

Migrations and apartheid

Voluntary Migration

Whites came to South Africa from Europe. Originally Dutch, they moved inland (Boers) when the British arrived in the Cape. The 'Great Trek' led to the creation of the three northern and eastern provinces.

Blacks are Bantu speaking, negroid stock who moved southwards shortly after the arrival of the Dutch (or Afrikaners as they became known).

Asians came from India and Malaysia during colonial times.

Seasonal migration

Many Bantus from surrounding countries (Figure 4.9) migrate to South Africa to work in factories and in mines. Legally they are only allowed to stay in the country for six months at a time.

Forced migration

Slaves were taken, and later political refugees were forced to leave countries such as India, Malaysia, Indonesia and Sri Lanka. White fathers and Asian 'slave' mothers had led to the creation of a new 'race', or ethnic minority – the *Cape Coloureds* – by the time slavery was abolished in 1834.

Many blacks had to move following the 'legalisation of apartheid' in 1959. Apartheid means separate development for whites and blacks. It created a system by which the whites had all possible rights and the blacks none (the Asians and coloureds were given very few). There was complete segregation in housing, transport, restaurants, schools, cinemas and at sporting and cultural events. Blacks had to carry passes at all times until 1986 and could be imprisoned without trial. They were not allowed any political party, and could only vote in tribal assemblies in their 'homelands'. The white South African government defended this policy by saying that the blacks had only come to work in South Africa and so were not permanent residents and that it followed that only basic necessities needed to be granted to them.

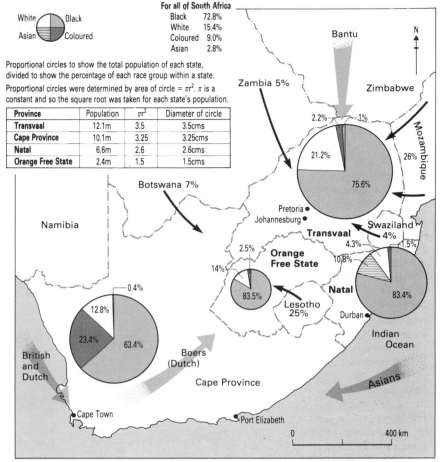

Province	Population	πr^2	Diameter of circle
Transvaal	12.1m	3.5	3.5cms
Cape Province	10.1m	3.25	3.25cms
Natal	6.6m	2.6	2.6cms
Orange Free State	2.4m	1.5	1.5cms

For all of South Africa
Black 72.8%
White 15.4%
Coloured 9.0%
Asian 2.8%

Proportional circles to show the total population of each state, divided to show the percentage of each race group within a state.

Proportional circles were determined by area of circle = πr^2. π is a constant and so the square root was taken for each state's population.

Voluntary migration mainly 18th and 19th centuries

Recent 'temporary' migration for work – per cent of total migrants

26%

――― province boundary

―·―·― national frontier

Transvaal name of province

△ **Figure 4.9** Distribution of compulsory race classification in South Africa, mid-1983

Homelands Blacks were further classified into nine tribal groups who had to live in one of ten reserves or 'homelands'. These were created after 1976, and by 1985 four had been given independence – though only South Africa recognises this independence. The homelands take up 13% of South Africa's land, hold 72% of the total population and create 3% of the country's wealth. It is estimated that 3½ million blacks have been forced to move to these homelands to live in areas of overpopulation which are disease ridden, drought affected, far removed from minerals, factories, jobs and power stations and which offer only overgrazed and eroded soils. Whereas the national infant mortality rate is 15 per 1000, on some homelands it is up to 250 per 1000. A black wishing for a job in the city is given a contract, but having lived in the city for a short time, he must return to the homeland before another contract can be signed.

Townships have been created for the 'urban blacks'. These are away from white residential areas, and the blacks have long and expensive journeys to work. Many of the original shanty settlements have been bulldozed and replaced by rows of similar houses (Figure 4.10). These houses are single storey with four rooms. Toilets are in backyards and only 20% of the houses have electricity. The corrugated roofs make the buildings very hot in summer and very cold in winter. The largest township, Soweto (Greater Johannesburg), had 1½ million inhabitants in 1985.

Figure 4.10 Housing in Soweto

Migration in the UK

The United Kingdom has experienced many waves of immigrants and our society has always been one of mixed races and cultures. Today's racial tension however is rooted in the fact that colour of skin has become an issue for the white population – a problem not encountered by previous immigrants and one which is not easily solved since it is a biological rather than a social difference.

☐ The late 1940s and the 1950s were a time when Britain was short of labour following the Second World War. Many West Indians arrived due partly to overpopulation and poverty in their own islands, but due mainly to the 'pull' of jobs in Britain. The British government invited many to apply for permission to enter the country for specific jobs, e.g. with London Transport. The number of immigrants rose and fell according to the number of job vacancies.

☐ Some Asians, such as religious and political refugees following the division of India and Pakistan, came to Britain during the 1950s; these included Sikhs, Hindus and Muslims.

☐ The Commonwealth Immigrants Act, 1962, reduced the number of non-white immigrants unless they were dependants of relatives already in Britain, or had specific jobs, especially those involving certain skills which were in short supply in Britain, e.g. doctors.

☐ In 1972 the law was temporarily relaxed to allow Asians with British citizenship who had been expelled from Uganda to move to Britain.

☐ During the 70s and 80s an increasing number of people of Asian or Afro-Caribbean origin were born in Britain. By 1977 about 40% were 'second generation' (i.e. British born) blacks.

☐ By AD 2000 the black and Asian population will probably have stabilised at about 6% of Britain's total population. Some 65-70% of these will have been born in Britain.

Uneven concentrations of ethnic groups

Immigrants avoided areas which had high unemployment levels (Scotland, Northern Ireland) and went to large cities and conurbations (not small towns) where there were greater chances of finding jobs. At the same time, many white people were moving out and so low quality housing was available. The greatest concentrations are in London, the West and East Midlands and West Yorkshire. There was also a tendency for one ethnic group to concentrate in a particular area, e.g. Pakistanis in West Yorkshire and West Indians in Birmingham.

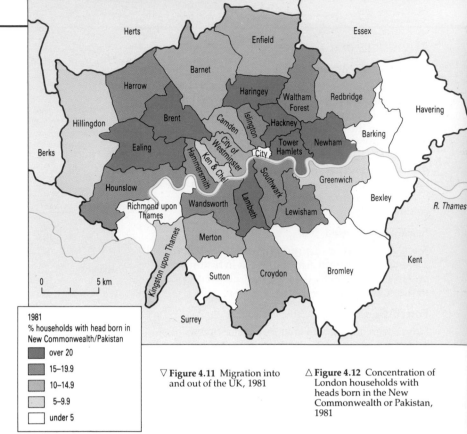

1981
% households with head born in New Commonwealth/Pakistan

- over 20
- 15–19.9
- 10–14.9
- 5–9.9
- under 5

▽ **Figure 4.11** Migration into and out of the UK, 1981

△ **Figure 4.12** Concentration of London households with heads born in the New Commonwealth or Pakistan, 1981

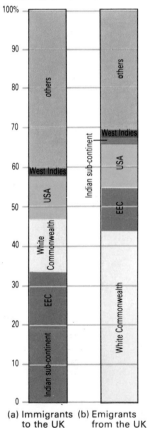

(a) Immigrants to the UK (b) Emigrants from the UK

Even in these larger urban areas, newcomers concentrated in particular parts of cities due to the availability of housing and access to jobs and in order to be with people of similar ethnic background. These areas (Figure 4.12) tend to be in the old inner cities. Although nowhere have the ghettos of New York developed in Britain, ethnic groups having a similar religion, language, diet, social organisation and culture tend to concentrate together for security, e.g. Jamaicans in Brixton, Anguillans in Slough, Sikhs in Southall and Bengalis in East London. Yet, as history has shown in many parts of the world, these concentrations tend to lead to fear, prejudice, and jealousy among rival communities.

Some longer-established immigrants in the higher socio-economic groups do find accommodation in the suburbs.

Problems facing ethnic minorities

The Scarman Report, following the 1981 riots in English cities, identified four main problems.

Housing Most blacks and Asians (80%) live in overcrowded buildings which they are able to rent or buy cheaply because they are sub-standard or in undesirable areas.

Education Blacks and Asians often experience language difficulties, making them more disadvantaged. In addition the schools they attend are often old and lack resources.

Group	% of England's population	% of own age group		% of own group			% of own group employed		
		under 16	over 60	living in conurbations	given new accommodation	lacking own bath, wc & hot water	professional managerial	semi and unskilled	unemployed 16–29 years old
White	96	24	17	32	64	18	40	18	15
Black and Asian	4	33	4	80	30	35–40	14	37	25

◁ **Figure 4.13** Inequality in England

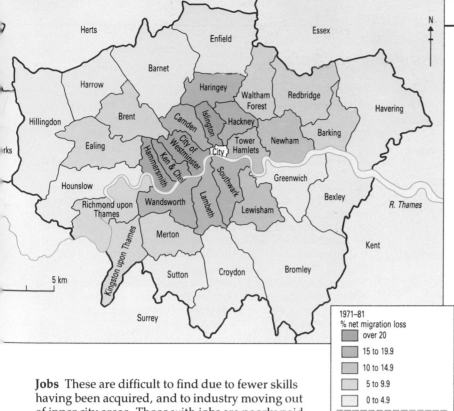

△ **Figure 4.14** Population movement in Greater London, 1971–81

Legend:
1971–81
% net migration loss
- over 20
- 15 to 19.9
- 10 to 14.9
- 5 to 9.9
- 0 to 4.9
- net increase

▽ **Figure 4.15** Population change in Belfast, 1971–81

Jobs These are difficult to find due to fewer skills having been acquired, and to industry moving out of inner city areas. Those with jobs are poorly paid and so cannot afford good housing – a vicious circle.

Discrimination This was regarded by Scarman to be (and still is) a major obstacle to assimilation.

Other problems include high birth rates and large families; crime and vandalism; a poor environment and strained police–community relations.

Movement out of large cities

The 1981 census showed an increasing trend among people who had previously lived in large cities and conurbations to move out into new towns, overspill towns and suburbanised villages. The biggest outward movement is taking place in the inner cities, and it is because of this movement outwards that newly arrived immigrants and people on low incomes can find accommodation.

Figure 4.14 shows the outward movement in London. The inner city areas, which are often adjacent to the River Thames, suffer the greatest loss. However, until the 1970s, many people initially moved into the outer suburbs. But the 1981 census showed that even these areas were beginning to lose population. The only anomaly (an instance which does not fit the usual pattern) is 'The City' which is still the commercial centre, but which now has such housing developments as the Barbican.

Who moves out?

☐ Those with higher incomes now capable of buying their own homes.

☐ Parents with young children who want gardens, parks and larger homes.

☐ Those with higher skills and qualifications who move to new towns where modern industry and offices tend to be located.

Why do they move?

Accommodation People will try to move away from small, terraced houses or high-rise flats. Older houses are of poorer quality, lack amenities, are often rented and are closely packed.

Employment People move either because of promotion, for better prospects or simply to find a job. As industry declines in the cramped, expensive inner city sites, most new jobs are created on the edge of town industrial (trading) estates, or in new towns.

Changing family status This may be the result of an increase in wealth or family size.

Environmental factors These include moving away from noise, air and visual pollution created by traffic or declining industry. People also prefer having access to more open space. In some cases redevelopment schemes force people out (page 20).

Social factors These include prejudice against neighbours and ethnic groups, and the above average crime and vandalism rate. It might mean moving nearer to friends and relatives.

Cycle of change Recently there has been a 'reversed' movement by wealthy people moving back into parts of inner London. Derelict property can be bought cheaply, refurbished and transformed into expensive houses and flats. This process is encouraged by property developers and estate agents. Schemes such as those in Islington and along the banks of the Thames (using disused warehouses) do not benefit the needs of the local inhabitants (page 75) who cannot afford the high prices of the new properties.

Belfast

1 Where is the only district to have increased its population between 1971 and 1981?

2 Which parts of Belfast have the highest percentage of people moving out? What does this suggest about the people who lived here in 1971?

3 Which parts of Belfast have well above the average population loss for the city? What do you think these areas will be like?

4 Why are the numbers moving out of Belfast greater than those moving out of London? Where do you think they will move to?

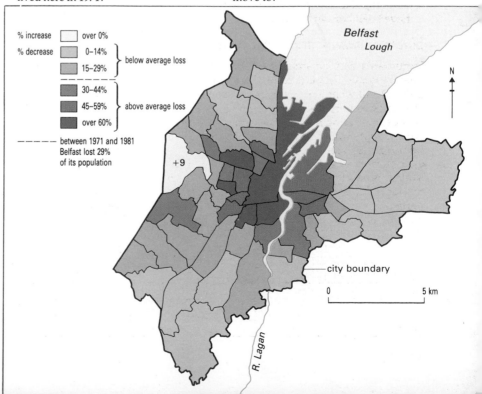

Legend:
% increase — over 0%
% decrease:
- 0–14% } below average loss
- 15–29%
- 30–44% } above average loss
- 45–59%
- over 60%
- - - - between 1971 and 1981 Belfast lost 29% of its population
— city boundary

Urbanisation and migration

1 *(Figure 3.4, page 17)*

a) Which was the largest city in the world in 1970?

b) Which continent contained two of the 12 largest cities in the world in 1970 and yet none in 1985?

c) By how many millions is Mexico City's population predicted to increase between 1970 and 2000 AD?

d) Give one point to describe the distribution of the 12 largest cities in the world in:
(i) 1970 *(ii)* AD 2000 (5)

2 *(Pages 18, 24 and 25)*

A feature of cities in the developing world is that they are growing very rapidly as people move to them from surrounding rural areas.

a) *(i)* What is this movement from the countryside called? (1)
(ii) Give three reasons why people may wish to move *into* a city from the surrounding countryside (urban *pull* factors). (3)
(iii) Give three reasons why people may have to move *away* from the countryside (rural *push* factors). (3)

b) *(i)* Name four problems likely to occur in urban areas when large numbers of people move into them. (4)
(ii) How are urban authorities trying to overcome these problems? (3)

3 *(Pages 20-21)*

Four residential environments are labelled A to D on pages 20-21.

a) For each area:
(i) Describe the type, appearance, age and ownership of its housing. (4)
(ii) Describe its road pattern. (2)
(iii) Give the approximate cost of housing (remembering there will be a difference between the south and the north of Britain). (1)
(iv) Describe and give reasons for its land use. (4)
(v) Describe its household and neighbourhood amenities. (4)
(vi) List the advantages and disadvantages of living in the area. (4)

b) What is meant by the following terms: socio-economic group; non–manual; housing tenure; owner occupied; suburbia; council estates; redevelopment; housing amenities; and housing density? (9)

c) Giving a reason for your answer in each case, say which of the four areas has (i) the least and (ii) the most of each of the following: elderly; young couples; young children; unemployed; immigrants; garages; open space; basic household amenities; housing density; professional and managerial. (10 × 3)

d) The four maps on pages 20-21 show different types of land use in each area.
(i) Take a piece of tracing paper 7cm × 7cm and divide it into 100 squares (1 square to equal 1%). Place the tracing paper over each map in turn, and determine the percentage of land use for each of the following categories: housing; open space and gardens; industry; transport; wasteland; services (schools, shops). (4 × 3)
(ii) Draw a histogram for *each* area to show your results. (4)

e) Make a journey along a main road from the CBD to the city boundary. Describe any changes in the housing that you see on your journey. (4)

4 *(Pages 20-21)*

a) *(i)* Which set of statistics, A, B or C is most likely to represent the area located at 1 on the map above? Give three reasons for your answer. (½ + 1½)
(ii) Which set of statistics A, B or C is most likely to represent the area located at 3 on the map? Give three reasons for your answer. (½ + 1½)

b) *(i)* Describe the differences you would expect to find in the design and layout of the housing in the residential areas located at 1 and 3. (2)
(ii) Suggest two reasons for these differences. (2)

c) *(i)* Give two advantages of living in area 1. (2)
(ii) Give two disadvantages of living in area 1. (2)
(iii) Give two advantages of living in area 3. (2)
(iv) Give two disadvantages of living in area 3. (2)

d) *(i)* How may changes in family wealth or family size affect the type of area in which people might live? (4)

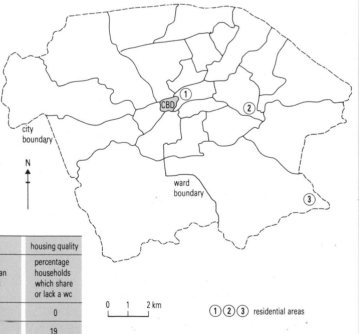

residential areas	housing tenure			housing density		housing quality
	% owner occupied	% owned by the council	% rented	households with over 1.5 persons per room	households with less than 0.5 persons per room	percentage households which share or lack a wc
set of statistics (a)	98	0	2	1	84	0
set of statistics (b)	24	34	42	19	35	19
set of statistics (c)	62	14	24	8	14	10

0 1 2 km

①②③ residential areas

5 *(Figure 3.22, page 25)*

The diagram opposite is an incomplete model of a city in the developing world.

a) Match up the following with letters A to F on the model (Figure 3.22):
   (i) Modern, luxury high-rise flats.
   (ii) Squatters who have built shanty towns (favelas).
   (iii) A large shopping centre with tall office blocks.
   (iv) A suburban luxury estate for professional workers.
   (v) Modern factories built alongside main roads leading out of the city.
   (vi) An area where some houses have had piped water and electricity added, yet are still of poor quality. (6)

b) Describe the housing conditions likely to be found in the shanty town (favela). (4)

c) Describe *two* different schemes which have been used to try to improve the housing of shanty towns. (4)

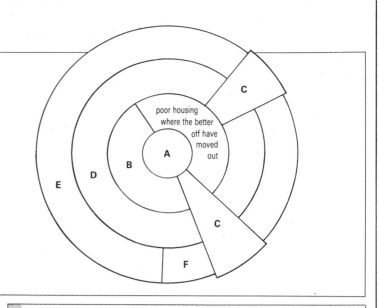

6 *(Page 30)*

a) *(i)* Put in rank order (the highest first) the five countries from which most migrant workers to West Germany came in the early 1970s. (5)
   (ii) What is the largest number of migrants from any one country (to the nearest 1000)? (3)

b) *(i)* Describe and suggest reasons for the pattern shown on the map. (6)
   (ii) State two of the problems which may arise in countries from which large numbers of migrants leave to work elsewhere. (2)

c) *(i)* Describe and suggest reasons for the types of work foreign workers in West Germany might be engaged in. (3)
   (ii) What probems do migrant workers create for the host country? (3)

d) By the mid-1980s the West German Government had almost stopped the inflow of migrant workers. Why do you think this was done? (2)

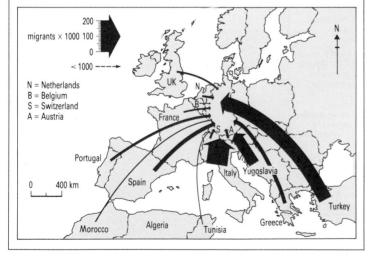

migrants × 1000

N = Netherlands
B = Belgium
S = Switzerland
A = Austria

0   400 km

7 *(Figure 4.7 and page 30)*

Using the population pyramid showing the age-sex structure of the migrant population into West Germany:

a) What percentage of the migrant population (males and females) is aged between 15 and 19? (1)

b) *(i)* Which are the four main age groups of immigrants? (4)
   (ii) Are there more male or female immigrants? (1)
   (iii) Suggest three reasons for your answers. (3)

8 *(Page 32)*

a) *(i)* Explain the meaning of the term 'new commonwealth immigrants'. (2)
   (ii) Name two new commonwealth countries. (1)

b) Four wards have been labelled A, B, J and K below.
   (i) Which ward has the greatest number of people living in it? (1)
   (ii) Which ward has the highest proportion of new commonwealth immigrants living in it? Why is this? (2)
   (iii) Which ward has the lowest proportion of new commonwealth immigrants living in it? Why is this? (2)
   (iv) Why does ward B have an above average number of new commonwealth immigrants for an edge-of-city ward? (1)

c) What are the problems any immigrant might face when he or she arrives in a new country as far as the following are concerned? (5)
   (i) Accommodation
   (ii) Employment
   (iii) Language
   (iv) Culture
   (v) Prejudice

20 000
15 000
10 000
7 500

0   1 km

main industrial areas

areas in which there is a serious lack of household amenities

proportion of population born in New Commonwealth

central business district

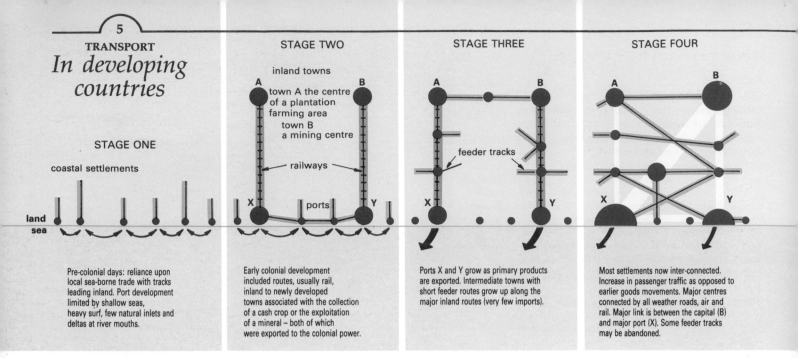

TRANSPORT
In developing countries

STAGE ONE

coastal settlements

land

sea

Pre-colonial days: reliance upon local sea-borne trade with tracks leading inland. Port development limited by shallow seas, heavy surf, few natural inlets and deltas at river mouths.

STAGE TWO

inland towns

A   B

town A the centre of a plantation farming area

town B a mining centre

railways

X   ports   Y

Early colonial development included routes, usually rail, inland to newly developed towns associated with the collection of a cash crop or the exploitation of a mineral – both of which were exported to the colonial power.

STAGE THREE

A   B

feeder tracks

X   Y

Ports X and Y grow as primary products are exported. Intermediate towns with short feeder routes grow up along the major inland routes (very few imports).

STAGE FOUR

A   B

X   Y

Most settlements now inter-connected. Increase in passenger traffic as opposed to earlier goods movements. Major centres connected by all weather roads, air and rail. Major link is between the capital (B) and major port (X). Some feeder tracks may be abandoned.

Transport systems in developing countries tend to be relatively simple and limited in coverage. They tend, in urban areas, to be over used and, in rural areas, to be outdated. The initial systems were often constructed by colonial powers seeking to obtain primary products for their own consumption, and were built for moving goods rather than passengers. Figure 5.1 attempts to show how transport patterns may have evolved in a developing country. Since independence, few countries have had sufficient money to improve and modernise their communication systems other than those between and within the major urban areas, and the building of a prestigious airport. As a result:

☐ Few roads are surfaced and tend to become dust tracks in the dry season and quagmires in the wet season.

☐ Public transport is heavily over used with passengers hanging onto or riding on top of trains and buses. Relatively few inhabitants can afford private cars.

☐ Railways, built during colonial days, were not designed for passenger traffic, and their rolling stock is outdated.

☐ Port development is often hindered by physical problems such as those listed in stage one in Figure 5.1.

☐ Airports tend to be built for overseas business persons and tourists rather than for the individual needs of the country.

Ghana

☐ Ghana, before colonial rule, had numerous coastal ports, mainly devoted to fishing. Until recently, they could not accommodate large ships due to the shallow sea and surf. Goods had to be loaded onto canoes and lighters for journeys between the land and ocean-going ships (stage one of Figure 5.1).

☐ Colonial development led to the establishment of cocoa plantations. Railways (stage two) were built to move the cocoa to the coast in readiness for its export to Britain.

☐ Later developments included roads between the south and the north, and the growth of intermediate towns (stage three).

☐ Before 1966 the River Volta had not been used due to rapids, low water levels during the dry season, and bars and the delta at its mouth.

☐ Recently piers have been built at Takoradi and Tema to accommodate large ships, with the resultant closure of the remaining surf ports. Internal air routes concentrate on the triangle between Accra, Kumasi and Takoradi (Figure 5.2).

△ **Figure 5.1** Model illustrating the evolution of routes and modes of travel in a developing country

▷ **Figure 5.2** Transport systems in Ghana. In 1966 the Volta was dammed at Akosombo, and a lake 500km in length was created offering opportunities for the development of cheap water-borne transport for heavy goods and to less accessible areas (page 55). Unfortunately, the main north-south road routes have been flooded, causing considerable congestion where ferries now have to operate, as at Yeji.

Using an atlas

1 Trace the present day railway network for the following countries: Angola, Nigeria, Tanzania and Brazil. Mark on your maps the main towns.

2 Have any of these countries, all of which are regarded as developing countries, reached stage four of the model shown in Figure 5.1?

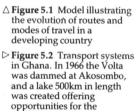

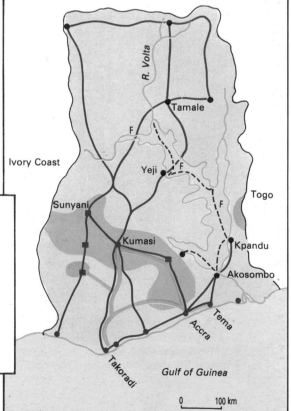

●	coastal ports
	cocoa belt
■	towns in cocoa belt
●	other towns
	Lake Volta
	Volta Delta
F	ferry
- - -	ferry routes
——	roads
～～	railways

R. Volta

Tamale

Ivory Coast

Yeji

Sunyani

Togo

Kumasi

Kpandu

Akosombo

Tema

Accra

Takoradi

Gulf of Guinea

0   100 km

Where traditional transport is best

The Sahara

Other than flying over the desert, the form of transport most suited to the extreme physical conditions of the Sahara is still the camel. Figure 5.3 shows how the camel is adapted to living in a desert environment and why it is so useful to the bedouin and other desert dwellers.

South America

Large tracts of South America still have no modern transport. This is partly due to a lack of money, and partly because much of the continent imposes severe physical constraints on the building of roads, railways and airports. The Incas, living high up in the Andes, are the only major civilisation in history to have developed without the use of the wheel. This was not because they were unaware of its existence but because of its limitations on the steep mountain sides. Instead the Incas used the donkey and the llama as beasts of burden, as do their descendants today.

▷ **Figure 5.3** The camel

▽ **Figure 5.4** Dugout canoes are still used by Lacandon Indians in Central America where vegetation is too dense for land routes

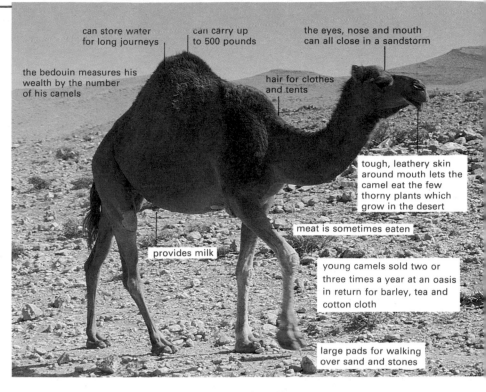

can store water for long journeys

can carry up to 500 pounds

the eyes, nose and mouth can all close in a sandstorm

the bedouin measures his wealth by the number of his camels

hair for clothes and tents

tough, leathery skin around mouth lets the camel eat the few thorny plants which grow in the desert

meat is sometimes eaten

provides milk

young camels sold two or three times a year at an oasis in return for barley, tea and cotton cloth

large pads for walking over sand and stones

Within much of tropical America large rivers have afforded the only easy routes into the interior. Even today many South American tribes still use the dugout canoe as their major form of transport in the forest (Figure 5.4). Even more traditional are the Totora reed boats which are used by the Oru tribe who fish in Lake Titicaca. Reeds also provide the 'ground' for this tribe to live on. As the bottom layers rot, the Indians spread new layers on top to form floating islands.

India

India is a land of stark contrasts. Modern jet aircraft cross its skies; fast electric trains connect its big cities; air-conditioned cars, buses and trucks move along its highways. The fast, air-conditioned Rajdhani expresses run at 150km an hour, covering the 1500km between Delhi and Bombay and Delhi and Calcutta in less than 17 hours, with perhaps only two stops. By contrast, local trains move at only 20km an hour with numerous stops every few kilometres.

Yet for most of the 75% of Indians who live in rural areas, the bullock cart remains the main vehicle. It carries the bulk of the farmer's produce to market, and is used to transport goods between villages and larger urban areas. It is an example of appropriate intermediate technology described on page 67. The Indian government is now making efforts to try to improve the wheels, carriage and harnessing devices to enhance the capability of this ancient vehicle. It is estimated that there are about 13 million animal-drawn carts in the country, which provide employment for about 20 million people. Planners now suggest that to encourage growth in the rural sector, efforts must be made to modernise bullock carts and develop roads. They also call for proper co-ordination between road transport and bullock carts, on the one hand, and rail and road transport on the other.

TRANSPORT
In developed countries

Commuting

Daily movement in all urban areas shows a distinctive pattern. There are two peak periods associated with the movement to work in the morning, and home again in the late afternoon. A commuter is a person who lives in a smaller town or village in the area surrounding a larger town or city, and who travels to that larger town or city for work. The term is also now applied to residents living in the suburbs of a large town or city. The increase in car ownership and the improvement in road networks means that more commuters live further from their place of work. This has led to increasingly large commuter 'hinterlands' (the areas around large cities) where commuters live.

Why do people commute?

While it is true that some people like commuting so that they can live away from their place of work, most resent the time and, especially in South East England, the cost involved. So why commute? Some commuters travel long distances so that they can live in a pleasanter environment. Travel time rather than cost may be a limiting factor for this group. Young people may commute because housing is cheaper in outlying towns and villages. Elderly commuters may have bought property in more rural areas in preparation for their retirement.

Whereas these groups commute 'voluntarily', others who have lived in towns for many years and who have lost their jobs may be 'forced' to look for employment in nearby urban areas.

Figure 5.6 shows, in the case of Amsterdam, how an increasing proportion of the city's workforce now commutes. A more recent trend is a 'reversed' flow of commuters. This group tends to be less skilled, to include members of ethnic minorities and to live in low cost inner city housing. These people have long journeys to work on the new edge-of-city industrial estates.

Problems caused by commuters in city centres

☐ Congestion, especially at peak hours, because most commuters prefer to travel by car (although, in London, most people do use public transport); and under-use of resources at off-peak times.

☐ Air pollution from car exhausts – a problem especially acute in Los Angeles and Tokyo where smog is a common occurrence. (Lead pollution from car exhausts can cause brain damage and mental retardation.)

☐ Noise pollution from cars and lorries.

☐ Visual pollution of motorways.

☐ Parking problems.

☐ Increased risk of accidents.

☐ Cost of building urban freeways, many of which are multi-lane.

☐ Destruction of houses and open spaces to create urban motorways.

☐ A reduction of public transport has meant increased hardship for the minority of non-car owning households (about 45% in the UK).

☐ Cost of energy consumption and the utilisation of oil supplies.

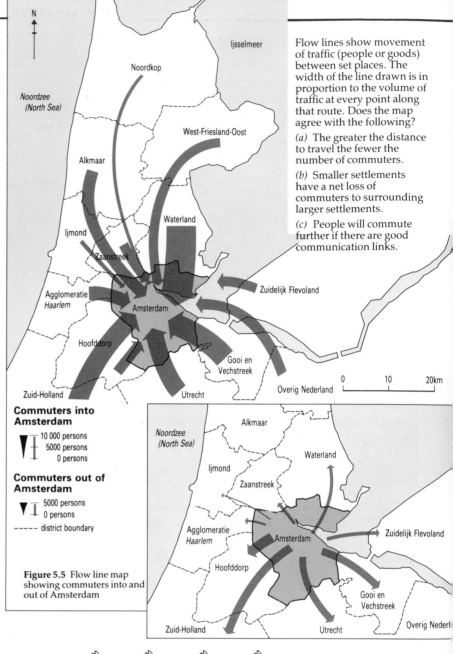

Flow lines show movement of traffic (people or goods) between set places. The width of the line drawn is in proportion to the volume of traffic at every point along that route. Does the map agree with the following?

(a) The greater the distance to travel the fewer the number of commuters.

(b) Smaller settlements have a net loss of commuters to surrounding larger settlements.

(c) People will commute further if there are good communication links.

Commuters into Amsterdam
- 10 000 persons
- 5000 persons
- 0 persons

Commuters out of Amsterdam
- 5000 persons
- 0 persons
- - - - - district boundary

Figure 5.5 Flow line map showing commuters into and out of Amsterdam

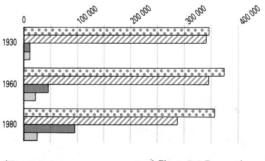

△ **Figure 5.6** Bar graph showing changes in population and commuting into and out of Amsterdam

- total employment
- employees living in Amsterdam
- incoming commuters
- outgoing commuters

▷ **Figure 5.8** The M25 – the pros and cons

▽ **Figure 5.9** Freeways in Los Angeles

Some urban transport solutions

Paris

Several schemes can be summarised as follows:

- An inner ring road (or *périphérique*) which surrounds the old city centre, and reduces traffic problems in 'Paris Ville'.

- Urban motorways such as the A86 (or *L'Autoroute Urbaine*). This encircles eastern Paris linking the two airports (Charles de Gaulle and Orly), and the motorways leading from the Channel Ports (*Autoroute du Nord*) to the south of France (*Autoroute du Soleil*).

- The Réseau Express Régional (RER) is a high speed (96km per hour) electric underground system (Paris already had a metro). The initial three routes will link both airports with each other and the CBD, the new commercial centre of La Défense, and the five new towns surrounding Paris.

London and the M25

This motorway, completed in 1986, encircles London, linking motorways and main roads from other parts of England. It is now much easier to drive from one side of London to the other without having to pass through the city itself (Figure 5.7). As with most new schemes, some groups of people were in favour of the M25 and others against it. Figure 5.8 lists seven groups of people who hold differing views as to the relevance and success of the motorway.

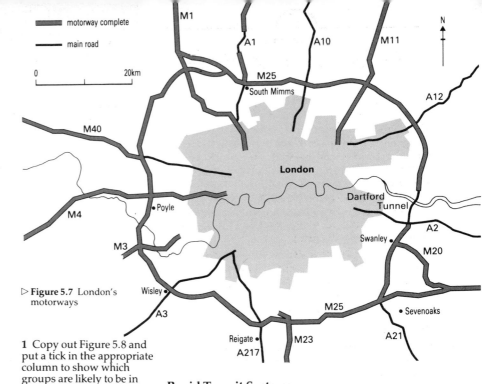

▷ **Figure 5.7** London's motorways

1 Copy out Figure 5.8 and put a tick in the appropriate column to show which groups are likely to be in favour of this scheme, and which against it. Give a reason for each of your answers.

2 Can you add to the list other groups likely to have views on the scheme?

3 What would your own decision be?

Group	For	Against	Reason
People living in houses alongside the new motorway			
Firms in towns north of London sending goods by road to places south			
People living in central London on streets used by heavy lorries			
Farmers whose land will be crossed by the motorway			
Firms in central London sending goods by road to the rest of Britain and the EEC			
Hospitals and traffic police in the middle of London			
Building workers			

Rapid Transit Systems

These are adopted increasingly in large urban areas. The first one in Britain was the Tyne and Wear Metro (Figure 5.10) which opened in 1980 and integrated public and private transport systems. The trains travel for over 55km, both overground (mainly linking the suburbs, coastal and commuter settlements) and underground (inner city and city centre areas). Much of the track used was formerly part of a British Rail system. Of the 46 stations, 15 are new (7 are underground), and the remainder have been modernised with special facilities for the elderly and disabled. Buses link with several Metro stations (tickets can be used on either form of transport) while other stations have free car parking facilities. Its advantages include speed, comfort and relative cheapness, together with cleanliness and the fact that it removes travellers from previously congested main roads.

Other Schemes These include Park and Ride, tidal (contra) flow, bus lanes, one way systems, computerised 'Dial a Bus' services and monorails.

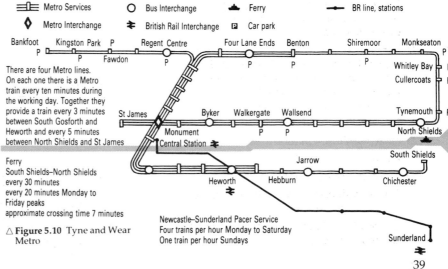

There are four Metro lines. On each one there is a Metro train every ten minutes during the working day. Together they provide a train every 3 minutes between South Gosforth and Heworth and every 5 minutes between North Shields and St James

Ferry
South Shields–North Shields every 30 minutes
every 20 minutes Monday to Friday peaks
approximate crossing time 7 minutes

Newcastle–Sunderland Pacer Service
Four trains per hour Monday to Saturday
One train per hour Sundays

△ **Figure 5.10** Tyne and Wear Metro

Ports

Traditional British ports

These grew up on the west and south coasts and were linked with the colonial trade. Glasgow, Liverpool and Bristol had connections with the Americas; Southampton and London with Africa and Australasia. However, in the last 30 years these ports have declined considerably due to such factors as the gaining of independence by the former colonies, the increase in rival merchant fleets (by 1984 Britain had fallen to eighth place in the world), an increase in containerisation, the introduction of Ro-Ro (roll on, roll off) loading, and greater links with the EEC. These factors, together with an increase in ship size, problems in labour relations and the decrease in world trade resulting from the recession of the early 1980s, have meant a shift in the importance of British ports. London and Liverpool, which still handled 59% of Britain's trade in 1960 handled only 15% in 1984.

Advantages of Felixstowe

From a near derelict site in 1950, Felixstowe is now Britain's premier container port. This is due to:

- Its being a deep water port capable of handling large vessels.

- Being sited on the coast, thus avoiding time-wasting journeys up river estuaries.

- Being on the major trade route between Britain and both the EEC and Scandinavia.

- Its modern equipment, and its efforts to gain container traffic (Figure 5.12). In 1986 a fourth container terminal was opened, and applications were made to purchase Trimley Marshes for a fifth terminal. The major European linked container ports are Rotterdam and Zeebrugge.

- The development of Ro-Ro facilities. These help speed up the turn-around of the ship (any merchant vessel in dock is losing money).

- Good industrial relations (it has only one union) which has earned the port a reputation for being efficient and reliable.

- Good road links with its hinterland which pass through mainly non-urban land and so are less congested than the approaches to other British ports.

△ **Figure 5.11** Aerial view of the port of Felixstowe

△ **Figure 5.12** Loading containers at Felixstowe

▷ **Figure 5.14** Topological map of British Rail, 1985

The Trimley container terminal (1986) consists of 550 metres of container quay, 28 hectares of storage space and 13.5 metres depth of water enabling the largest of container ships to dock.

	1957	1969	1973	1979	1984	1986	1990 (approx)
Number of employees	100	650	1032	—	1600	1900	2500
Tonnage handled (000s tonnes)	—	2019	3463	5497	8989	—	—
Number of containers (000s)	0	74	135	231	496	—	1000

TRANSPORT
British Rail
Three major projects

West Coast Main Line (WCML) The tilting Advanced Passenger Train (APT), introduced in December 1981, ran into major technological difficulties. It was designed to reach speeds of 250km per hour (155mph) and to negotiate tighter bends and steeper inclines than existing locomotives. New trials began on a revised model in mid-1984 with the coaches still tilting, but drawn by a lightweight, streamlined locomotive which will not exceed 225km per hour (140mph) – hence its name, 'Intercity 225'. It is hoped that 30 new locomotives will have been ordered by 1989 to run from London to Glasgow and North West England.

East Coast Main Line (ECML) The Secretary of State for Transport approved, in mid-1984, a £306 million investment in the electrification of the ECML (see Figure 5.13). Electrification is expected to reach Peterborough by 1987, and York, Newcastle and Edinburgh by May 1991. The entire route will be controlled from only seven modern signalling centres. Estimates suggest the scheme should create 3000 jobs. Although there are no plans to increase train speeds over the existing 200km per hour (125mph), the 31 proposed new Electra locomotives have the ability to reach 225km per hour (140mph).

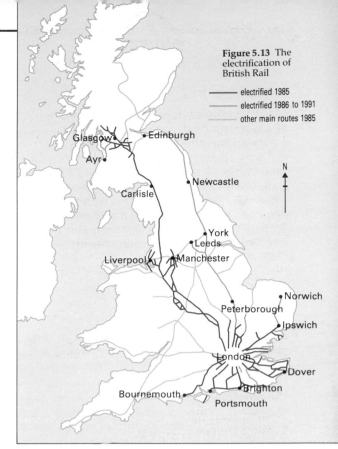

Figure 5.13 The electrification of British Rail

— electrified 1985
— electrified 1986 to 1991
— other main routes 1985

Channel Fixed Link (CFL) The British and French governments agreed, in January 1986, to accept a scheme which involved building two rail tunnels. Each would have a diameter of 7.3 metres, linked by a central service tunnel, with a diameter of 4.5 metres bored in advance to overcome geological problems. The tunnels are to connect Cheriton (north west of Folkestone) and Frethun (south west of Calais). Of the 50km of tunnel, 37km will be underwater. Although early hopes were for the first shuttle trains to be running by mid-1991, many expect even 1993 to be an optimistic date. This scheme had political advantages in that it had relatively low costs (compared with other schemes), was paid for by private investors, should have comparatively few technological risks, and could provide as many as 5000 British jobs on the tunnel construction and another 25 000 in associated industries (e.g. concrete tunnel linings, and tunnel boring equipment). As yet no decision has been made regarding which high speed train (expected to travel through the tunnel at 160km per hour (100mph) will be used. Will it be France's TGV (*Train à Grande Vitesse*) or Britain's new Electra?

Topological maps

Figure 5.13 shows British Rail's major routes with correct directions and distances. However, these routes have been drawn differently, as a topological map, in Figure 5.14. Topological maps eliminate irrelevant information and concentrate on one characteristic, such as time, cost or linear distance between various nodal points (see 'Nodes', page 43). These maps use straight lines. Two further examples of such maps are the London Underground and the Tyne and Wear Metro (page 39) (see Question 4, page 46).

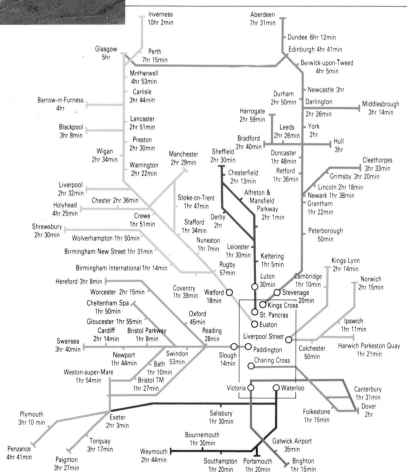

Flows and networks

Flows

These are affected by a wide range of factors:

Physical The relief of the land can determine both the density of communications (i.e. lengths of roads or railways per square km) and the actual routes taken by those communications. Flatter areas like the Fens in South East England are likely to have a high density compared with the more dispersed pattern of an upland area such as central Wales. Routes usually avoid marshy and mountainous areas, and concentrate in low lying areas and along valleys.

Climate Heavy snowfalls can block routes, such as the Snake Pass in Derbyshire, causing considerable delays and detours. Flooding can have a similar impact.

Economic Routes are needed in areas providing or using raw materials, particularly farming and mining in rural areas. Industrial areas and ports have high densities.

Urbanisation Higher densities and a wider range of communications are needed the more urbanised a region, or the greater the number of settlements in an area. Demand and densities are less in rural areas.

Social The affluence of an area can also affect traffic flows. Communications are likely to be greater in developed than in developing countries, and in urban rather than in rural areas. Another factor is the desire or necessity of some people to live close to or away from their place of work.

Region	Mode of transport						
	car	bus	train	under-ground	cycle (motor, pedal)	foot	others or at home
UK mean	50.7	16.1	3.8	1.8	6.4	15.4	5.8
North	48.0	23.0	1.0	0.4	4.0	18.0	5.6
Yorks and Humberside	47.7	23.0	1.0	0	7.0	15.7	5.6
East Midlands	53.3	15.6	0.7	0	8.5	16.5	5.4
East Anglia	56.0	7.5	1.0	0	15.3	12.9	7.3
South East	48.6	12.0	8.7	5.5	6.7	13.2	5.3
(Greater London)	37.4	16.8	10.7	12.7	4.5	12.8	5.1
South West	56.8	8.8	0.7	0	9.1	16.7	7.9
West Midlands	54.4	18.1	1.5	0	5.8	15.3	4.9
North West	51.6	19.5	2.3	0.3	5.6	15.9	4.8
Wales	56.6	14.0	1.2	0	3.7	16.3	8.2
Scotland	45.1	24.6	2.8	0.3	2.6	19.3	5.3
Northern Ireland	53.8	15.5	1.0	0	2.5	16.6	10.6

Political Modern communications are expensive to build and to run. Often only the government has money to finance and operate such schemes.

Using the above ideas, and Figure 5.15, how do you account for the following?

1 Fewer car users in Greater London

2 Fewer buses in East Anglia and South West England

3 Most train users in the South East and fewest train users in the South West and East Anglia

4 Most underground users in Greater London, and a few in Scotland and the north of England

5 Most cycle users in East Anglia

6 Fewest pedestrians in Greater London

7 Most people appearing to work at home in Wales, the South West, East Anglia and Northern Ireland

△ **Figure 5.15** Means of travel to work

▽ **Figure 5.16** Accessibility matrices

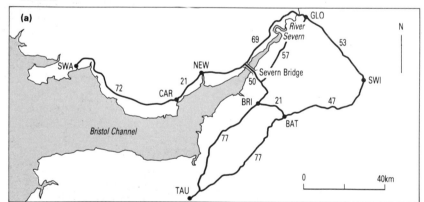

Note places north and west of the Bristol Channel have (i) a shorter distance to Swindon via the Severn Bridge but (ii) have fewer nodes to Swindon via Gloucester

Networks

A network can be defined as a set of geographical places which are joined together in a system by a number of routes. Networks vary between and within countries, and so there is a need to find a method by which to compare these different networks. The network can be divided into:

1 **Links** The lines of transport between places. On the topological map (Figure 5.14) these links were converted into straight 'edges' but in Figure 5.16(a) they have been left as 'arcs'.

2 **Nodes** The points (towns) which the links join together.

(b)	Bat	Bri	Car	Glo	New	Swa	Swi	Tau	Total
Bat	0	21	92	78	71	164	47	77	550
Bri	21	0	71	57	50	143	68	77	487
Car	92	71	0	90	21	72	139	148	633
Glo	78	57	90	0	69	162	53	134	643
New	71	50	21	69	0	93	118	127	549
Swa	164	143	72	162	93	0	211	220	1065
Swi	47	68	139	53	118	211	0	124	760
Tau	77	77	148	134	127	220	124	0	907

route distance matrix (km)

(c)	Bat	Bri	Car	Glo	New	Swa	Swi	Tau	Total
Bat	0	1	3	2	2	4	1	1	14
Bri	1	0	2	1	1	3	2	1	11
Car	3	2	0	2	1	1	3	3	15
Glo	2	1	2	0	1	3	1	2	12
New	2	1	1	1	0	2	2	2	11
Swa	4	3	1	3	2	0	4	4	21
Swi	1	2	3	1	2	4	0	2	15
Tau	1	1	3	2	2	4	2	0	15

accessibility matrix

BAT = Bath
BRI = Bristol
CAR = Cardiff
GLO = Gloucester
NEW = Newport
SWA = Swansea
SWI = Swindon
TAU = Taunton
77 distance in kms

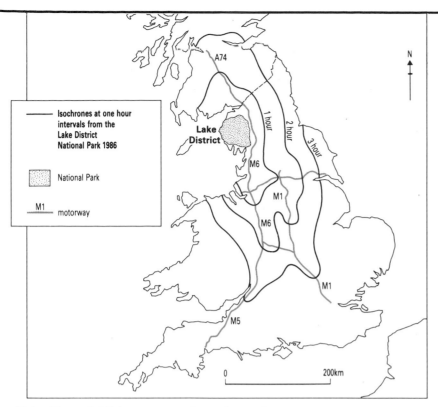

△ **Figure 5.17** Isochrones showing travel times to the Lake District National Park. How many conurbations are within a three-hour drive?

Isolines

These join places with equal characteristics (e.g. isobars join together places with equal pressure, isotherms places with equal temperature, and isochrones places with equal travelling time). Figure 5.17 gives travelling times to the Lake District, and illustrates the impact of such motorways as the M6, M5, M62 and even the M1 on that National Park.

Radial graphs

These graphs are used to compare and contrast movements of people. They can be used to show differences in either distance, time or cost. Figure 5.18 shows how far two families living in different parts of the same city have to travel to places of work, shops, schools and entertainment.

1 Describe and give reasons for the differences in the six movements shown in Figure 5.18.

2 Now look at Figure 5.19. Mr and Mrs Brown and their two children live near the western edge of a city. Mr and Mrs Brown both work 7km away in the city centre. Their two teenage children attend a school 2km to the south of their home. On Saturdays the weekly shopping is done in a hypermarket 2km to the north west of their home, and a visit is made to a local park on the northern edge of the city. Which graph, A or B in Figure 5.19, shows the movements of the Brown family?

3 Construct a labelled radial chart to show the following journeys made by the Green family. They live 4km to the north of the city centre where Mr Green works. Mrs Green does most of her shopping at a supermarket 2km to the south west of her home, and has to walk 1km east from her home to collect her two young children from school. At weekends they often visit an adventure playground which is located 4km to the north west of their house.

Using Figure 5.16(a) as an example, nodes can be: a point of origin or destination (e.g. Swansea); a significant town en route (e.g. Cardiff); or a junction of two or more routes (e.g. Bristol).

This division into links and nodes determines the accessibility of a place and the efficiency of the network. Accessibility is the ease of travel between various points. Figure 5.16(b) shows the shortest distance in kilometres between places and Figure 5.16(c) shows the 'shortest path matrix'. The aim is to follow a route between two places passing through as few nodes as possible, as nodes can mean congestion and delay. In the example in Figure 5.16 Bath to Bristol is only one nodal point, Bath to Newport (using the Severn Bridge) two, Bath to Cardiff three and so on. The total from Bath to all places is 14. After totalling up all the places on the map, that with the lowest number is said to be the most accessible on the network, and the place with the highest total is the least accessible. Question 5 on page 46 uses Figure 5.16, as well as referring to a problem which arose on 24 March 1986 when, for the first time since the Severn Bridge was opened in 1966, traffic crossing it was stopped due to hurricane force winds. Vehicles from South West England and London had to make a detour via Gloucester.

$$\text{Detour index} = \frac{\text{Shortest possible route distance}}{\text{Direct (straight line) distance}} \times \frac{100}{1}$$

The lowest possible index is 100, whereas an index of 300 would mean that the shortest possible route is three times longer than the straight line path. The higher the index the less efficient the system. A developed country has numerous routes linking many places, making journeys more rapid; whereas developing countries have fewer routes with many terminal, isolated points, making journeys slow and costly.

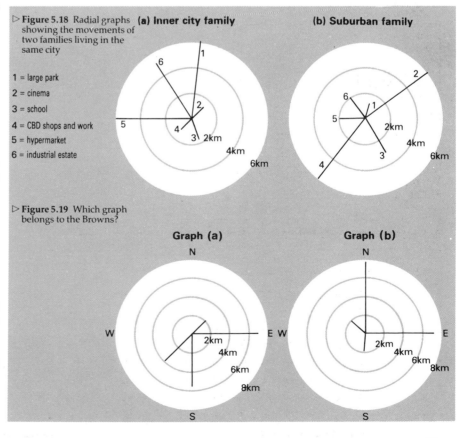

▷ **Figure 5.18** Radial graphs showing the movements of two families living in the same city

1 = large park
2 = cinema
3 = school
4 = CBD shops and work
5 = hypermarket
6 = industrial estate

▷ **Figure 5.19** Which graph belongs to the Browns?

Recent trends

Hierarchies

In a region

Each shop or service has a threshold population (page 13). This threshold population will indicate how many potential customers or clients that shop or service will have. It may also indicate the size and number of shops and services required to serve that population. For example, it is estimated that a small Boots the Chemist needs a threshold of 10 000, a multiple shoe shop 20 000, Marks & Spencer 50 000, some Sainsburys 60 000 and a John Lewis department store 100 000. Figure 6.1 attempts to suggest a hierarchy of shops and services (see also Figure 2.4).

Order	Type	Approx. threshold	Shops and services
1st	village	1000	store, post office
2nd	small town	10 000	small Boots, doctors, Spar, part-time bank
3rd	large town	20 000	Boots, Tesco, Burtons, shoe shop, bank, doctors
4th	regional shopping centre	50 000	Marks and Spencer, Tesco, Woolworth, Currys, Boots, furniture shop, Burtons, banks, shoe shop, department store, accountant, hospital, solicitors

In an urban area

1 Using Figure 6.2, describe carefully the location of the following shopping areas: (a) a corner shop or local shopping area (b) a suburban or district shopping area (c) a ribbon development along a main road (d) a warehouse-type DIY shop (e) a city centre covered precinct (Figure 6.3) (f) a hypermarket (g) an edge of town/regional shopping centre (page 45).

2 What is meant, in Figure 6.2, by the following terms? (a) comparison goods (b) convenience goods (c) specialist shops (d) service goods (e) low and high order goods (f) bulk buying (g) trade areas.

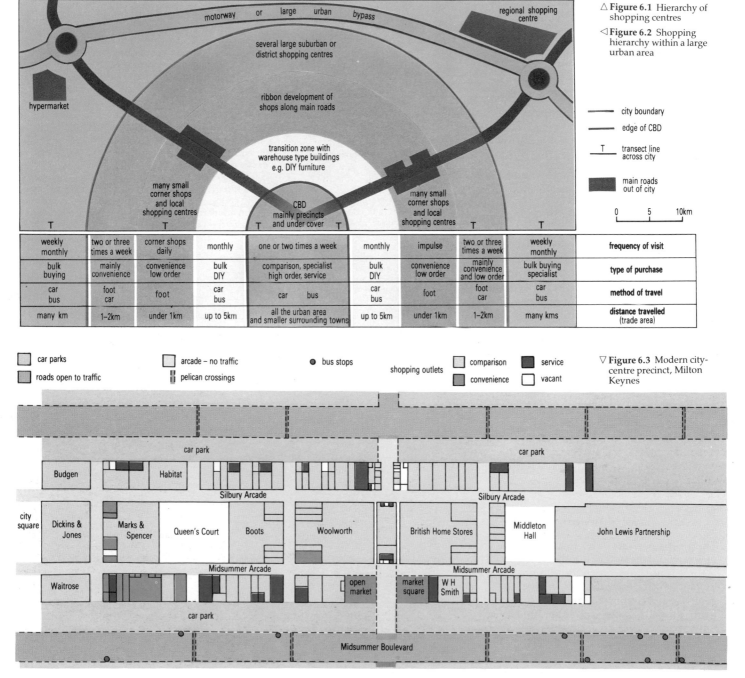

△ **Figure 6.1** Hierarchy of shopping centres

◁ **Figure 6.2** Shopping hierarchy within a large urban area

▽ **Figure 6.3** Modern city-centre precinct, Milton Keynes

Out-of-town shopping centres

MetroCentre in Gateshead

Family shopping has evolved from the corner shop to the supermarket, and from the hypermarket to the 'out-of-town' shopping centre. John Hall, whose brainchild is the MetroCentres, claims that since the 1960s shopping has evolved in three stages around central malls:

1 The Arndale Centres of the 1960s.
2 The Brent Cross, Eldon Square complexes of the late 1970s and now.

3 MetroCentres, where the emphasis is laid on family shopping and associated leisure activities. This concept is aimed at a day out for the family.

The site for Gateshead's MetroCentre (Figure 6.4) was surveyed in 1980, and at that time received little interest from the city centre 'magnet' (or 'anchor') shops. However, by the time plans were published in 1983, retailing had changed and the success of out-of-town DIY shops led such retailing outlets as Marks & Spencer to reconsider their future policy. Indeed MetroCentre will be Marks & Spencer's first out-of-city location.

The scheme

There will be free parking for 7800 cars. The disabled will have special parking facilities, and a bus station caters for the non-motorist. There will be 200 shops with Carrefour and Marks & Spencer at opposite ends.

Much attention has been paid to creating a pleasant shopping environment (Figure 6.6) – wide, tree lined malls, air conditioning, one kilometre of glazed roof to let in natural light, (supplemented by modern lighting in 'old world' lamps), numerous seats for relaxing, window boxes, hot air balloons, escalators and lifts for the disabled. A market effect has been created by traders selling goods from decorative street barrows and there is a wide variety of places to eat in. Leisure is a vital part of the scheme. There is a ten-screen cinema, a crèche for children, a space city for computer and space enthusiasts, a covered fantasy-land with all the attractions of the fair without the worries of the British climate, and a children's village with children's shops. Later stages of the development will include a luxury hotel and further leisure amenities.

▷ **Figure 6.5** The location of MetroCentre, Gateshead

Advantages of the site

☐ It is in an Enterprise Zone (see page 68) which allows relaxation in planning controls.

☐ The Enterprise Zone also means tax allowances and exemption from rates until 1991.

☐ The area was previously marshland and so was relatively cheap to buy, and the 47 hectare site has possibilities for future expansion.

☐ It is adjacent to the western bypass (2km of frontage) which links with the North East's modern road network — essential for an out-of-town location (Figure 6.5).

☐ 1.3 million people live within 30 minutes drive.

☐ It is adjacent to a main railway line, and is soon to have its own railway station. A future possibility is a link with the Tyne and Wear Metro (Figure 5.10).

△ **Figure 6.4** The site of Gateshead's MetroCentre beside a dual carriageway (foreground), mainline railway and the River Tyne (behind)

▷ **Figure 6.6** The emphasis inside the MetroCentre is on a pleasant, bright layout based on two-tiered malls

Transport and shopping

1 (Page 36)

a) (i) Why were railways built in Ghana?
(ii) Why is the railway network so thin in Ghana?
(iii) Is Ghana's railway network typical of other developing countries? (3)

b) Say how each of the following limits the construction of an efficient road network in a developing country such as Ghana,
(i) Physical problems
(ii) Economic difficulties (4)

2 (Figures 5.5 and 5.6, page 38)

a) What is a commuter? (1)

b) (i) How many commuters travel into Amsterdam from Zuid-Holland?
(ii) How many commuters travel *from* Amsterdam *to* Zuid-Holland?
(iii) Which district loses most commuters to Amsterdam?
(iv) Why do you think so few people commute from Noordkop to Amsterdam? (4)

c) Why has Amsterdam more incoming than outgoing commuters? (2)

d) In 1980 there were fewer of Amsterdam's employees living in the city than in 1960, and more of Amsterdam's employees travelling into the city for work (Figure 5.6). How do you account for this change? (3)

e) (i) List three problems which large-scale commuting has created in large urban areas. (3)
(ii) Describe three planning solutions which have been designed to try to overcome these problems. (3)

3 (Figure 5.11, page 40 and the map below)

a) (i) Which direction was the camera facing in Figure 5.11?
(ii) How many metres of waterfront has the Sealand container terminal? (2)

b) On a tracing paper overlay of the map mark and label:
(i) Sealand, Dooley and Trinity container terminals.
(ii) Trimley Marshes and the Townsend Thoresen passenger terminal.
(iii) The tanker jetty and Calor Gas Ltd. (8 × ½)

4 (Figure 5.14, page 41)

a) If you lived in London, which stations would you use to catch trains to the following places?
(i) Glasgow (ii) Edinburgh (iii) Cardiff (iv) Plymouth (v) Brighton (vi) Norwich (3)

b) (i) If you lived in Sheffield and were going on holiday to the Netherlands, which two stations would you pass through in London on your journey from home to the port of Harwich?
(ii) If you lived in Liverpool and wished to see your football team playing at Southampton, which two London stations would you pass through? (1)

c) (i) How long does it take to travel by fastest train between London and Inverness?
(ii) How much quicker is the journey between York and Edinburgh than the journey between Rugby and Carlisle?
(iii) If you left on the fastest train from London Kings Cross to Aberdeen at 0800 hours, what time would you reach York, Newcastle, Edinburgh, and Aberdeen? (4)

d) What are the advantages and disadvantages of a topological map? (3)

5 (Figure 5.16, page 42)

a) (i) Which two places were the most accessible after the opening of the Severn Bridge?
(ii) Which place was the least accessible after the opening of the Severn Bridge? (2)

b) On 24 March 1986, hurricane force winds closed the Severn Bridge to all traffic for the first time since it opened in 1966. Drivers had a choice of either waiting for the winds to subside, or making a detour via Gloucester.
(i) Redraw Figure 5.16(b) to show the route distance matrix while the bridge was closed. (2)
(ii) Redraw Figure 5.16(c) to show the new accessibility matrix assuming drivers went via Gloucester. (2)
(iii) Which place was the most accessible during the time the bridge was closed? (1)
(iv) Which place was the least accessible during the time the bridge was closed? (1)

c) Apart from the extra distance, what other problems faced the driver travelling between Bristol and Cardiff? (2)

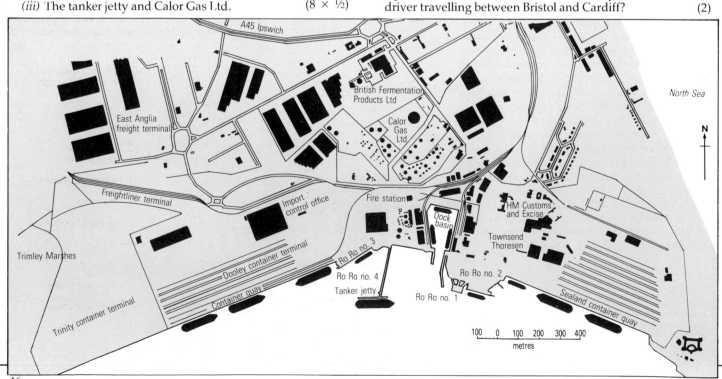

7 *(See the map below)*

a) (i) Give three points describing the distribution of department stores in the city. (3)

(ii) Give three reasons for this distribution. (3)

b) (i) Give three points describing the distribution of fish and chip shops in the city. (3)

(ii) Give three reasons for this distribution. (3)

c) Why are there more fish and chip shops than department stores in the city? (2)

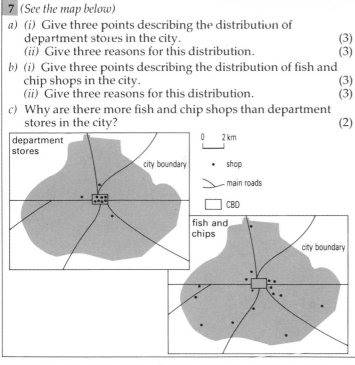

8

	Items to be bought			
Type of shopping centre	Bread	Clothes	Furniture	Jewellery
Corner shop (local)	24	0	0	0
Suburban parade (neighbourhood)	28	8	5	0
City centre (CBD)	25	66	75	100
Hypermarket (edge-of-city)	23	26	20	0

The table above shows the percentage of each item bought in each type of shopping centre.

a) (i) Draw a histogram to show where people buy their bread. (2)

(ii) Draw a percentage bar graph to show where people buy their clothes. (2)

(iii) Draw a pie chart to show where people buy their furniture. (2)

b) (i) Which of the four items can be bought only in the city centre?

(ii) Which product can be bought in all four shopping centres? (2)

---

6 *(Page 44 and the map below)*

a) (i) Describe the location of the corner shops. (2)

(ii) Why are there so many corner shops? (2)

(iii) Why have so many corner shops closed in recent years? (2)

b) (i) Describe the location of neighbourhood (suburban) shopping parades. (2)

(ii) How far are people prepared to travel to these shops? (1)

(iii) How often might people shop here? (1)

(iv) Give two advantages and two disadvantages of neighbourhood shopping areas. (4)

c) (i) What types of shopper use the inner city shops along the main roads? (1)

(ii) What types of goods are sold there? (1)

d) In the CBD of most British cities is a large, modernised, covered, air-conditioned, pedestrianised shopping centre.

(i) Why were such shopping centres built? (2)

(ii) What are the advantages of these centres for shoppers and shopkeepers? (2)

e) In many towns and cities the newest shopping centres are located on the very edge of the urban area. These centres usually include hypermarkets.

(i) What is a hypermarket? (1)

(ii) Using the map, give three reasons why site H is a good one for a hypermarket. (3)

(iii) What will be the views of the following groups of people to the building of a hypermarket at H?

Town planners; city councillors; people living near to the proposed site; chamber of commerce representing shopkeepers in the city centre; the elderly and the disabled; and long distance delivery drivers. (6)

(iv) How has the growth of hypermarkets and edge-of-city shopping centres changed the shopping patterns in an area? (2)

(v) Draw a sketch map to show the location of a hypermarket or edge-of-city shopping centre that you have studied. (3)

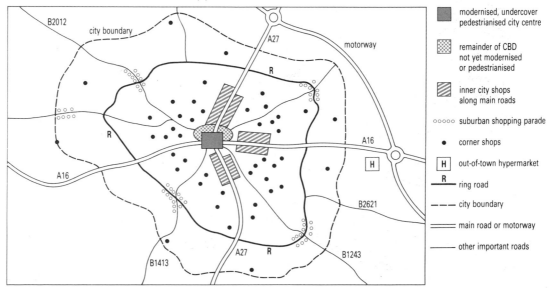

Distribution of resources

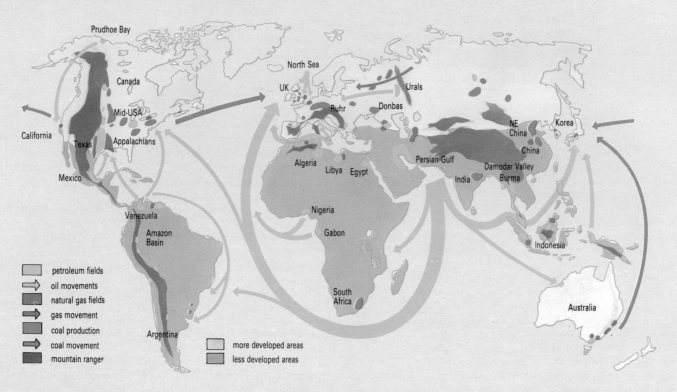

△ **Figure 7.1** Location and movement of the world's fossil fuels

petroleum fields
oil movements
natural gas fields
gas movement
coal production
coal movement
mountain ranges

more developed areas
less developed areas

About 85% of the world's supply of energy comes from three fossil fuels – coal, oil and natural gas. In some areas electricity generated by nuclear power and hydro-electricity is important. Although other forms of energy account for only a small percentage of the world's total, they can account for 90% in some of the less developed countries. Figure 7.1 shows the uneven distribution of the three fossil fuels.

□ Developed countries usually have insufficient oil to meet their demands (except the UK and Norway) and so need to import vast quantities. Even the USA, the world's second major producer (Figure 7.2(a)), had to import 45% of its requirements in 1985. Several developing countries produce oil, but few refine and use the oil themselves.

□ Coal, which gave the impetus to the industrial revolution of the 19th century, is mined, largely, in the developed countries and communist bloc countries (Figure 7.2(b)). Few developing countries have reserves of coal and this has been partly the cause of their delayed industrial development.

□ Nuclear power has become increasingly important since the 1970s yet, again, only the developed countries and communist bloc have the money to invest in this controversial form of energy (Figure 7.3(a)).

□ Hydro-electric power, the only major renewable form of energy, is more widespread – though developing countries (Figure 7.3(b)) tend to have large prestige schemes not always suitable to their stage of development.

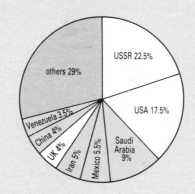

(a) Crude oil production 1983
total 2 756 687 (thousand tonnes)

USSR 22.5%
others 29%
USA 17.5%
Venezuela 3.5%
China 4%
UK 4%
Iran 5%
Mexico 5.5%
Saudi Arabia 9%

(b) Coal production 1982
total 2 861 000 (thousand tonnes)

others 7%
West Germany 3.5%
Australia 3.5%
UK 4.5%
India 4.5%
South Africa 5%
Poland 6%
USSR 18%
USA 26%
China 22%

△ **Figure 7.2** World production of crude oil and coal

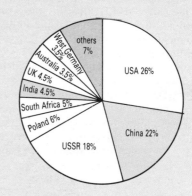

▽ **Figure 7.3** The importance of nuclear and hydro-electric power

40% and over	30–39%	20–29%	10–19%
France 40 (over 50% by 1985)	Sweden 37 Finland 36	Switzerland 28 Belgium 25 Bulgaria 25	Japan 15 West Germany 14 UK 14 USA 12 East Germany 12 Canada 10 (USSR 5)

(a) Reliance upon nuclear power 1982
(% of country's energy from nuclear power)

50% and over	30–49%	10–29%
Norway 99 Brazil 92 Austria 72 Canada 70 Switzerland 70 Colombia 69 North Korea 68 Sweden 58	Turkey 48 Yugoslavia 42 Venezuela 40 India 39 Argentina 37 Finland 34 Mexico 34	France 26 Italy 25 China 21 Spain 21 Australia 18 Japan 16 USSR 14 USA 11

(b) Reliance upon hydro-electric power 1982
(% of country's energy from HEP)

□ The unevenness in distribution, the fact that developed countries use, on average, 15 times more coal, oil and gas than developing countries and technological improvements in transport mean that energy can be moved great distances (Figure 7.4).

Distribution of energy resources in Britain

Britain has always been fortunate in its energy supplies. In the Middle Ages the many fast-flowing rivers, resulting from heavy rainfall in hilly areas, were used to drive waterwheels. The invention of the steam engine, which enabled Britain to become the first industrialised country in the world, was dependent upon heat derived from coal. During the 19th century coalmining regions (Figure 7.4.) saw the most rapid growth in towns and in jobs. When, by the mid-20th century, the most accessible reserves had been exhausted, new forms of energy were discovered. In 1965 natural gas was found in the North Sea, off the coast of Norfolk and in 1970 oil was discovered off the east coast of Scotland. At a time when world oil prices reached their maximum, Britain became self-sufficient in that form of energy. At the same time, Britain took a lead in the development of nuclear power – although fears over its safety and the availability of other fuels meant, in the 1980s, that the industry grew less quickly than in other developed countries.

Oil and gas were only expected to last until about 2000 AD, but now, due to a falling demand for energy and the discovery of new fields, these two forms of energy should last until 2035 AD. However, after 2000 AD, oil at least may have to be imported in increasingly large amounts. Coal reserves are likely to last for another 300 years, though their exploitation is likely to be limited to East Yorkshire, East Nottinghamshire and Leicestershire.

Yet even when fossil fuels become less available, Britain's seas and weather provide the potential to produce 'alternative' or renewable sources of energy based on waves, tides and wind. Experiments are also being carried out into geothermal energy. Of the future forms of energy only solar power is unlikely to become a major source in 'cloudy' Britain.

1 Using Figure 7.5 calculate the percentage of each type of energy used in the UK in (a) 1963 (b) 1983 (c) 2000 (estimated).
2 Having obtained these percentages, use two different types of graph to show the importance of each type of energy in 1983.
3 As a class, how do you account for the changes in UK energy consumption between 1963 and 1983?

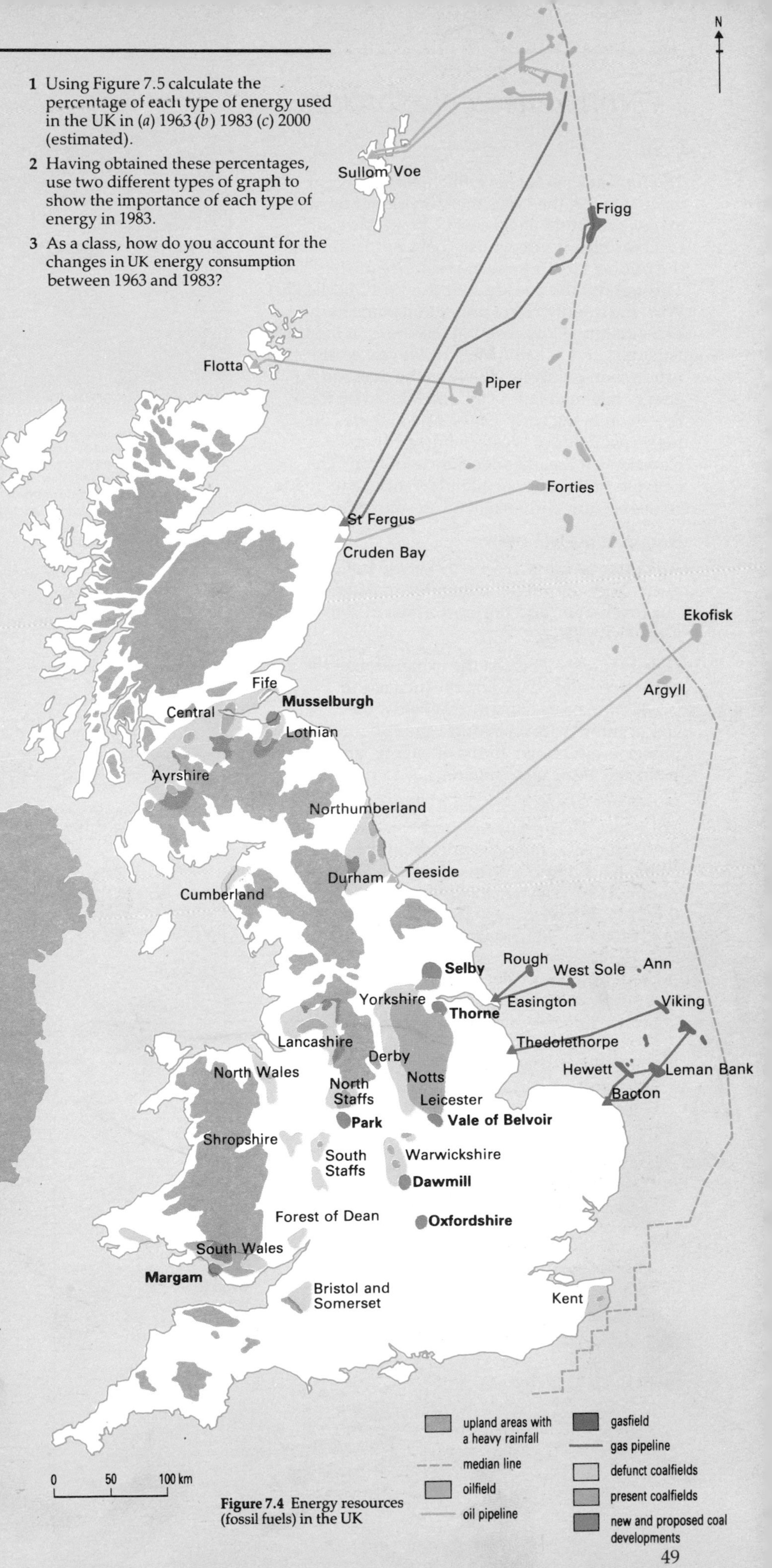

Figure 7.4 Energy resources (fossil fuels) in the UK

upland areas with a heavy rainfall	gasfield
median line	gas pipeline
oilfield	defunct coalfields
oil pipeline	present coalfields
	new and proposed coal developments

	Million tonnes oil equivalent				
	1963	1973	1983	1990	2000
				projected	
Oil	61	114	72	69	63
Natural Gas	—	26	44	51	54
Coal	116	78	66	61	68
Nuclear	1	5	12	16	19
Hydro-electric	2	2	2	2	2
TOTAL	180	225	194	199	206

△ **Figure 7.5** UK primary energy consumption

49

Non-renewable sources

Coal

The fortunes of coal have fluctuated in recent years. During the 1960s the low price of oil and the exhaustion of the most easily obtainable coal reserves meant a decline in coal production and the mining labour force in Western Europe. Throughout the decade after the 1974 Middle East War, the rapidly rising price of oil enabled the exploitation of low cost coal resources in the USA, Australia and South Africa. However, world production rose only slowly as the demand for energy began to fall – a fall accelerated by the recession of the early 1980s. Again, it was the high-cost fields of Western Europe that experienced the major decline in output. The collapse of the price of oil in 1986 has again made coal less competitive than other sources of energy.

Britain in the late 1980s

Advantages Large reserves likely to last over 300 years, high output per miner due to technological improvements, and the more efficient conversion into electricity.

Disadvantages Include the exhaustion of the most easily accessible deposits, the increase in production costs of many coalfields, the competition from oil, natural gas and nuclear power as alternative forms of energy, and coal's pollution of the atmosphere.

By 1987 most of Britain's coal came from the Yorkshire, Derby and Nottinghamshire coalfields, with relatively small amounts from the traditional fields in Scotland, Northumberland, Durham and South Wales. The two most recent developments (Figure 7.4) have been Selby in Yorkshire and the Vale of Belvoir in Leicestershire – both following long public enquiries resulting from concern over the environment.

△ **Figure 7.6** The Alaskan oil-field, typical of many found in sedimentary rocks which have been gently folded in areas fairly close to mountain ranges. The oil is obtained in winter temperatures of −50C, causing frostbite and making breathing and working conditions difficult. Machines have to be left running constantly to prevent them freezing. There are 22 hours of darkness a day, and permafrost (permanently frozen ground) hampers the drilling.

Oil in Alaska

Oil was discovered at Prudhoe Bay in 1968 (Figure 7.1). Despite adverse environmental conditions (Figure 7.6) production began due to the then rising demand for oil and its by-products. Because the Beaufort Sea is frozen for eight months of the year, the oil has to be sent by pipeline over mountain ranges and earthquake belts to Valdez on the south coast of Alaska (Figure 7.18).

Advantages of oil include its being more efficient and cleaner than coal, safer than nuclear power, relatively easy to transport over vast distances and essential for most forms of transport.

Disadvantages include its limited life span, the expense of finding and exploiting new oilfields and transporting the oil, the expense of large oil refineries with possible dangers of spillage and explosions, the fluctuation in world prices and oil's vulnerability to political, economic and military pressures.

Nuclear power in France

France has probably the most ambitious nuclear power programme in the world. The country has little of its own coal, oil or natural gas and so has had to rely upon expensive oil imports from the politically unstable Middle East and North Africa. France had over 50 nuclear reactors operating by the mid-1980s. In 1980, 37% of France's electricity came from nuclear power; by 1986 the figure was in excess of 50%. It was expected to reach nearly 75% by 1990, although recently the French President called a halt to the construction of five new reactors. Figure 7.7 shows the location of French reactors, and it can be seen that such power stations are mainly sited along inland rivers (the Loire, Rhône and Garonne) and coasts (the English Channel).

Advantages of nuclear power include its greater efficiency than rival fuels, its cleanliness and its use of little raw material. The raw material for its production (uranium) should last for decades.

Disadvantages are headed by its doubtful safety and the possibility of explosions and leakage of radioactivity (as at Chernobyl in the USSR in 1986), the impact on local communities and environments, and the disposal of radioactive waste.

▽ **Figure 7.7** Nuclear power stations in France, 1984

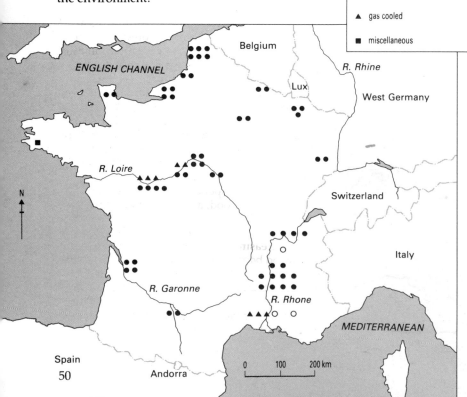

Type of reactor

● pressurised water

○ breeder

▲ gas cooled

■ miscellaneous

Electrical power in the UK

Electricity is supplied through the National Grid – a technically sophisticated system of power stations, electricity storage schemes and transmission lines. The location of major power stations in the late 1980s is seen in Figure 7.8. The future will probably witness an extension in two fields:

Electricity generation facilities

1 Coal-fired power stations consisting of plants with ash and dust disposal facilities, and usually with cooling towers, are located either:
   (a) along main inland rivers, e.g. Trent, or
   (b) on estuaries with rail or sea access to fuel sources and with the availability of cooling water, e.g. Thames.

2 Oil-fired power stations are located near deep, sheltered coastal estuaries for tanker access and the availability of cooling water, e.g. Milford Haven. However, present government and EEC fuel policies make it unlikely that further oil-fired power stations will be built.

3 Nuclear power stations are more likely to be located, as at present, on coasts and estuaries because of access to cooling water, and away from highly populated areas and hazardous industries for safety reasons, e.g. Sizewell. They require transport facilities for fuel inputs and radioactive waste outputs.

Electricity storage schemes

Electricity generation will have to be supported by the storage of off-peak electricity from power stations both to:

1 Level the changes in the daily demand for electricity (peak times in early morning and early evening) and possibly in seasonal demand (peak time in winter).

2 Smooth the availability of energy from intermittent sources such as waves and wind.

Facilities could include an extension to pumped water storage dams, reservoirs and power/pump houses located in hilly and mountainous areas.

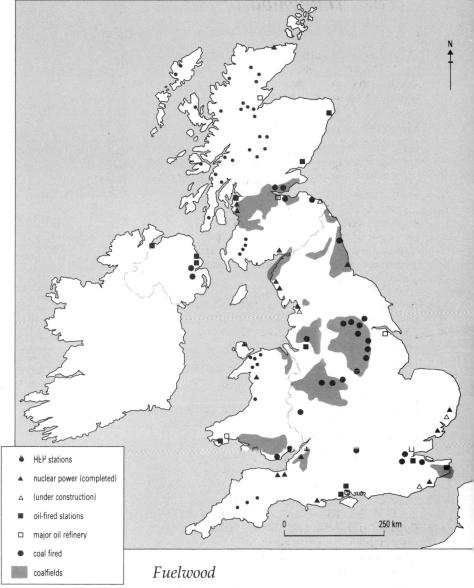

Legend:
- HEP stations
- ▲ nuclear power (completed)
- △ (under construction)
- ■ oil-fired stations
- □ major oil refinery
- ● coal fired
- coalfields

△ **Figure 7.8** Locations of the UK's main power stations

▷ **Figure 7.9** In rural areas of Africa, collecting fuelwood is a daily task for the women and children. They may have to travel all day to find sufficient wood for the following day, or will have to buy wood at rapidly rising prices.

Fuelwood

In Africa, trees have often been called the staff of life because of their vital role in preserving the environment and in providing rural communities with the necessities of life (fuel, shade, food, building materials and furniture). Yet here, as throughout the developing world, trees are being removed at an ever faster rate (pages 127 and 137). As in many developing countries, fuelwood in Tanzania, for example, accounts for over 90% of the nation's energy consumption. However, as the population of such areas grows, trees are cut down and fuelwood becomes scarcer. Many Africans have to spend 25% of their meagre income on firewood, a position which is worsened as their traditional diets of maize, cassava and peas all need lengthy cooking periods.

As increasing numbers drift to the towns, fuelwood becomes scarcer there too. The typical African cooking stove has been notoriously inefficient, and even newer models are considered to be only 35% efficient. It may seem incredible to inhabitants of the developed world that, in some poorer countries, wood is almost as expensive as paraffin.

51

ENERGY
Renewable and alternative energy sources

As fears have risen that fossil fuels may be used up, and as the cost of their extraction and transfer to usable forms of energy has increased, attempts have been made to harness new forms of energy which can be used over and over again. Some authorities suggest a division into:

1 Renewable energy in the form of hydro-electricity which is already widely used in many parts of the world.

2 Alternative forms of energy, which may eventually come to rival the existing types of energy, but which as yet are not widely adopted, e.g. tidal, solar, wind, geothermal and biogas. At present, research into alternative forms of energy is at the mercy of political decision makers.

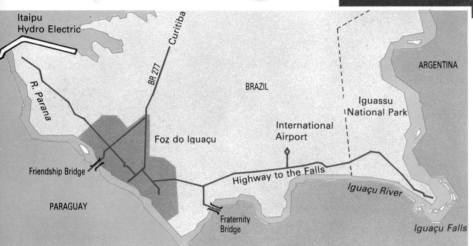

△ **Figure 7.11** The Itaipu Dam, 190m high and built to be the largest hydro-electricity power station in the world

△ **Figure 7.10** Location of the Itaipu Dam

disappear when the scheme is completed), the building of new houses, towns and services (which will not be needed once the workers have left) and the bringing of money into a relatively poor, isolated area (although wildlife was lost and some rich farmland was flooded). Although the Paraguayan government now receives much needed income and São Paulo its energy, how much do you think the local inhabitants of Itaipu have benefited?

Tidal

River estuaries with large tidal ranges have the potential to generate significant amounts of electricity. Despite this, only one scheme is operational – the Rance-Barrage in Brittany, France. Tides in the Rance Estuary can have a range of over 11 metres, and enter and leave the estuary at speeds of up to 20km per hour. The incoming tide turns turbines, the blades of which can then be reversed to use the receding tide. The other two schemes being tested are in the Bay of Fundy in Canada and in the USSR. In the UK, with its considerable potential, investigations into the Severn Estuary continue.

Waves

The Atlantic approaches to most of the British Isles have higher wave energy levels than any other sea area in the world, and they are adjacent to areas of high energy consumption. Though only at an early research stage, it is envisaged that strings of wave machines could possibly be positioned off the coasts of North West Scotland and North West Ireland to generate electricity. Transmission lines would be needed to bring the electricity ashore so that it could be connected to the National Grid. Gales, which produce the biggest waves, occur most frequently in winter, at the time of peak energy demand. A drawback, however, is that these are not continuous.

Hydro-electricity

The Itaipu scheme – Paraguay/Brazil

The largest waterfall in the world, by volume, was once the Guaira Falls on the border of Paraguay and Brazil (Figure 7.10). This had a flow twice that of Niagara but the waterfall is now submerged beneath the waters of a lake 180km long and 5km wide, formed by damming the Parana river at Itaipu (Figure 7.11). Completed in 1982, the dam is 190m high, and by the time the eighteenth and last turbine has been fitted in 1988 it will be the largest hydro-electric power station in the world (producing 12.6 million megawatts a year compared with the 9.7 million produced by the Grand Coolee in the USA). By mid-1986 four turbines were working. Although the scheme was a joint one between Paraguay and Brazil, Paraguay already receives more than her annual requirement from just one turbine. By agreement, Brazil can purchase the remainder of Paraguay's share at a cheap price, and transmit the power to the São Paulo industrial area. The scheme involved rehousing 42 000 people (many did receive some compensation), the creation of thousands of new jobs (most of which will

Solar

The amount of solar energy reaching the outer atmosphere far exceeds the total amount of all other forms of energy on earth. Solar energy has the advantages of being safe, pollution free, efficient and of limitless supply. But it is expensive to construct solar 'stations' which, in any case, are still only at the research stage. For the UK, the solar energy option is perhaps hindered by the weather. The UK receives less sunshine than most places on earth and, in winter, when demand is highest, it gets more cloud and shorter hours of daylight – and, when the sun does shine, its angle is very low and so less effective.

Before 1984, most research involved the collection of heat, rather than light, from the sun, and was achieved by using large numbers of solar panels. In 1984, the EEC and Japan decided to concentrate their efforts on developing the photovoltaic cell. This is a device for converting the sun's energy directly into electricity (without producing heat). In 1985, Europe's first factory producing photovoltaic cells was opened in Bridgend in South Wales, and Europe's largest solar housing project was opened at Bournville.

Research is now directed towards finding the best methods of using the energy produced:

1 In developed countries this will be to feed solar energy into the National Grid.

2 In developing countries energy will be collected for use in isolated, rural areas where mains electricity is too expensive to be practical. The 'solar village' concept was first used in Mali (Africa) in 1978 and is beginning to spread rapidly. In India, with the fastest proposed growth, the 220 villages served in 1985 were expected to increase to 18 000 by 1987.

Geothermal

Nicaragua, along with Mexico and El Salvador, produces geothermal power – a source of energy which is likely to contribute 10% of Latin America's energy requirements by 2000 AD. In Nicaragua, hot rocks lie relatively near the earth's surface, and water in contact with these rocks soon becomes steam. The steam is brought to the surface, through stainless steel pipes, where it is used to drive turbines. At present Nicaragua has four generators producing 55% of the country's power. The largest, at Momotomro, provides 35 megawatts. Nicaragua plans to have ten more stations working by 1988.

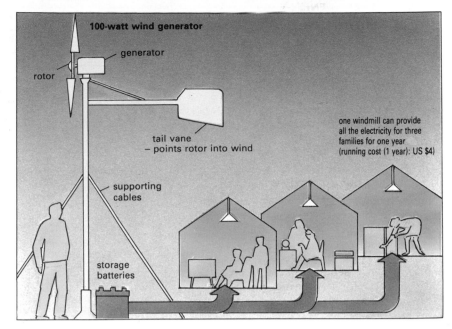

△ **Figure 7.12** Power from the wind, China

Wind

China first began using the wind to provide power for irrigation 2000 years ago, but only began mass production of wind-powered water pumps in the late 1960s, and to experiment with land generators in the late 1970s. Seven prototype wind generators, capable of producing up to 100 kilowatts, were being tested by 1985. However China has placed greater emphasis on the production of mini-wind generators (Figure 7.12) of 50 to 100 watts, which can be used on isolated farms and villages.

Biogas

Alcohol in Brazil

A national programme was launched in 1975 to try to reduce Brazil's dependence on imported oil. Manioc and the surplus from sugar-cane factories are used to produce alcohol. This alcohol can either be mixed with petrol up to a ratio of one-in-four without changes to existing car engines, or used by itself in specially built cars. By 1985, 3% of Brazil's energy requirements was met by alcohol, and there were over one million specially built cars (Figure 7.13).

Advantages include the reduction of the cost of, and reliance on, imported oil; the employment of one million workers in sugar-cane fields and alcohol distilleries; and the reduced lead-based additives which lessen atmospheric pollution (down 18% in São Paulo).

Disadvantages include the vast clearances of the Amazon Forest – partly for new sugar plantations; the exceptionally low wages paid to plantation workers; the destruction of other forms of agriculture; the money borrowed for such schemes from the World Bank which has increased Brazil's already high national debt; and the fact that alcohol is only economic if the price of oil is over US $28 a barrel (in early 1987 it was US $15 a barrel).

▽ **Figure 7.13** Petrol and alcohol pumps at a Brazilian garage

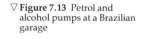

Energy and development

The two graphs attempt to illustrate any link between the wealth of a country and the amount of energy it uses (Figure 17.14).

GNP (Gross National Product) per capita is the amount of money earned by a country divided by the number of people living in that country. It is expressed in American dollars. (GNP is not the only accepted method of determining the level of development of a country (pp. 98-99)).

Energy consumption is measured in kilograms of coal (or oil) equivalent, i.e. the amount of energy obtained from a kilogram of coal (or oil) whether it is produced by oil, coal, gas, nuclear power etc.

In graph (a) the figures for 21 countries have been plotted, e.g. Mexico has a GNP of US $1290 and an energy consumption per capita (person) of 1380 kilograms of coal equivalent. The resultant graph shows a scatter of 21 points – hence it is called a scattergraph. To this can be added a best fit line. Notice that this line does not pass through all the points, but is the line drawn nearest to most of the points. Occasionally one or two points, in this case countries 18 and 21, lie a long way from this best fit line. These are anomalies in that they do not fit in with the pattern. If, as in this case, this best fit line goes from bottom left to top right there is a positive correlation, i.e. the amount of energy consumed does increase as the GNP increases. If it goes from top left to bottom right then there is a negative correlation – for example, here it would have shown that, as the amount of energy consumed increased, then the GNP decreased.

Arithmetical and semi-log graphs

Arithmetical scattergraph Both scales are divided into equal divisions. Usually the perfect correlation would be a straight line with all the points on the best fit line.

Semi-log The vertical scale (the ordinate) is divided into cycles, each beginning and ending ten times greater than the previous cycle, e.g. a range of 1 to 10, 10 to 100 and so on. The base can begin with any multiple of 10, e.g. 0.1, 1.0, 10.0. The steeper the line the greater the rate of change. Note that the line can be drawn as a smooth curve, and that there is no room for a 'zero' value. It is also used to measure earthquakes (the Richter scale), e.g. an earthquake reading 5.0 on the Richter scale is ten times stronger than one registering 4.0, and another measuring 6.0 would be 100 times bigger than the one which registered 4.0 (p. 131).

Logarithmic scales are used when:

☐ There is a great range in the data, as this scale compresses values.

☐ There is more data at one end of the range than the other (notice the bunching at the bottom left on graph (a)).

☐ Rates of increase need to be shown rather than the amount of change.

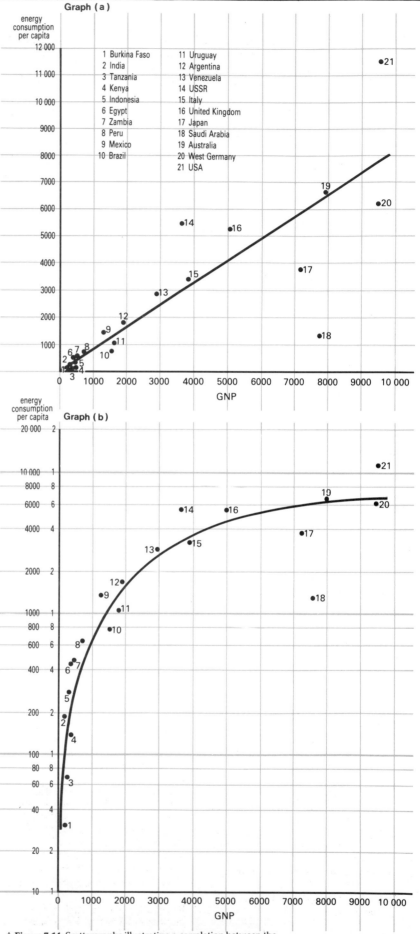

△ **Figure 7.14** Scattergraphs illustrating a correlation between the wealth of a country and its energy consumption

Energy and development

Most of the world's energy is consumed by a fairly small number of developed countries which have reached a high standard of living and which need energy for their industry, transport systems and heating. The graphs do show a very close correlation between GNP and energy consumption, with the USA having the greatest wealth and consuming most energy, and the poorer countries of Burkina Faso, India, Tanzania and Kenya consuming the least energy. Yet there are anomalies, for example:

☐ The USA uses even more energy than its GNP suggests.

☐ Japan has a high GNP but, being short of its own energy resources, has industrialised with a relatively low energy consumption.

☐ Saudi Arabia has a very high GNP because it sells most of its oil and consumes very little itself.

Energy in Ghana

In the mid-1950s, Ghana's first President, Dr Kwame Nkrumah, saw the River Volta as his country's chance to improve its economy. Before then, Ghana had been a British colony, the Gold Coast, relying mainly on the export of one crop, cocoa, for its income. Dr Nkrumah believed that with a limitless supply of cheap electricity his country could develop – but, as in all developing countries, the problem was how to obtain sufficient money for the scheme.

The solution appeared in the form of a multinational (page 70) called Valco (Volta Aluminium Company). It agreed to build a smelter in return for duty and tax exemptions on the import of bauxite and the export of aluminium, and for the purchase of cheap electricity.

In order to supply the energy necessary for the creation of jobs, the development of secondary and service industries, and the money needed to

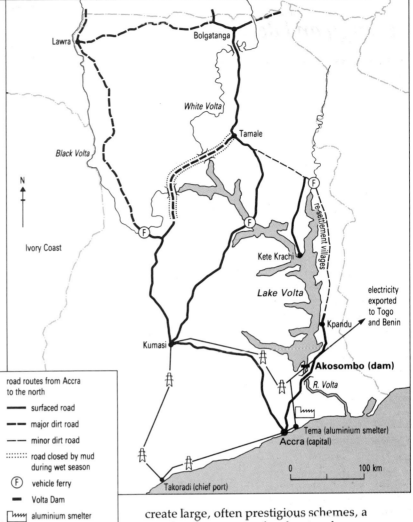

road routes from Accra to the north

▬▬▬	surfaced road
▬ ▬ ▬	major dirt road
— — —	minor dirt road
⋯⋯⋯	road closed by mud during wet season
Ⓕ	vehicle ferry
▬	Volta Dam
〰	aluminium smelter
〈T〉	new electricity grid fed from the dam

△ **Figure 7.15** Ghana's Volta power scheme

create large, often prestigious schemes, a developing country often has to rely upon a multinational company to provide such resources. In return they must grant that firm favours.

The Volta Scheme (Figure 7.15) included the building of a dam at Akosombo in a gorge on the River Volta. This created a huge lake. A power station provided electricity for the newly built aluminium smelter, situated on the coast at Tema. Although the scheme has brought many advantages to Ghana, it has also created many problems.

The project in the mid-1980s

Just as 30 years earlier, Ghana had suffered from having only one main export, cocoa, so in 1985 its economy was again affected by its reliance on one main project. The drought, which had led to the famine in Ethiopia and Sudan, had caused the drying up of rivers which fed Lake Volta. Power supplies from Akosombo to Togo and Benin were cut by half (each country had received 95% of its electricity from Ghana), the Valco Aluminium Smelter had to close making its workforce redundant, and all other factories were restricted to a three-day week in an attempt to conserve energy. So, until the rains come in sufficient quantity to refill Lake Volta, Ghana will be unable to repay loans to the World Bank, will use up more of her dwindling wood supply as an alternative form of energy and will have to delay any further possible hydro-electric schemes.

Advantages	Disadvantages
☐ Prestigious project for Ghana.	☐ Much land, even if of poor quality, was flooded.
☐ Long term cheap electricity and a new electricity grid.	☐ Seasonal variations in lake levels leave swampy areas around its edges.
☐ Created a pool of skilled Ghanaian technicians.	
☐ Ghanaians obtained top jobs.	☐ 80 000 people had to be rehoused.
☐ Growth of industry, i.e. aluminium, boat building, construction.	☐ Loss of wildlife under the lake.
☐ New jobs in fishing on Lake Volta and refrigerator plants.	☐ The main north-south road was flooded.
	☐ Relatively few jobs, only 2500 at Tema, in return for the huge amount of money spent on the scheme.
☐ Fish from the lake improved the local diet.	
☐ The lake provided an assured water supply for domestic use, farming and industry.	☐ All profits overseas – not to Ghana.
	☐ None of Ghana's bauxite used – imported from the Americas, just as all the aluminium is exported.
☐ Development of water transport on the lake.	
☐ Electricity exported to Togo and Benin.	☐ 65-70% of Akosombo's power goes to Valco.
	☐ Electricity is only available for towns in the south, not for villages in the north.

ENERGY
Energy and the environment

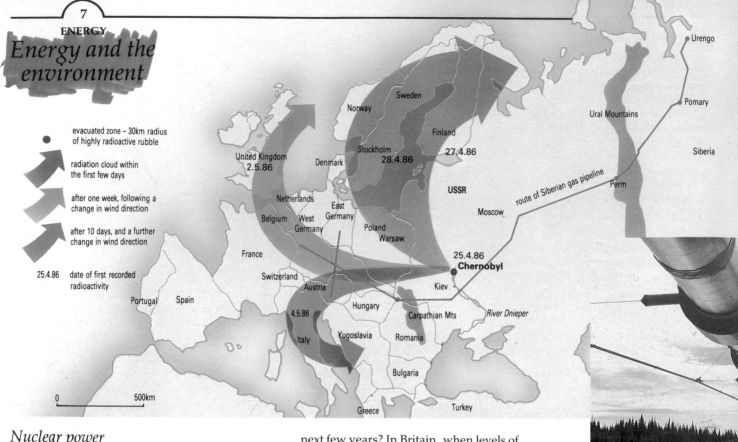

- ● evacuated zone – 30km radius of highly radioactive rubble
- radiation cloud within the first few days
- after one week, following a change in wind direction
- after 10 days, and a further change in wind direction
- 25.4.86 date of first recorded radioactivity

0 ——— 500km

Nuclear power

Chernobyl (USSR)

On 25 April 1986, the core of one of the four reactors at the Russian showpiece nuclear power station at Chernobyl, 100km north of Kiev, overheated causing gas to explode (Figure 7.16). The roof of the reactor was blown off, causing radioactive material to be deposited around the plant and releasing a radioactive cloud which drifted north west over Poland and towards Scandinavia. No news of this explosion was released by the Soviet Union until three days later when, 1500km away in Sweden, alarm signals were set off at a nuclear power station south of Stockholm. At first the Swedes thought that their reactor was leaking and they evacuated the site – only to realise later that it was the radioactivity from Chernobyl which had activated their alarms. Radioactivity readings soon rose ten times in Sweden and five times in Denmark and Finland, though experts said that those levels were well below those which would threaten human life. It took two weeks for the fire at Chernobyl to be put out – a task achieved by dropping sand and lead from helicopters. Action was taken just in time to stop radioactivity contaminating underground water supplies which drained into Kiev's main reservoir. The explosion killed only two people, though within four months this total had risen to 31, following the deaths of several who had been most severely exposed to radiation. Four settlements, including the new town of Pripyat (built to house the workers at Chernobyl), were evacuated.

How much damage was done? Were water supplies contaminated? Was the Ukrainian wheat crop affected? Will the incidence of leukaemia and other forms of cancer increase in the area in the next few years? In Britain, when levels of radioactivity rose 12 days after the accident, the transportation of sheep was restricted in North Wales, the Lake District and parts of South West Scotland.

Lappland, November 1986 Lichens, which cover large areas of Lappland and provide a basic diet for reindeer, are very sensitive to pollution. They receive their nutrients from the atmosphere and are therefore vulnerable to nuclear fall-out. As the Chernobyl cloud passed over they absorbed rain like a giant sponge and were then eaten by the reindeer herds which underpin the Lapp economy. The early autumn slaughter showed that the animals contained radiation levels 33 times higher than the Swedish permissible level for human consumption. The Lapps must either destroy their herds (cultural suicide) or ignore government health warnings and eat contaminated meat.

Sellafield (Cumbria)

A series of leaks and discharges from Sellafield, and the question of the disposal and storage of nuclear waste led to major concern about the environment in Britain in the mid-1980s. An independent authority claimed, after Chernobyl, that 'radioactivity released from coal burning power stations is twice that released at nuclear stations' (and that it only made up 0.15% of radiation in the atmosphere). He also said that 'a winkle at Seascale (the beach next to Sellafield) contained less radiation than that present naturally in a Brazil nut'. Anti-nuclear campaigners point to increases in radiation in the Irish Sea and on Cumbrian beaches and ask what would happen in Britain if one of our reactors exploded (Figure 7.19).

△ **Figure 7.16** Chernobyl – a nuclear disaster. (The map also shows the extent of the Siberian gas pipeline (see page 57) (top left)

△ **Figure 7.17** The environmental problems of the Alaskan pipeline (top right)

△ **Figure 7.18** The pipeline cannot pass through the frozen ground and so has to be suspended above this Alaskan river

▷ **Figure 7.19** Two views of nuclear power. Which one most closely reflects your own view?

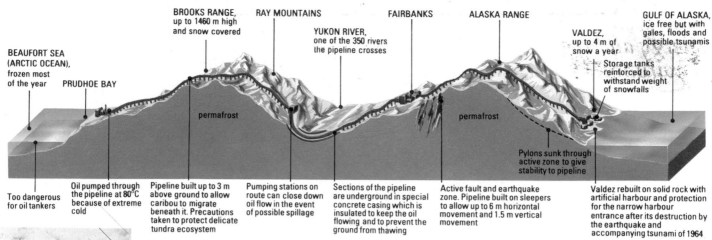

BEAUFORT SEA (ARCTIC OCEAN), frozen most of the year

PRUDHOE BAY

BROOKS RANGE, up to 1460 m high and snow covered

RAY MOUNTAINS

YUKON RIVER, one of the 350 rivers the pipeline crosses

FAIRBANKS

ALASKA RANGE

VALDEZ, up to 4 m of snow a year

GULF OF ALASKA, ice free but with gales, floods and possible tsunamis

Storage tanks reinforced to withstand weight of snowfalls

permafrost

permafrost

Pylons sunk through active zone to give stability to pipeline

Too dangerous for oil tankers

Oil pumped through the pipeline at 80°C because of extreme cold

Pipeline built up to 3 m above ground to allow caribou to migrate beneath it. Precautions taken to protect delicate tundra ecosystem

Pumping stations on route can close down oil flow in the event of possible spillage

Sections of the pipeline are underground in special concrete casing which is insulated to keep the oil flowing and to prevent the ground from thawing

Active fault and earthquake zone. Pipeline built on sleepers to allow up to 6 m horizontal movement and 1.5 m vertical movement

Valdez rebuilt on solid rock with artificial harbour and protection for the narrow harbour entrance after its destruction by the earthquake and accompanying tsunami of 1964

Transcontinental pipelines

Alaska

The Alaskan oilfield, discovered in 1968, is the largest in North America. The oil is essential to the economy of the USA and now provides 33% of that country's oil and 12% of its natural gas. However, before the oil could be used, it had to be transported south. Two routes were suggested:

1 By tanker from Prudhoe Bay (Figure 7.17). But the Beaufort Sea is frozen for most of the year; the route is dangerous and would require too many tankers; and the risk of spillage was too great.

2 A pipeline 1300km southwards to the ice-free port of Valdez. This would have to be built in the face of great difficulties and to the satisfaction of a highly organised lobby of conservationists.

The pipeline was decided upon, but was not opened until 1977, partly due to the many physical problems which had to be overcome (p. 50). Conservationist arguments had also to be satisfactorily resolved.

Threats to the environment included:

□ Concern that, once the tundra vegetation was removed, regeneration would be very slow – a fear partly confirmed by some of the destruction caused in the early days of oil exploration.

□ The pipeline had to cross the caribou migration routes, a problem overcome by raising the pipe on stilts.

□ The change to the habitat of foxes, wolves, bears and moose.

□ Fears that as the pipeline had to cross an earthquake zone, a major earth movement might break the pipe causing a massive spillage. The oil companies claim that the pipeline is built to bend rather than break; in addition several pumping stations were built to close down sections in the event of any spillage.

□ Fears that the storms and tsunamis (tidal waves), in the Gulf of Alaska might cause coastal flooding and, together with fogs, cause a major hazard to oil tankers.

Siberia

In 1981, despite major opposition from the USA, several western European countries signed the largest ever east-west trade deal when they agreed to supply equipment for the Siberian pipeline in return for natural gas from the USSR. The world's largest gas field is at Urengo (Figure 7.16) and, from here, a 4500km pipeline has been built across 120km of permafrost, 1000km of waterlogged tundra, through coniferous forests, over the Ural Mountains, and into Czechoslovakia. Indeed six lines run parallel to Perm (Fig. 7.16) before branching to serve different areas. Unlike the Alaskan pipeline, where oil is heated to 80°C to prevent it freezing as it passes through pipes built above the ground on stilts, the Siberian gas is sent underground at −2°C to stop the permafrost melting. The first gas reached West Germany in 1984.

The Sellafield saga

The chattering classes in this country have never shown much interest in the creation of new wealth. That is seen at its starkest today in their attitude towards the nuclear power industry. Somebody only has to sneeze at the Sellafield nuclear waste reprocessing plant these days to get on to the front page of the nation's press. An alliance of anti-nuke environmentalists, opportunist politicians and a media establishment which cannot tell the difference between press vigilance and press vendetta seems determined to have Sellafield closed down, despite the fact that it employs 15,500 people, invests £1m a day and has won international orders worth £2.7 billion to keep it in work into the next century. Of course, nuclear safety is of crucial importance and Sellafield has to be held to account when its safety procedures are not up to scratch, and when it tries to cover up past mistakes. This paper will continue to subject Sellafield to the utmost scrutiny. But its safety record must be seen in perspective. As far as we know, nobody has died because of Sellafield. Yet every year during this decade about 40 people have died in coal, oil and gas, with barely a footnote in the newspapers or television. Much urgent research remains to be done, of course, on the possibility of any link between radiation leaks at Sellafield and the incidence of forms of cancer in the surrounding area. But even if such a link is ever established it again has to be seen in perspective. All the evidence suggests that, even on the very worst assumptions, nuclear power is far less dangerous to your health than most other types of mass-produced energy. Since it is an international industry that Britain happens to be rather good at we should not be in such a rush to destroy it.

The factory as a system

Industry as a whole, or a factory as an individual unit, can be regarded as a system. This system can be represented in the following way:

Inputs	→	Factory	→	Outputs
(raw materials and human inputs) Expenditure		(manufacturing processes)		(end products) Income

In this model, outputs (income) minus inputs (expenditure) will give that industry or firm a profit or a loss. For a firm to remain profitable, some of the income must be re-invested to modernise the factory.

Industrial location

Before building a factory, the manufacturer should consider the major elements in the system diagram (Figure 8.1). It is unlikely that the manufacturer will find all the elements operating at one site, and so a decision must be made as to which site has the greatest advantages. (Presumably in a capitalist country that means where there would be profit and in a communist country where there would be most benefit to the state).

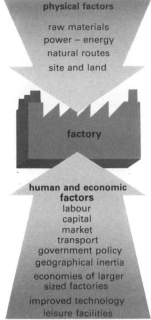

△ **Figure 8.1** Factors influencing the location of industry

physical factors
raw materials
power – energy
natural routes
site and land

factory

human and economic factors
labour
capital
market
transport
government policy
geographical inertia
economies of larger sized factories
improved technology
leisure facilities

Human and economic factors

Labour This includes both quantity (large numbers in 19th century factories) and quality (as some areas developed special skills).

Capital Early industry depended on wealthy entrepreneurs. Now banks and governments may provide the money.

Markets The size and location of markets have become more important than the source of raw materials.

Transport Costs increase when items moved are bulky, fragile, heavy or perishable.

Geographical inertia This is when an area becomes known for its products (e.g. cutlery at Sheffield, pottery at Stoke). Any new firms will locate there to benefit from the name, tradition and skills of that area.

Economies of scale Small units may become unprofitable and so merge with, or be taken over by, other firms.

Government policies As governments tend to control most wealth, they can influence industrial location.

Improved technology Newsprint and teletext are examples.

Leisure facilities Both within the town and the surrounding countryside, leisure activities are becoming more desirable.

Period of time		Location of early 19th century iron foundries in South Wales (e.g. Ebbw Vale)	Location of integrated steelworks of the 1980s at Port Talbot and Llanwern (Newport)
Physical			
Raw Materials	Coal	Mined locally in valleys	Limited reserves in West Wales, some now imported
	Iron ore	Found within the coal measures	Imported from North Africa and North America
	Limestone	Found locally	Found locally
	Water	For power and effluent – local rivers	For cooling – coastal site
Energy – fuel		Charcoal for early smelting, later rivers to drive machinery and then coal	Electricity from national grid (using coal, oil, natural gas and nuclear)
Natural routes		Materials mainly on hand. 'Export' routes via the valleys	Coastal sites
Site and land		Small valley floor locations	Large areas of flat, low capacity farmland
Human and Economic			
Labour		Large numbers of unskilled labour	Still relatively large numbers but with a higher level of skill. Fewer due to high tech.
Capital		Local entrepreneurs	Government. EEC.
Markets		Local	Tin plate industry (Llanelli) and the car industry
Transport		Little needed, some canals	M4. Purpose-built ports
Geographical inertia		Not applicable	Tradition of high quality goods
Economies of scale			Two large steelworks more economical than numerous small iron foundries
Government policy			Having the capital they can determine locations and closures
Technology		Small scale – mainly manual	High technology – computers, lasers etc.

△ **Figure 8.2** Changing location factors for iron and steelworks in South Wales

▷ **Figure 8.5** Japan's main industrial centres. Notice industry's strong preference for the coast and plains. The pattern is the geographical need for accessibility, flat land, the possibility of offshore reclamation and deepwater transport.

▷ **Figure 8.6** Labour relations in Japan

Physical factors

Raw materials The bulkier and heavier these are to transport, the nearer the factory should be located to the raw materials. This was even more important in times of poorer transport.

Power – energy This is needed to work the machines in the factory. Early industry needed to be sited near to fast flowing rivers or coal reserves, but today electricity can be transported long distances.

Natural routes River valleys and flat areas were essential in the days before the railway, car or lorry.

Site and land Although early industry did not at first take up much land, it did need *flat* land. As the size of plant increased (e.g. steelworks), more land was needed. Ideally such sites should be on low quality farmland where the cost of purchase is lower. Last century many sites were in today's 'inner city' areas whereas now they tend to be on edge-of-city 'greenfield' locations.

Modern industrial location

The car industry

Unlike the older, heavier industries where physical factors determined their location (e.g. shipbuilding, steel), the car industry is 'market orientated' and it is usually found near to large centres of population, e.g. Detroit in the USA, and Wolfsburg in West Germany. The important location factors include:

- Availability of raw materials e.g. steel.
- Large areas of land for the production line, offices, car parks and car storage.
- Availability of energy.
- Large labour force, both skilled and unskilled.
- A central location for the assembling of parts from the many subsidiary factories.
- A large local market.
- A coastal site for the export of cars.

Manufacturer	1984
General Motors	6.33
Ford	3.62
Toyota	2.49
Nissan	2.05
Volkswagen Audi	1.88
Renault	1.55
Peugeot-Citroen Talbot	1.46
Fiat	1.39
Chrysler	1.27
Honda	1.02
Toyo Kogyo (Mazda)	0.77

◁ **Figure 8.4** Vehicle production (in millions) – manufacturers and countries

△ **Figure 8.3** The Mizushima works of the Kawasaki Steel Corporation, built on land reclaimed from the sea

The Mazda car factory, Hiroshima (Japan)

Hiroshima is one of many large cities lying in a zone 1100km long between Tokyo and northern Kyushu (Figure 8.5). 70 million people crowd together on limited areas of flat land which are intensively used for housing, agriculture and industry. How has Japan, with only 15% of its land flat enough for development, and lacking in raw materials and sources of energy, become such an industrialised giant?

	1972	1977	1982
USA	8.6	9.2	5.1
Japan	3.7	5.4	6.9
West Germany	3.7	3.8	3.7
France	2.7	3.1	2.7
Italy	1.7	1.4	1.3
UK	1.7	1.3	0.9

(World production 27.5)

The Mazda car factory at Hiroshima employs 30 000 workers, and produces 0.8 million cars a year, of which 63% are exported (Figure 8.4). It has achieved this position due to:

- Reclamation of land from the sea (Figure 8.3). While much of the city is built on the flat delta of the Ota River, land for the 3km production line was only obtained, as in many other areas of Japan, by creating new land from the sea.
- Numerous natural harbours including the area around Hiroshima which lies on the 'inland sea'. The port is protected from typhoons and heavy seas by the island of Shikoku. Many semi-processed materials for the car industry are imported, and finished cars exported. Most of Japan's internal trade is carried out by coastal ships.
- Hiroshima being on the new 'Bullet Train' route which has to be built on stilts as it passes through the city before disappearing into tunnels in the surrounding highlands.
- The amalgamation of companies into large scale firms.
- Labour shortages in the 1960s led to the introduction of labour-saving machines and robots. However there is still a large workforce checking both the machines and each other.
- Good labour relations (see Figure 8.6).

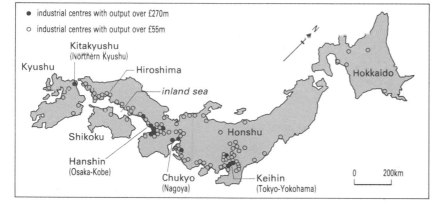

- industrial centres with output over £270m
- industrial centres with output over £55m

Japanese cars and world markets

Due to the high level of automation, the high level of productivity (three times the number of cars per worker compared with western Europe), good labour relations, and the ability to produce the type of car likely to sell in world markets, the Japanese have begun to flood the American and European markets. To try to overcome this criticism, the Japanese have built branch factories in several countries (e.g. Nissan at Washington in Tyne and Wear) and have joined forces with foreign manufacturers to gain access to overseas markets (e.g. Honda-Rover in the UK).

A Mazda car worker does not only have a *job* with the company, he has a *relationship* with it. The company supplies medical and social facilities to a worker and his family on a grand scale. Mazda has its own hospital, its own gymnasium and swimming pool, and its own company holidays to company 'retreats'. The umbrella of some car manufacturers is even *more* all-embracing: Toyota operates from a town called Toyota where the probability of being born in a Toyota hospital, living in a Toyota flat and being buried in a Toyota grave is very real indeed. Most Mazda workers will expect to spend their whole lives working for the company. Chopping and changing jobs is a risk most people are not prepared to take because so much of an individual's security is tied up with a company (and not with the State) and because it is difficult for an individual to fit into an organisation he did not join at the 'right' age.

To our eyes, this two-way loyalty between worker and company may seem paternalistic, stifling and restrictive. But it suits the Japanese need to see themselves as part of a well-defined group with a clear set of objectives. No Mazda assembly line worker would deny that the actual work he does is not repetitive. But once this inevitability is accepted, he would claim that it is fundamentally more interesting and rewarding to work within a system where the well-being of everybody is intimately tied up with the quality and quantity of the vehicles leaving the assembly line. This kind of work ethic – possibly questionable and indigestible to us – is arguably *the* most important force behind Japan's industrial performance.

Japan, The Overcrowded Islands – Industry, BBC Publications

Employment structures

Classification of industries

Traditionally, industry has been broken down into three groups (primary, secondary and tertiary), although during the 1980s a fourth group has been added (quaternary).

Primary industries extract raw materials directly from the earth or sea. Examples are farming, fishing, forestry and mining.

Secondary industries process and manufacture the primary products (e.g. steelworks, shipbuilders or furniture-makers). They include the construction industry and the assembly of components made by other secondary industries.

Tertiary industries provide a service. These include health, education, office work, local and national government, retailing, entertainment and transport.

Quaternary industries provide information and expertise. The new microchip and micro-electronics industries come into this category.

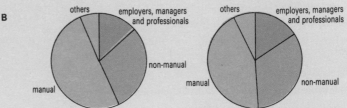

A

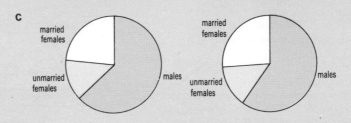

B

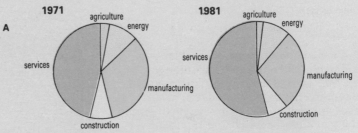

C

Changing employment structure in Britain

A Using Figure 8.7:

1 In A, why has there been a decrease in manufacturing (secondary) employment and an increase in employment in services (tertiary)?

2 What, in B, is meant by manual, non-manual and professional? Which type of job has decreased, and which two have increased? Why?

3 Why, in C, has the percentage of working married females increased, while the percentage of working males has decreased?

B Using Figure 8.8:

4 Describe and account for the distribution of primary industry in Britain in 1975.

5 Describe and account for the distribution of secondary industry in Britain in 1975.

6 Describe and account for the distribution of tertiary industry in Britain in 1975.

7 How many more people had jobs in 1985 than in 1975?

8 Between 1975 and 1985:
   (a) What change has taken place in the primary sector?
   (b) Which areas have lost most jobs in the secondary sector? Why has this happened?
   (c) Which areas have seen the largest increase in the tertiary sector? Why?

C Try to find employment figures for your own city or county.

9 How have these figures changed during the last 100 years?

10 How and why do these figures differ from the national average?

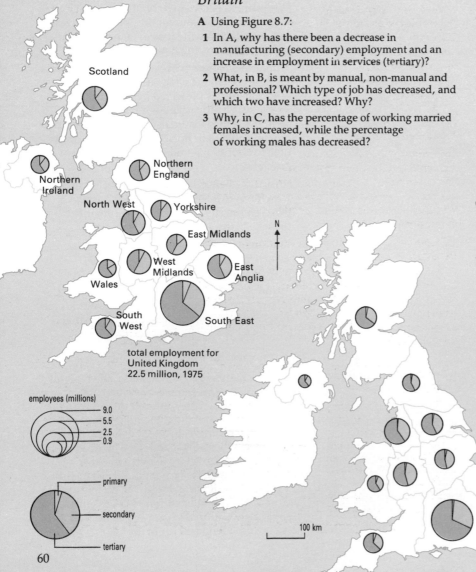

total employment for United Kingdom 22.5 million, 1975

employees (millions)

- 9.0
- 5.5
- 2.5
- 0.9

— primary

— secondary

— tertiary

100 km

total employment for United Kingdom 23.2 million, 1985

△ **Figure 8.7** The changing nature of employment in Britain 1971–81

◁ **Figure 8.8** Changing employment structures in Britain 1975–85

Triangular graphs

One method of illustrating the percentages employed in primary, secondary and tertiary industries is to present these three variables on a triangular graph. This is an equilateral triangle with each 'base' divided into percentage scales to represent each variable. It may be more convenient, though not essential, to have the sides of the triangle 10cm in length. Figure 8.9 shows how the three variables are plotted for the employment structure of Town A. The figure for primary is found by using the left hand scale (see 'green' graph), for secondary by using the right hand scale (see 'blue' graph) and for tertiary the base (see 'orange' graph). The answer for Town A is given in the table underneath the graph. Complete this table (Figure 8.9) for Towns B and C. These three towns represent, but not necessarily in this order, a small market town, a holiday resort and an industrial town. Which figures do you think fit each letter? Give reasons for your answer.

Differences between developed and developing countries

As can be seen in Figure 8.10, developing countries have a high percentage of their workforce in the primary sector (e.g. Niger 91%, Tanzania 83% and India 71%). Most of these workers will be employed in farming, which is labour intensive, or in mining, forestry or fishing. Countries in an early stage of economic development have a concentration in subsistence agriculture (page 81). As countries reach a more intermediate stage of development (e.g. Brazil) the numbers in primary occupations fall, as mechanisation increases, until in a developed country they are very small (UK and USA 2% each).

Developing countries have a relatively low percentage engaged in secondary industries. This may be due to such reasons as a lack of capital to establish industry, a more limited education system leaving a less skilled workforce, a lack of technological knowledge, a lack of mechanisation, the export of most primary products, a lack of energy supply to operate factories, and a limited local market not wealthy enough to buy manufactured goods. At a more intermediate level, the numbers in the secondary sector increase (e.g. Brazil 22%, Italy 42%) although there does seem to be a point in development beyond which numbers begin to decrease (e.g. USA 32%).

Developing countries have very small numbers in the tertiary sector (Niger 6%, Tanzania 11%) due to limited developments in education, health, commerce, transport, recreation and tourism. In the more developed countries the numbers employed in service industries are greater than in both the primary and secondary industries combined (UK 56%, USA 66%). The one anomaly in Figure 8.10 is Jamaica where the development of the tourist industry is shown by 55% employed in the tertiary sector.

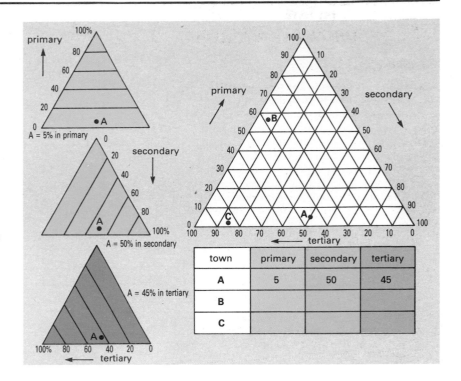

town	primary	secondary	tertiary
A	5	50	45
B			
C			

Employment structures in a developing country – Ghana

Primary industry Nearly two-thirds of Ghanaians are employed as subsistence farmers, with a few still employed on the cocoa plantations established under British colonial rule. Gold, manganese and diamonds are mined, and timber is obtained from forests in the south of the country. Agriculture accounts for 61% of Ghana's gross domestic product (GDP). As in many developing countries, most of Ghana's raw materials are exported to developed countries.

Secondary industry Less than 20% of Ghanaians are employed in this sector, and most are employed in the coastal zone between Accra and the port of Tema (page 55). Here there is some oil refining, and the manufacture of steel, cement and aluminium.

Tertiary industry As in secondary, there are less than 20% employed in service industries. Although commerce and administration have grown in the larger, southern cities, there are still relatively few schools, hospitals and offices; the transport system is mainly concentrated in the south (page 36), and no important tourist industry has developed.

△ **Figure 8.9** Triangular graph showing employment structures

▽ **Figure 8.10** Employment structures in selected countries

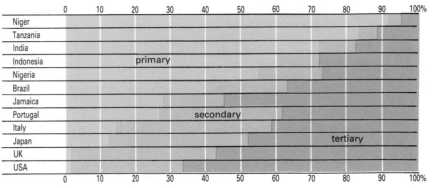

Industrial decline

National levels

Exhaustion of resources The most profitable and accessible coal seams in such areas as Central Scotland, Northumberland, Durham and South Wales have long been used up. Iron ore is no longer worked in Furness (Cumbria) or in the Cleveland Hills, and tin mining in Cornwall received a last-minute reprieve. Problems of unemployment in such areas are accentuated by the fact that many people have no alternative form of work.

Increasing costs of raw materials This can also include component parts.

Automation and new technology The industrial revolution in Britain saw the replacement of workers by machines. Recently the introduction of robots (e.g. car industry) and computers have accelerated the replacement of labour by capital. In transport and in the docks, containerisation has led to a rapid decline in the workforce.

The introduction of a rival product Examples are: aluminium replacing steel, synthetic fibres replacing natural fibres and coal, as a source of energy, threatened by oil and nuclear power.

Fall in demand Examples are the reduced consumption of sugar and tobacco.

Overseas competition This can include the flooding of the market with cheap clothes, or high technology electrical equipment.

Rationalisation Small firms are taken over by larger firms (sometimes by overseas companies). In the UK, the numerous iron works of the early industrial revolution have been reduced to five major steelworks.

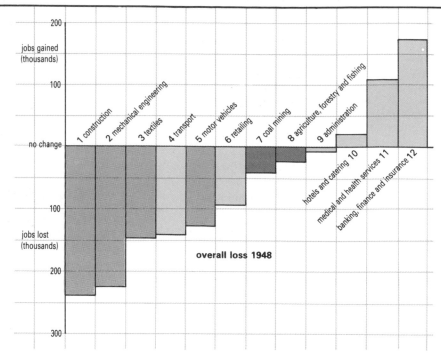

tertiary

secondary

primary

△ **Figure 8.11** Changes in employment in the UK 1979–82

▽ **Figure 8.12** The job market and the future (forecast for the Federal Republic of Germany, 1978–90)

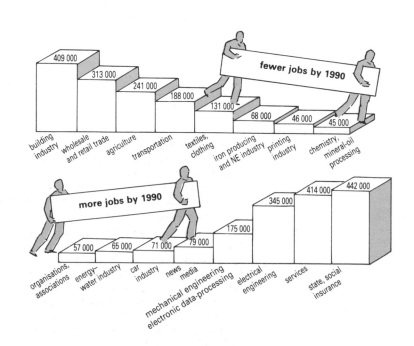

A decline in public transport or isolation An efficient transport system is essential for modern industry, and areas lacking such a system will be at a disadvantage. Coupled with this is the tendency for places furthest from the capital city or 'largest market' to have the highest rates of unemployment, e.g. Northern Ireland and Scotland in the UK (see page 63), and the Mezzogiorno (South Italy) in the EEC.

A rise in production costs causing a fall in production Contributory factors here include old, inefficient machines in a cramped old factory, and high wage bills.

A lack of capital investment In times of recession, less money is put back into industry, and this will make it less efficient.

Inner city clearances These have had some impact within conurbations, increasing unemployment there.

Political decisions The government is one of the few remaining sources of wealth. At a time of reduction in public expenditure, fewer grants have been given to ailing industries (e.g. cars, shipbuilding). British Leyland has long been subsidised by British governments, while the steelworks of Ravenscraig (Scotland) has only remained open due to a government decision – a decision which could just as easily be reversed.

Strikes These can cause loss of markets – the arguable point is who is at fault. The government? Inefficient management? Undemocratic trade unions? A lack of dialogue and trust between management and the workforce (see the section on Japan, page 59)? Your response to this will probably be determined by your own political views.

Rapid population growth This is not applicable to the UK, but is the major cause in developing countries such as Brazil and India. Here migrants from rural areas move to São Paulo and Calcutta in the vain hope of finding employment.

Regional levels

The increase in unemployment in Britain has not been evenly distributed (Figure 8.13).

The North and West, which already had the highest levels of unemployment in 1980, have continued to experience the most rapid increase. This can be explained partly by:

☐ The exhaustion of raw materials (coal, iron ore).

☐ The decline in the 'heavy' manufacturing industry (steel, ships, textiles and engineering) (Figure 8.11).

☐ The greater distance and remoteness from the largest market (London) and the EEC.

☐ The recession hitting manual workers more than non-manual, with the North having had the majority of manual jobs.

☐ A greater loss of jobs in the older industries which tended to be located in inner city areas of conurbations – and most conurbations are in the North and West.

The exception to this continued decline has been the north-east of Scotland where over the last decade there has actually been a decrease in unemployment due to North Sea oil.

The South and East have also had an increase in unemployment, but the levels are much lower because:

☐ London, being the capital, has job opportunities in government (administration) and in offices (there is prestige value in locating a firm's headquarters in the capital city). It is the centre of commerce (Figure 8.11).

☐ Having the largest market, the area has most service industries (e.g. shops, schools, hospitals).

☐ The South is perceived as having a 'cleaner' environment and a more amenable climate.

☐ This area has more cultural and social attractions.

☐ People are moving out of London, leaving fewer inhabitants seeking work.

☐ The more rural counties surrounding London never had large numbers in the secondary sector and so have been less affected by the recession.

☐ Larger numbers are employed in tourism – a growth industry.

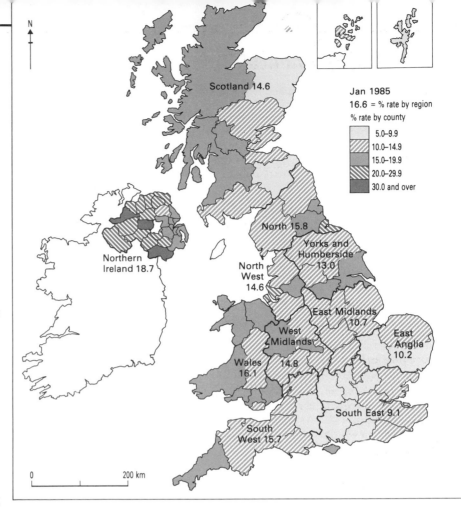

△ **Figure 8.13** Unemployment in the UK 1985

▽ **Figure 8.14** Unemployment in Birmingham, 1981

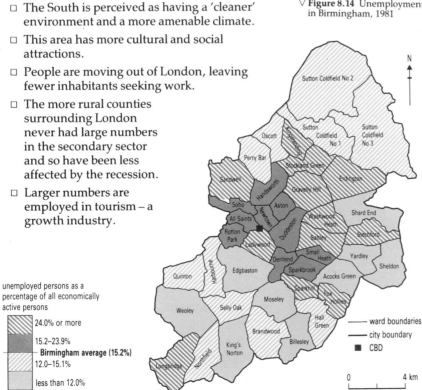

Summary Although the map does show the increasing gap in job opportunities between 'the North' and 'the South', this is not a new problem. Disraeli, a British prime minister writing in the 1840s subtitled one of his novels *The Two Nations*. However the map does disguise local pockets of exceptionally high unemployment (e.g. 30% in the former steel towns of Consett and Corby), and the collapse of manufacturing in the West Midlands.

Local (city) levels

Using Birmingham as a typical example, Figure 8.14 shows how unemployment is also unevenly distributed in large cities and conurbations.

Notice:

☐ That unemployment is highest in inner city areas, where people with fewest skills tend to live. The fact that there is a greater concentration to the north of the CBD is linked to the fact that the north is the centre of the car and engineering industries.

☐ The decrease in unemployment towards the city boundaries. The inhabitants of many suburbs tend to work in service industries and so have been less affected by the recession. Where unemployment is higher on the outskirts this can be accounted for by a predominance of outer city council estates (page 21) and the declining workforce of the British Leyland car factory (Minis and Metros) at Longbridge.

63

Footloose industries

The term 'footloose' is applied to those firms which have a relatively free choice of location. Many of these newer industries provide services for people and are therefore market orientated. The raw materials are often component goods made elsewhere, and the finished product is usually light and easily transportable by road or air.

Location Two prime sites for these footloose industries are:

1 On large trading or industrial estates built on former greenfield sites on the edges of towns and cities (Figure 8.15).

2 Alongside major motorways to capitalise upon efficient transport links (e.g. M4 in Figure 8.20).

Advantages of an edge-of-town location
(Figure 8.15)

☐ Cheaper land values away from the CBD as competition for land is lower near to the city boundary (lower rents and rates).

☐ Ample space for the construction of large buildings, car parks and lorry unloading bays, together with room for possible future expansion.

☐ Well planned, modern estates, often with local roads, services and factory units built in advance.

☐ A good internal road system linked by main roads to motorway intersections.

☐ Adjacent to modern, suburban housing estates, both private and council, as well as access to commuter villages which provide a local labour force – an increasing proportion of which is female.

☐ A pleasant working environment, and these new industries provide very little air or noise pollution.

☐ Access to urban markets.

▽ **Figure 8.16** The layout of Euroway Industrial Estate, Swindon

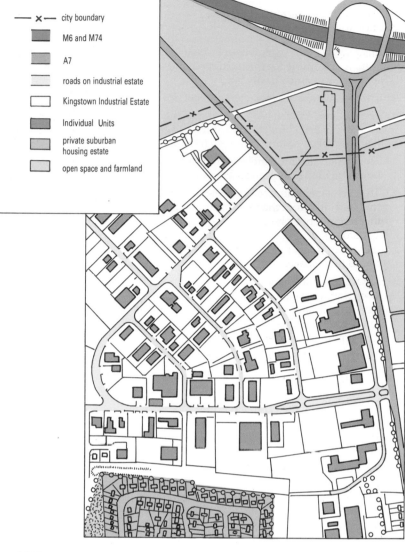

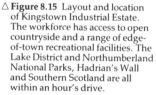

△ **Figure 8.15** Layout and location of Kingstown Industrial Estate. The workforce has access to open countryside and a range of edge-of-town recreational facilities. The Lake District and Northumberland National Parks, Hadrian's Wall and Southern Scotland are all within an hour's drive.

Legend:
— ×— city boundary
M6 and M74
A7
roads on industrial estate
Kingstown Industrial Estate
Individual Units
private suburban housing estate
open space and farmland

Layout of estates (Figure 8.16)

☐ Roads are usually wide and straight, or gently curving, to allow easy access and turning for large delivery lorries.

☐ Each factory unit is in its own relatively large area of land with room for expansion, its own car and lorry park.

☐ Some vacant sites have been designated to try to attract firms in future years.

Types of firm

☐ Distributive firms which can warehouse their goods either for dispatch by motorways to other parts of the country or for later delivery to the CBD (e.g. food, drink, car parts).

☐ Food processing firms.

☐ Light, small scale, manufacturing industries.

☐ High technology firms.

☐ The more recent addition of offices, hotels and hypermarkets.

The demand for leisure and social activities is now an important consideration in locating new firms.

Office location

City centres Until recently it had become a tradition for offices to locate in city centres. The high streets consisted of banks and building societies, post offices and estate agents, insurance companies and solicitors, betting shops and employment agencies. In the larger cities competition for space resulted in the upward growth of office blocks (Figure 8.17). The advantages of being located in the CBD included:

□ The centre of communications both within that city, and with other cities (e.g. rail).

□ The centre of the supply of staff.

□ Offices being able to afford the high rates and rents resulting from the high cost of land. As offices do not need bulk deliveries nor require large storage space, they can be built upwards, unlike warehouses and shops which need ground floor space.

□ Exchange of information between firms and other commercial linkages (e.g. banks). If head offices are situated close to each other, time and money could be saved. This is increasingly important in data collecting firms.

□ Near to international airports, restaurants, hotels and entertainment for contacts with overseas branches or other businesses.

□ The prestige of a city centre site and address.

□ Property developers make greater profits by building office blocks in city centres rather than in the suburbs.

Out-of-town suburban locations Since the 1970s there has been, both in Britain and North America, a movement away from the CBD to the suburbs (Figure 8.19). In New York it is claimed that over 100 of the 200 major companies found in the CBD in 1960 had moved out by 1985, leaving mainly the most successful firms such as the American Express Credit Card Company, and leading oil companies. The advantages of the suburbs include:

□ Lower rates and rent. The cost of a square metre of floorspace is usually less than half that in the CBD.

□ Less traffic congestion surrounding the office block.

□ Nearer to motorways.

□ Room for expansion and car parks.

□ As data/information can now be readily transferred by such methods as telex, the need to be close to other firms has lessened.

□ Pleasanter working environment (see Science Parks, page 66).

□ Easier access for staff who, being mainly professional, managerial and skilled, will live in local, expensive suburban estates or commuter villages.

△ **Figure 8.17** High-rise office blocks in São Paulo. Notice the heliport and underpass

Decentralisation

Decentralisation is when a large firm or the government decides to move its office (or factory) from the capital city to another location in Britain. In 1983, 458 of Britain's largest 1000 companies had their headquarters in London, followed, a long way behind, by the West Midlands with 46, West Yorkshire with 34 and Strathclyde with 31. As office jobs account for over 25% of all jobs in Britain, this helps to account for the lower levels of unemployment in the south-east of England, and the increase of females in paid employment (Figure 8.7). Since the 1970s governments have attempted, mainly by offering grants, to decentralise offices. The new locations are found either in development areas of northern and western Britain, or in towns in the south-east of England, away from London with its high land values.

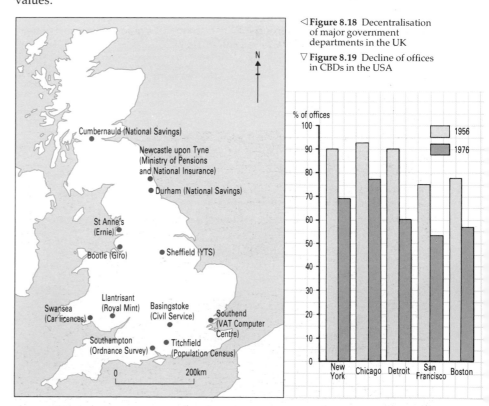

◁ **Figure 8.18** Decentralisation of major government departments in the UK

▽ **Figure 8.19** Decline of offices in CBDs in the USA

High technology industries

The term 'high technology industry' (or hi-tech) refers, usually, to industries developed within the last 20 years and whose processing techniques often involve micro-electronics. These industries have been the 'growth' industries of recent years though unfortunately they employ few people in comparison with the older, declining heavy industries. Two possible subdivisions of hi-tech industries are:

1 The 'sunrise industries' which have a high technology base.

2 Information technology industries involving computers, telecommunications and micro-electronics.

As a highly skilled, inventive, intelligent workforce is essential, and as access to raw materials is relatively unimportant, these hi-tech footloose industries tend to become attracted to areas which the researchers and operators find attractive – from a climatic, scenic, health and social point of view. Such areas include:

☐ Silicon Glen in central Scotland.

☐ Silicon Valley in California.

☐ Sunrise Strip which follows the route of the M4 from London westwards towards Newbury (locally known as Video Valley) and more widely to Bristol (Aztec West) and into South Wales (Figure 8.20).

Legend:
═══ motorways
┼┼┼ railways
▨ towns
--- county boundaries
✈ Heathrow Airport
▨ hills
(H) high technology firms and research centres

Figure 8.20 The 'Sunrise Strip'. Many hi-tech industries have located around Bristol, especially at Aztec West at the junction of the M4 and M5, where expertise had already developed through such firms as Rolls Royce and British Aerospace.

The majority of new industries have tended to locate along the Berkshire section of the M4 where the nearness to Heathrow Airport has been a vital extra advantage

Figure 8.21 Windmill Hill Business Park, Swindon. In all, three large business parks have been developed, each offering facilities and accommodation in a landscaped, parkland environment

Figure 8.22 Press advertisement for a hi-tech park in the county of Gwent, South Wales

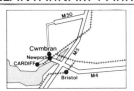

LLANTARNAM PARK

Llantarnam Park is on its way to becoming one of the most advanced high-tech parks in Europe.

At the southern edge of Cwmbran New Town (pop. 45,000) and linked to the M4 motorway by expressway, Llantarnam Park lies at the heart of the West's major communications network.

Enterprises involved in research and light manufacture, will find the stunning landscaping, low density of buildings and carefully controlled environment ideal. The park soon will be fully serviced by its own banks, shops and an international hotel.

Existing high technology tenants include the Parrot Corporation, Data Type, Cifer and Isomet Lasers. Available on the 110 acre park are:-
– Factory units from 750 sq.ft. to 20,000 sq.ft. and larger.
– Serviced greenfield sites for the construction of buildings to meet specific needs.

The Cwmbran Development Corporation offer a variety of helpful options: freehold sale, long and short leases and leasebacks.

Generous Development Area financial incentives, can mean substantial savings in setting up costs for most companies moving to Llantarnam Park.

YEARS AHEAD IN HIGH TECH,
5 MINUTES OFF
THE M4 CORRIDOR

Cwmbran
Britain's best located Development Area

'Sunrise Strip'

The advantages of this area for spontaneous, unplanned growth of micro-electronics industries include:

☐ The proximity of the M4 and main line railways.

☐ The presence of Heathrow airport.

☐ The previous location and existence of government and other research centres.

☐ A large labour force, many of whom have moved out of London into new towns and overspill towns.

☐ The proximity of other associated industries with which ideas and information can be exchanged.

☐ Nearness to universities with expertise and research facilities available. A science park is located near to a university so that hi-tech firms can work closely with that university.

☐ An attractive environment. Figure 8.20 names the Cotswolds, Mendips, Chilterns and Marlborough Downs. Nearby are the North Downs, three National Parks (Brecon Beacons, Dartmoor and Exmoor) and, through the centre of the area, the Thames Valley.

▷ **Figure 8.23** The sunbelt
states: population change,
1970–80

The 'Sunbelt' of North America

Figure 8.23 locates the states in this sunbelt, and
shows how rapidly the population of five of them
grew between 1970 and 1980. The rapid growth of
these states has been attributed to:

□ Investment under which sunbelt states impose
low taxes and spend little on welfare
provision. A redundant worker receives below
average compensation (trade union closed
shops are illegal) though luckily unemployment
in these states is low.

□ A highly skilled workforce is migrating here
from the industrially declining northern
states, while poorly skilled labour (for
construction work) is continually swelled by
Mexicans (page 30), many of whom are illegal,
yet essential, immigrants.

□ The climate is seen most favourably by
northerners. The milder winters and hot
summers draw people of all ages, with the less
humid western states seen as the most
attractive (e.g. Arizona).

□ Retirement communities in which wealthy
northerners bring income and the need for
more service to the area.

□ Changing industrial trends from 'the smoke
stack to hi-tech' have favoured the sunbelt. The
recession has hit the manufacturing areas of the
north-east of the USA, allowing the footloose
and hi-tech industries to develop in the oil-rich
areas, with the added advantage of a pleasant
living environment.

Phoenix City (Arizona) is one of the fastest
growing cities. Relative humidity is nearly always
less than 50%, and the city is within easy range of
the Grand Canyon, forested plateaux and rocky
deserts – the out-door image so attractive to
modern Americans. Recreational amenities are
found in abundance. Phoenix's three leading
manufacturing activities are hi-tech, electronics
and aerospace. In turn these industries have
helped the growth of tourism, food processing
and service industries.

Appropriate (intermediate) technology for developing countries

In developing countries, not only are hi-tech
industries too expensive to develop, they are also
usually most inappropriate to the inhabitants.
Appropriate technology means innovations
suitable to the resources of those countries.

Appropriate technology should:

□ Try to avoid high capital investment by not
using expensive machinery and sources of
energy. It must be at a price which the country
can afford.

□ Be labour intensive as the majority of people in
developing countries are either unemployed or
under-employed. With so many people
needing an income, it is of limited value to
replace these people with robots.

□ Be suited to the levels of skills of the people.

□ Try to develop, rather than to replace, local
industries and methods of farming.

□ Try to use local resources instead of those from
outside the area or country. It is preferable that
such resources are renewable, such as the use
of biogas plants, or that the product, once used,
can be recycled.

□ Help to conserve the local environment.

△ **Figure 8.24** Possible
applications of appropriate
technology.
Animals (**1**) provide dung
and pull carts. The dung
ferments in ditches (**2**) and
methane gas is given off
and stored (**3**).

A biogas plant (**4**) converts
animal waste into gas for
cooking, while compost
toilets (**5**) improve sanitation
and provide biogas fuel.

Fast-growing neem and
eucalyptus trees (**6**) provide
fuel for the gasifier (**7**) which
generates electricity for water
pumps.

Solar panels (**8**) and
photovoltaic cells (**9**) provide
power to heat water.

Improved cooking stoves (**10**)
and water filters (**11**) are also
used.

Government aid and industrial location

▷ **Figure 8.25** Assisted areas in the UK, 1987

▽ **Figure 8.26** Changing employment in Corby

Successive British governments have tried, since 1945, to encourage industry to move to areas of high unemployment. The size and location of these areas of high unemployment have changed over a period of time. Figure 8.25 shows the areas which were regarded as needing the most assistance in 1986. Over the years governments have tried to encourage new industries to reduce unemployment by:

☐ Industrial development certificates which control where a firm can locate. These were first issued by the British government in 1947.

☐ The creation of new towns in order to take work to the unemployed.

☐ Providing 'advanced factories' and industrial estates with services already present (e.g. roads, electricity).

☐ Financial aid in the form of removal grants, rent-free periods, tax relief on new machinery, and reduced interest rates.

☐ Decentralising government offices (page 65).

☐ Improving communications and accessibility.

☐ Subsidies to keep firms going which otherwise would close down.

☐ Retraining schemes.

☐ Job Creation, Manpower Creation Schemes (MCS) and Youth Training Schemes (YTS).

☐ Enterprise Zones.

☐ Assistance from the EEC.

Enterprise Zones (EZs)

The first Enterprise Zones came into operation in 1981. They were planned for areas in acute physical and economic decay, with the aim of creating conditions for industrial and commercial revival by removing certain tax burdens and administrative controls. Initially eleven Enterprise Zones were established, and by 1986 there were 25 of these (Figure 8.25). They tend to fall into two main groups:

1 Old inner city areas where factories had closed, causing high unemployment, and where old houses had been pulled down and the land was derelict (e.g. Isle of Dogs (page 74), Clydebank).

2 Towns that had relied upon one major industry which had been forced to close (e.g. Corby, Figure 8.26).

The inducements to new firms that might locate in Enterprise Zones include:

☐ Rate-free premises until 1991.

☐ Maximum grants for machinery and buildings.

☐ Planning applications from firms wishing to locate there are given top priority.

☐ Employers are exempt from industrial training levies.

☐ Allowances of 100% are given for the construction, extension, or improvement of commercial and industrial premises.

☐ No industrial development certificates are needed.

Corby Enterprise Zone

In 1934 Corby was only a small village situated on a large deposit of iron ore. Stewarts and Lloyds decided to convert the ore found on the spot into steel, and then the steel into tubes in one continuous process. The demand for a large workforce led to the rapid growth of Corby with many new families coming from Scotland (Figure 8.26). By 1956, 70% of the workforce was connected with the steel industry, and Corby had virtually become a one industry town.

In 1980, the British Steel Corporation (BSC) had to close the steel-making side at Corby. This was because the strip which it produced was so expensive that the tube works found it impossible to compete on world markets. The largely unskilled workforce had either to move, commute or join the dole queue. Following the closure, the tube works obtained steel strip from elsewhere in BSC at a lower price enabling it to become competitive again – although by 1985 only 10% of the working population of the town was now linked with steel.

In 1981, Corby was designated an Enterprise Zone. Money came not only from the British government, but also from the EEC. Improved road links have been made with the M1 and A1, while government grants and a vigorous advertising policy (Figure 8.27) have encouraged new firms to locate here (e.g. Weetabix, Avon Cosmetics and Golden Wonder Crisps). Although the average workforce for each new firm is only 50 (compare that with the peak workforce at BSC), Corby has become a more balanced town with a wider industrial base.

Using Figure 8.27:

1 List four sources of aid available to Corby.

2 Why is Corby 'strategically placed for any business that needs fast, inexpensive and easy access to the big South East and Midland population centres'?

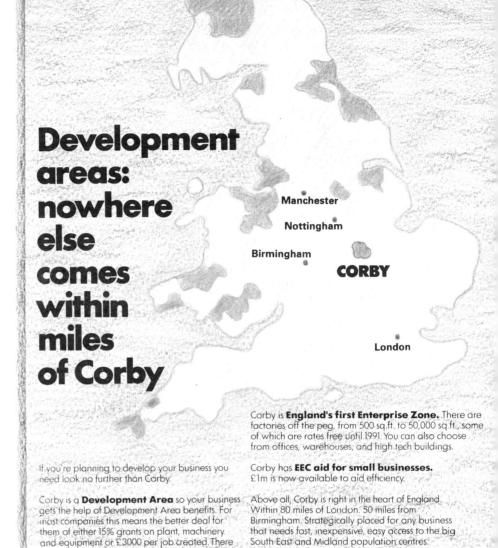

Development areas: nowhere else comes within miles of Corby

Manchester
Nottingham
Birmingham
CORBY
London

Corby is **England's first Enterprise Zone.** There are factories off the peg, from 500 sq.ft. to 50,000 sq.ft., some of which are rates free until 1991. You can also choose from offices, warehouses, and high tech buildings.

If you're planning to develop your business you need look no further than Corby.

Corby is a **Development Area** so your business gets the help of Development Area benefits. For most companies this means the better deal for them of either 15% grants on plant, machinery and equipment or £3000 per job created. There is also selective assistance for some job creating projects.

Corby is also a **Steel Opportunity Area,** and this means even more incentives.

Corby has **EEC aid for small businesses.** £1m is now available to aid efficiency.

Above all, Corby is right in the heart of England. Within 80 miles of London. 50 miles from Birmingham. Strategically placed for any business that needs fast, inexpensive, easy access to the big South East and Midland population centres.

However far you look, you will find that, as a total package for the success of your business, nowhere else comes within miles of Corby.

△ **Figure 8.27** An example of Corby's publicity material

Nissan comes to Washington

Washington, in a development area, had been designated a new town in 1964 due to the high rate of unemployment in the North East, following the decline in the traditional industries of that area – steel, ships and engineering. By 1984 Nissan (Japan) had become the fourth largest car producer in the world (Figure 8.5), with the majority of cars being exported to North America and western Europe. Countries such as the UK negotiated voluntary agreements with Japan to the effect that, for example, the volume of Japanese cars imported into Britain would not exceed 11% of Britain's passenger car market. Following this, Japanese car manufacturers began to look for ways to overcome this barrier, and to produce cars within Britain.

When, in 1981, the British government decided to allow Nissan to build a factory to assemble cars, several areas with high unemployment began a highly active campaign to attract Nissan. The former Tyne and Wear council successfully lobbied the Japanese by showing that Nissan could get grants to cover one-third of their building costs by being in a development area, that a huge area of flat land (formerly Sunderland airport) was already available, that the site was adjacent to the AI(M), near to the Tyne and Wear for the import of parts for car assembly and the export of finished cars, and in an area with a tradition in engineering.

At the opening in September 1986, it was announced that the initial workforce of 500 needed to assemble 24 000 cars a year was to be increased by 2000 (and extra jobs would be created in component factories elsewhere in Britain). The local council hopes that by landing such a prestigious company other firms will be attracted to the area.

INDUSTRY
Multinationals

A multinational company, sometimes now called a transnational company, is one which operates in many countries, regardless of national frontiers. The headquarters are usually in developed countries with, increasingly, the 'branch' factories in developing countries. The multinational companies directly employ about 30 million people around the world, and indirectly influence an even larger number. Many companies have annual sales larger than the GNP of some European countries. The largest 100 firms (led by oil companies and car firms) controlled one-fifth of the world's manufacturing output in 1965, and one-third by 1985. The four largest ones had, in 1980, a bigger turnover than all of Africa's GNP. Recently some multinational companies have grown in developing countries with their 'branches' in other developing countries. Many people attack multinationals as exploiters of poor countries but as an Indian from Manaus (Brazil) said, 'It is more important to have jobs'. Study Figure 8.28. Do you think multinationals are, on balance, a blessing or a curse to a country?

Union Carbide is an American multinational with a factory at Bhopal in India (Figure 8.29). In late 1984 it was the scene of the world's worst industrial accident.

Why was Bhopal chosen? It was centrally placed in India, and also centrally placed in a large agricultural area. The city had a population of 700 000, many of whom had no jobs, was a state capital, and was on the main Bombay to Delhi railway line.

Why was it welcomed by Bhopal and India? Union Carbide designed and built the factory, provided the equipment, introduced a high level of technology, trained the workforce, employed many local workers, brought more money into the local economy, improved some local services and satisfied the demand for fertilisers and pesticides needed by the many Indian farmers.

What problems were raised in Bhopal? So keen were the authorities for the factory that it was allowed to be built in a residential area. A large agricultural labour force migrated to the city for work, putting more pressure on Bhopal, at a time of world economic recession and falling sales. Union Carbide spent less money on safety, and due to the distance from the head office little notice was taken of local claims concerning the leak of toxic gas.

December 1984 A sudden release of toxic gas into the air resulted in 2500 deaths, over 100 000 injured (of whom thousands will have been left irreversibly blind or deranged) and the loss of animals and crops.

Advantages to the country	Disadvantages to the country
Brings work to the country and uses local labour	Numbers employed small in comparison with amount of investment
Local workforce receives a guaranteed income	Local labour force usually poorly paid
Improves the levels of education and technical skill of the people	Very few local skilled workers employed
Brings welcome investment and foreign currency to the country	Most of the profits go overseas (outflow of wealth)
Companies provide expensive machinery and modern technology	Mechanisation reduces the size of the labour force
Increased gross national product/personal income can lead to an increased demand for consumer goods and the growth of new industries	GNP grows less quickly than that of the parent company's headquarters, widening the gap between developed and developing countries
Leads to the development of mineral wealth and new energy resources	Minerals are usually exported rather than manufactured and energy costs may lead to a national debt
Improvements in roads, airports and services	Money possibly better spent on improving housing, diet, and sanitation
Prestige value (e.g. Volta project)	Big schemes can increase national debt (e.g. Brazil)
Widens economic base of the country	Decisions are made outside the country, and the firm could pull out at any time
Some improvement in standards of production, health control and recently in environmental control	Insufficient attention to safety and health factors and the protection of the environment

△ **Figure 8.28** Advantages and disadvantages of a multinational company

▽ **Figure 8.29** Map: location of Bhopal.
Photo: workmen spray water on a section of tarpaulin fencing erected around the Union Carbide factory in Bhopal, to prevent further leakage of poisonous gas as technicians began to convert the remaining gas to pesticide

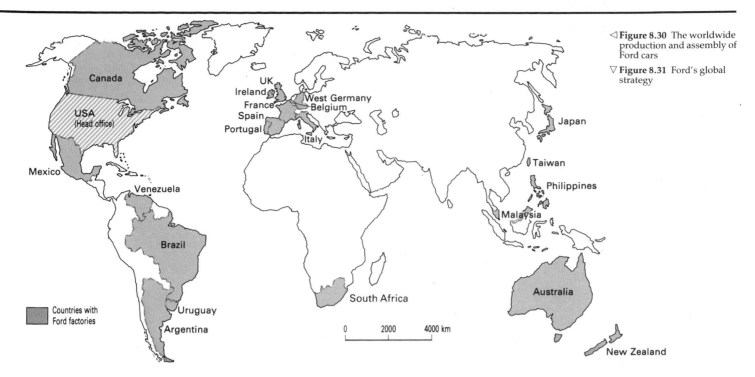

Countries with Ford factories

Ford – a multinational car company

The global factory is a relatively new term applied to those multinationals which see the world, rather than the local area, as their supplier of labour and area for sales. In other words they are creating a world market for their products. By the mid-1980s the Ford Motor Company was:

☐ Manufacturing and/or assembling its cars worldwide (Figure 8.30), even if the bulk of the parts were still produced in the more developed areas of North America, western Europe and Japan.

☐ Increasingly locating new factories to manufacture cars (e.g. São Paulo) or to assemble parts made elsewhere (e.g. Malaysia, the Philippines) in the developing countries.

☐ Increasingly making parts in several countries (less prone to strikes) so that a particular model was no longer made in just one country. Figure 8.31 shows that a Ford car sold in Britain may have been assembled here or in another West European country, and that its parts may have come from up to six different countries.

☐ Facing, as were other car companies, the problems of overproduction by which the number of cars being produced exceeded the world demand for those cars. Together with the increased competition from rival companies, especially those based in Japan, this has led to a saturation of the market, and redundancies. When Ford is forced to close assembly factories, it is more likely to be in the less developed countries where the local market is smaller than in the more developed countries.

☐ Facing rapidly increasing costs as the need for a more efficiently produced car meant a greater use of computers and robots.

☐ Aiming at the production of a 'world vehicle'.

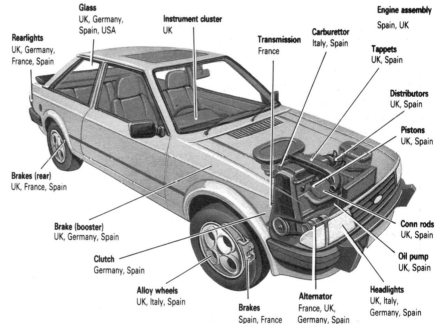

Glass UK, Germany, Spain, USA

Instrument cluster UK

Engine assembly Spain, UK

Rearlights UK, Germany, France, Spain

Transmission France

Carburettor Italy, Spain

Tappets UK, Spain

Distributors UK, Spain

Pistons UK, Spain

Brakes (rear) UK, France, Spain

Conn rods UK, Spain

Brake (booster) UK, Germany, Spain

Oil pump UK, Spain

Clutch Germany, Spain

Alloy wheels UK, Italy, Spain

Brakes Spain, France

Alternator France, UK, Germany, Spain

Headlights UK, Italy, Germany, Spain

In the 1970s there were hopes that a 'world car' would evolve – not only would parts be made in many countries, but it was thought that the resulting vehicle would be universally accepted. This has not happened – the trend is rather towards more variety in cars – but in the early 1980s it seems that a world truck may be acceptable. The Ford Motor Company's world truck, the Cargo, will have a driver's cab and cab panels made in Europe, a North American chassis, a Brazilian gearbox and a diesel engine developed for tractor use in the USA. About 40 000 a year are expected to be produced. The truck will be assembled in Brazil and initially sold throughout North America as well as in Brazil itself; other export markets are being considered, especially in south-east Asia. The Ford world truck programme has been under development since 1982, and is expected to take another ten years to complete. At that time Ford anticipates that 'components for our heavy trucks will be of a single, world-class design and will be built in a number of countries. We will buy from those international suppliers who can supply in the countries where we assemble trucks and need the components.'

(*Financial Times*, 16 January 1985)

Employment in a third world city

In third world cities, the number of inhabitants greatly outweighs the number of jobs available. With the rapid growth of these cities the job situation is continually worsening (Figure 8.32).

The 'informal sector' is sometimes referred to as the 'third sector' (i.e. linked to the third world) as it does not fit into:

1 The profit-making enterprises of the capitalist western world, or

2 The central planning ideology of communist countries.

In many developing cities there are now publicly and privately promoted self-help programmes to support, but not to direct, these self-help efforts. Yet with or without this support, the numbers engaged in the informal sector are growing (Figure 8.33).

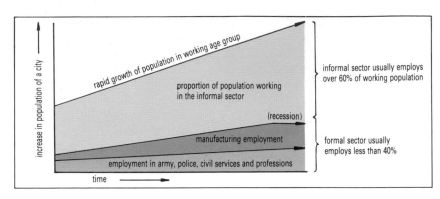

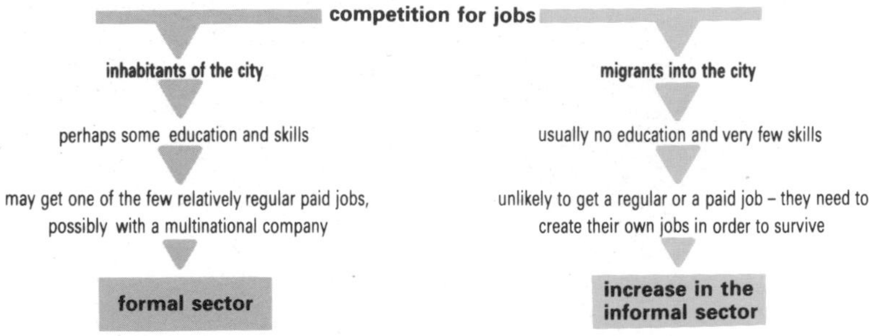

competition for jobs

inhabitants of the city — perhaps some education and skills — may get one of the few relatively regular paid jobs, possibly with a multinational company → **formal sector**

migrants into the city — usually no education and very few skills — unlikely to get a regular or a paid job – they need to create their own jobs in order to survive → **increase in the informal sector**

△ **Figure 8.32** Competition for jobs in a developing city

△ **Figure 8.33** The formal and informal sectors of employment

▷ **Figure 8.34** Main photo: Copacabana beach and Sugarloaf Mountain. Inset: shoe-shine boys, Mexico; girl selling shuttlecocks in Rio de Janeiro; beach vendors on Copacabana beach

Differences between the formal and informal sectors

Formal	Informal
Description	
Employee of a large firm	Self employed
Often a multinational	Small scale/family enterprise
Much capital involved	Little capital involved
Capital-intensive with relatively few workers. Mechanised	Labour-intensive with the use of very few tools
Expensive raw materials	Using cheap or recycled waste materials
A guaranteed standard in the final product	Often a low standard in quality of goods
Regular hours (often long) and wages (often low)	Irregular hours and uncertain wages
Fixed prices	Prices rarely fixed and so negotiable (bartering)
Jobs done in factories	Jobs often done in the home (cottage industry) or on the streets
Government and multinational help	No government assistance
Legal	Often outside the law (illegal)
Usually males	Often children and females
Type of job	
Manufacturing — both local and multinational industries	Distributive, e.g. street pedlars and small stalls
Government-created jobs such as the police, army and civil service	Services, e.g. shoecleaners, selling clothes and fruit
	Small scale industry, e.g. food processing, dress repairs, furniture repairs
Advantages	
Uses some skilled and many unskilled workers	Employs many thousands of unskilled workers
Provides permanent jobs and regular wages	Jobs may provide some training and skills which might lead to better jobs in the future
Produces goods for the more wealthy (cars, food) within their *own* country so that profits may remain within the country	Any profit will be used within the city
Waste materials provide raw materials for the informal sector	Uses local and waste materials
The products will be for local use by the lower paid people

Our small group of 11 tourists from Britain was staying at the Rio Palace, a five star hotel overlooking the famous Copacabana beach in Rio de Janeiro. Walking along the beach one afternoon, I noticed numerous beach vendors. These form part of Rio's large informal sector. Several vendors carried large umbrellas (Figure 8.34) from which dangled an assortment of sun hats, suntan lotion or tangas (bikinis). One vendor carried pineapples in a basket perched on his head and, in his hand, a large knife with which to cut the fruit. Some vendors carried cooler boxes in which were ice cream, Coca Cola, coconut water and other drinks, while others carried large metal drums which contained maté (a local drink). These people drew attention to themselves by shouting, blowing whistles, beating metal drums or whirling a metal ratchet that clattered loudly. On the pavement next to the beach were small children trying to sell sweets and chocolate, and numerous kiosks with fruit and drink available.

Returning to the hotel, several of us were tempted to buy a brightly feathered shuttlecock from a girl who had a most enchanting smile (Figure 8.34) but we resisted other sellers of cheap jewellery and Copacabana T-shirts. That evening as our group ate in a restaurant next to the Rio Palace, other pedlars poked their heads through the open door and windows trying to sell not very musical instruments, monkey-puppets and T-shirts. As we left the restaurant at 9.30 pm to visit one of Rio's famous Samba shows, we saw a small boy of four or five years with sad, appealing eyes trying to sell roses individually wrapped in cellophane. How could one fail to buy a rose which, he indicated by his fingers, were only 15 crusadas (about 50p)? However by the time the money was produced, he had raised his price to 20 crusadas – and shown us that his eyes had been trained and his brain sharpened for business. When we returned at 1.00 am, he was still outside the hotel with the remainder of his roses.

Role of children

Children, many of whom are under ten years old, make up a large proportion of the informal sector workers. Very few of them have schools to go to, and from an early age go out onto the streets to try to supplement the family income. One such 'worker', who has become well known in British schools, was a shoe-shine boy called Mauru who lived in São Paulo, and was seen in a TV programme *Skyscrapers and Slums*. He would try to earn money during the day, and try to study, to become an airline pilot, at night.

Re-arrange the jobs listed below, which were noted during a study of a city in the developing world, into (a) primary, secondary and tertiary occupations and (b) formal and informal occupations by completing the accompanying table.

Shoe-shiner; maker of sandals from old wood and tyres; policeman; bus driver; tinsmith using old beer cans; soldier; self employed fisherman with a fish stall; car-factory worker; snake-charmer; bottler at a Coca-Cola works; hotel waitress; tour guide; smallholder with a few goats; worker on a coffee plantation; cool-drink vendor; gardener in a city park; and machine operator at a textile mill.

	Formal	Informal
Primary		
Secondary		
Tertiary		

PLANNING
Old industrial areas

Planning takes place throughout the world on a variety of scales and levels, ranging from the almost randomly established bustees in Calcutta, where the individuals are responsible for the housing layout, to the highly organised city layout of Brasilia, where planners, developers and architects work together as one.

The London Docklands: the LDDC development plan

One major planning development taking place today is in the old docklands of East London. The area available for development covers 21 square kilometres and had become, due to the decline of the docks, an almost derelict area (Figure 9.1).

The London Dockland Development Committee (LDDC) was set up in 1981 and is responsible for the regeneration of the area. To achieve this, the committee hopes to bring land and buildings in the dockland area into effective use, to encourage the development of the few existing industries as well as new industry, and to ensure that housing, social and recreation facilities are available, so creating an attractive environment in which to live and work. There are four areas of development planned in the docklands (i) business (ii) housing (iii) shopping (iv) leisure and recreation.

Attracting business to the area Of the four categories listed above, this offers the greatest challenge. In 1982, London's only enterprise zone was set up in the Isle of Dogs and to encourage rapid building throughout the whole docklands area there are few planning restrictions (Figure 9.2).

New firms include newspaper works, many City finance firms and hi-tech industries. The LDDC also hopes that the docklands could become an extension of the City, where all the banks are situated at present. London's invisible market, that of finance, is the biggest in the world, but is rapidly running out of space in the 'square mile' of the City, and so the docklands offer an ideal opportunity to expand eastwards.

In August 1986, London's financial system changed dramatically (known as the *big bang*) with the rearrangement of the stock market. At the moment London acts as a mediator between the time gaps of New York and Tokyo and has more banks than those two put together. However, if London is to remain a leader of the financial world, more office space is required, and the docklands provide a prime site. Yet if the financial market is to extend into the docklands, development must be rapid, hence the few restrictions imposed on planning in the area.

An American consortium is in charge of the development programme and plans three office blocks up to 270m high (Figure 9.3). Also, it is thought large dealing floors (required due to the change in the stock market) of up to 40 000m² in area will have to be built. The docklands are one of the few areas in London where such space is available.

◁ **Figure 9.1** The derelict and undeveloped docklands of East London

▽ **Figure 9.2** Aspects of the London Dockland Development Scheme

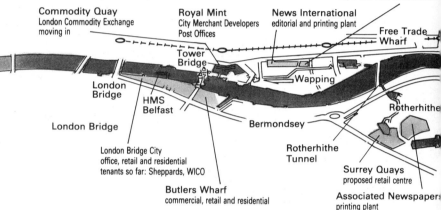

Commodity Quay
London Commodity Exchange moving in

Royal Mint
City Merchant Developers
Post Offices

News International
editorial and printing plant

Tobacco Dock Grade 1 building developed into retail and recreation

Free Trade Wharf

Tower Bridge

Wapping

London Bridge

HMS Belfast

London Bridge

London Bridge City
office, retail and residential
tenants so far: Sheppards, WICO

Butlers Wharf
commercial, retail and residential

Bermondsey

Rotherhithe

Rotherhithe Tunnel

Surrey Quays
proposed retail centre

Associated Newspapers
printing plant

◁ **Figure 9.3** Model of the proposed Canary Wharf development, the Isle of Dogs Enterprise Zone

▷ **Figure 9.4** Rolling stock for the new docklands light railway

▷ **Figure 9.5** The de Havilland Canada Dash 7 landing in London docklands during demonstrations of the aircraft's performance and noise during June 1982. The airport is due to come into operation in mid-1987.

Transport and communications

There have been two phases in development:

1 Communications to the City

2 Communications throughout the docklands and to other areas.

Phase 1 has centred mainly on a light railway which runs above ground level on conventional tracks (DLR). It is intended that this line will run from the centre of the present City, at Bank, to the eastern side of the docklands, thus reducing transport time dramatically (Figure 9.4).

Phase 2 has involved the building of a new road network throughout much of the docks, with fibre optic cable laid beneath it, to allow instant access to other parts of London and Britain. British Telecom has installed satellite dishes to allow immediate contact with any city in the world including the two other major financial centres of Tokyo and New York.

A short take off and landing airport (Stolport) is being built on a wharf in the east docklands to connect with other parts of Britain and major cities in Europe within a 650km radius. It is only a 20 minute drive from the City, whereas Gatwick and Heathrow take over an hour to reach. It is hoped that waiting times in the Stolport itself will also be reduced (Figure 9.5).

Problems

As with any new development there are problems and objections. Although it is next to the City, many feel it is still too far away from the centre for it to become an extension to the traditional banking sector. Even if did, the close-knit banking community and the City's characteristics would be destroyed, leading to an environment like that in Manhattan, where personal contact is replaced by telephone calls and telexes between offices.

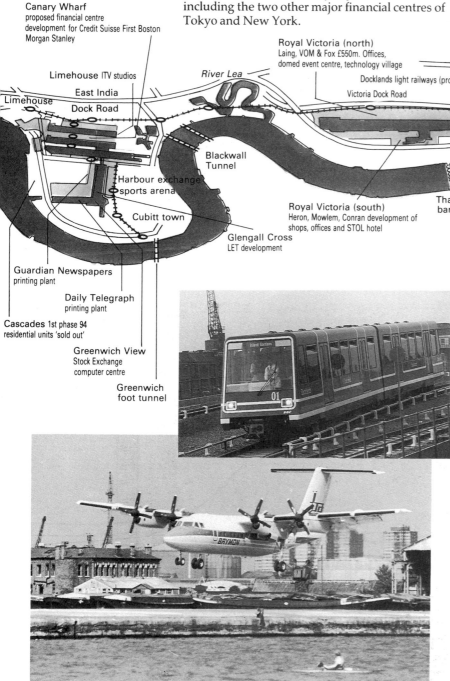

Canary Wharf
proposed financial centre development for Credit Suisse First Boston Morgan Stanley

Limehouse ITV studios

East India

Limehouse

Dock Road

River Lea

Royal Victoria (north)
Laing, VOM & Fox £550m. Offices, domed event centre, technology village

Docklands light railways (proposed)
Victoria Dock Road

Royal Albert (north)
Rosehaugh Stanhope
£750m leisure, shopping, business park and marine centre

M11

Blackwall Tunnel

Harbour exchange sports arena

Cubitt town

Royal Docks

River Thames

Woolwich foot tunnel

proposed Thames crossing

Royal Victoria (south)
Heron, Mowlem, Conran development of shops, offices and STOL hotel

Thames barrier

British Telecom
UK Satellite Station

Royal Albert (south)
City Stolport

Glengall Cross
LET development

Guardian Newspapers
printing plant

Daily Telegraph
printing plant

Cascades 1st phase 94 residential units 'sold out'

Greenwich View
Stock Exchange computer centre

Greenwich foot tunnel

Many people are opposed to the development, feeling that it has been left to the eleventh hour, as development here has been possible since the Second World War. The 40 000 residents in the area are worried for their homes (96% are council houses at present) despite assurances that this number will remain together with an increase in owner occupied houses (which will be expensive due to the rapid rise in land values in the area). They are also worried that all the jobs in the area will be hi-tech and skilled, and thus there will be few opportunities for the present low skilled population.

The plans for high rise buildings have attracted complaints, often from residents south of the river, that they will be an eyesore in what is now a flat dockland. It is also thought they will pose hazards to planes landing at the Stolport. Others feel the enterprise zone is too big and that if the project does not work, East London will be left with yet more tower blocks, leaving a new 'wasteland'.

In 1986 it was claimed that the success to date was a decade ahead of earlier predictions. Over 9000 homes had been built or were under construction; 1.2 million square metres of the office floor was in use; 400 new business had moved in, creating 8000 jobs; and Stolport (now called London City Airport) and the extension to the light railway were on schedule for a mid-1987 opening. Future plans include a shopping centre two-and-a-half times larger than the one at Brent Cross, a marina and a technology village.

New towns

These have been built for a variety of reasons. In the United Kingdom they were created mainly to take the overspill from expanding conurbations, to attract new industries into areas of high unemployment, and to try to create a more pleasant environment in areas of old, declining industry. Most new towns in western Europe were created for similar reasons. In South Africa new townships have been established to house and segregate black workers (page 31), while in Israel new communes are built to try to colonise the desert and to ensure the land becomes part of their state.

USSR

Many new towns have also been built since 1917:

- East of the Ural Mountains they have been created to exploit the vast energy reserves and mineral wealth of the area (oil, natural gas, HEP, iron ore, etc.)
- West of the Urals to encourage the growth of large industrial areas.
- Around the older cities of Moscow, Leningrad and Kiev where there was a demand for more and newer housing (e.g. Chernobyl).
- In the Arctic areas to the north and in the deserts to the south to colonise new areas, sometimes for minerals, and sometimes to increase food production (irrigation).

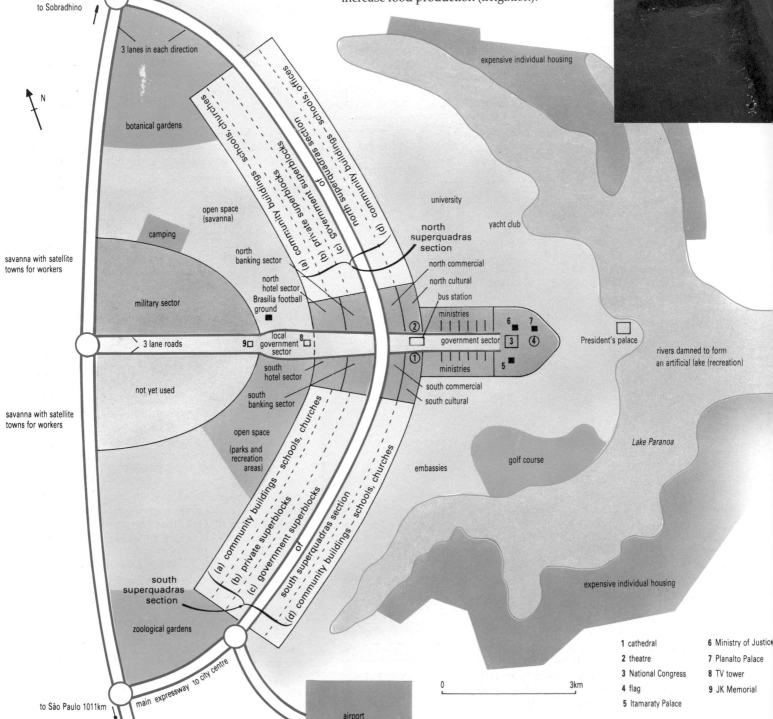

to Sobradhino

3 lanes in each direction

N

botanical gardens

open space (savanna)

camping

savanna with satellite towns for workers

military sector

north banking sector

north hotel sector
Brasilia football ground

north superquadras section of government superblocks — community buildings — schools, churches

(a) community buildings
(b) private superblocks
(c) government superblocks
(d) community buildings — schools, churches

university

yacht club

north superquadras section

north commercial

north cultural

bus station

ministries

government sector

3 lane roads

local government sector

9 ☐   8 ☐

② ☐

① ☐

ministries

6 ■   7 ■
3   ④
5 ■

President's palace

rivers damned to form an artificial lake (recreation)

savanna with satellite towns for workers

not yet used

south hotel sector

south banking sector

open space (parks and recreation areas)

south commercial

south cultural

embassies

golf course

Lake Paranoa

expensive individual housing

(a) community buildings — schools, churches
(b) private superblocks
(c) government superblocks
(d) community buildings — schools, churches

south superquadras section

south superquadras section

zoological gardens

expensive individual housing

to São Paulo 1011km

main expressway to city centre

airport

expensive individual housing

0   3km

1 cathedral
2 theatre
3 National Congress
4 flag
5 Itamaraty Palace

6 Ministry of Justice
7 Planalto Palace
8 TV tower
9 JK Memorial

▷ **Figure 9.7** A view of the northern wing of the aeroplane, showing the many superblocks

▽ **Figure 9.8** Inside one of the superblocks, Brasilia

▽ **Figure 9.9** Plan of part of the south superquadras (residential) section

Figure 9.6 Plan of Brasilia

The superblocks (superquadras)

The wings of the 'aeroplane' are used for housing and are divided into superblocks (superquadras), each of which is meant to be a complete unit in itself (Figure 9.9) (similar to a neighbourhood unit in a British new town). Each superblock is approached by a slip road, and at each entrance is a post box, public telephone and a newspaper kiosk. Inside the superblock are nine to eleven apartment blocks, each ten storeys high, and housing about 2500 people. The apartments are luxurious, unlike most British high rise flats, and are well looked after. The apartments shown in Figures 9.7 and 9.8 belong to the Bank of Brazil and are occupied by its employees. Almost all the other apartments are inhabited by local or national government workers, all of whom have well paid jobs. The apartments' rear windows are covered by a grid for privacy, and the fronts have shutters which can be opened or closed. The whole area is very clean and well maintained. Many flowering trees and shrubs have been planted (Brasilia has 30 000 new trees planted each year). The inhabitants favour living in these apartments as it gives them security (although Brasilia's crime rate is well below the national average), the environment is attractive, services are nearby, and those working in the town centre can easily travel home at lunch time (unlike other Brazilian cities). Each superblock has its own kindergarten, to save the children crossing roads. Each pair of super-blocks has a play area and a self contained shopping area. On the edge of the housing area are community buildings with a Catholic church, a senior school and a community centre for each set of four superblocks.

How do the (a) type of housing (b) services and (c) quality of the environment of the superblocks of Brasilia and the neighbourhood units of a British new town differ?

Brasilia

This is perhaps the most famous example of an elaborately planned new town. For decades, concern had been expressed at the relative richness and overpopulation of the south east of Brazil (São Paulo and Rio de Janeiro) compared with the rest of the country. In 1952 Congress approved by only three votes the move of the capital from Rio de Janeiro (where most politicians preferred to live) inland to Brasilia to try to open up the more central parts of the country. Building began in 1957.

Brasilia was built like an aeroplane. The two wings, each 6.5km long, were used for housing (superblocks), and the fuselage, 9km long, has been divided into sections for local government, hotels, commerce, culture and national government (Figure 9.6). Each section is paired along the length of the fuselage. Many of the cultural and civic buildings are noted for their futuristic architecture.

Brasilia was built for the motorist. The idea was to have a road network enabling people to get to work and shops without having to use traffic lights and in safety. The result has been great distances between places (often too far to walk), adding danger to those wishing to walk (as they have to cross three lane expressways), and an increasing number of accidents. Recently several sets of lights have been introduced.

Several local rivers have been dammed to form a large artificial lake (mainly used for recreation). Around this lake are the very expensive, individual houses, and foreign embassies. By 1986 there was still much building to be done, but the city had already reached one million inhabitants – a figure initially planned for the year 2000. Brasilia is a bureaucratic city with little industry.

Key:
- apartments
- community buildings
- open space
- shops
- car parks
- **P** = post box, telephone and newspaper kiosk
- **K** = kindergarten
- trees and shrubs

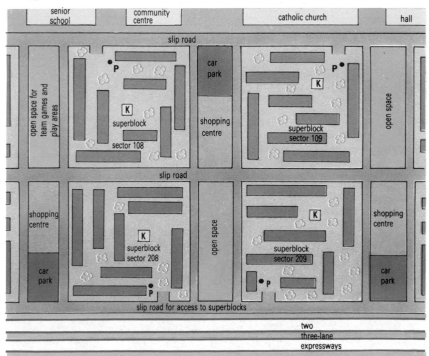

PLANNING
Urban renewal

In an attempt to improve living conditions in old inner city areas of Britain, local community housing associations have been set up. These are non-profit making societies run by voluntary committees, often under guidance from the local city or district council, to provide accommodation for people in need of housing and to improve existing housing. By registering with the Housing Corporation, a community housing association can obtain government loans and/or grants. The Housing Corporation is a government agency with statutory duties to promote, assist, supervise and finance local community housing associations.

In Glasgow the 'GEAR' project included five housing associations which have helped to improve the old tenement buildings, encouraged the building of new properties and tried to improve the quality of the environment by creating areas of open space. This has meant much voluntary effort by local residents, but it is hoped that by involving members of the community, such areas will not be further neglected in the future.

1 List some of the (a) social (b) environmental (c) economic problems found on the map in Figure 9.10.
2 How is urban renewal different from urban redevelopment?
3 In drawing up any new plan for an area, all groups living there should be considered, e.g. young children, teenagers, couples, the elderly, the disabled, pedestrians, car-drivers, etc. Study Figure 9.11 which shows the changes that have been made to this area.
   (a) Which of the groups in the community do you think have been catered for, and which have not?
   (b) How successful do you think the planners have been in trying to overcome the social, environmental and economic problems of the area?
   (c) If you were on the local housing association, what further ideas would you put forward to improve the area – bearing in mind that inner city areas are usually short of money?

▽ **Figure 9.10** An old inner-city area before urban renewal
▽ **Figure 9.11** An old inner-city area after urban renewal

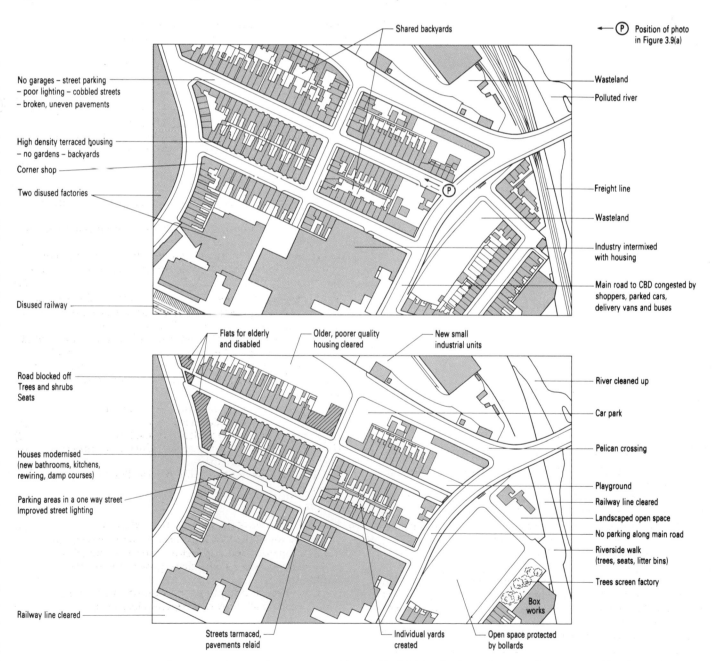

78

Energy, industry and planning

1 *(Figures 7.2, 7.3, 7.4 and 7.5 on pages 48–49)*

(a) (i) Which two countries produced most crude oil in 1983?
(ii) What percentage of the world's crude oil did they produce?
(iii) How many countries produced more coal than the UK in 1982?
(iv) Which two of those countries are said to be 'developing'?
(v) Which types of energy named in Figure 7.5 are 'non-renewable'?
(vi) What does the term non-renewable mean? (6)

b) Why do solar energy and geothermal power have limited use in Britain? (2)

2 *(Figure 7.8, page 51)*

a) (i) Give two points to describe the location of nuclear power stations.
(ii) Give two reasons for the location of nuclear power stations. (4)

b) Give two reasons for, and two reasons against an increase in the number of nuclear power stations. (4)

3 *(Pages 60-61)*

Study the triangular graph (Figure 8.9) which shows the percentage of workers in each of the main sectors of industry in selected countries during 1981.

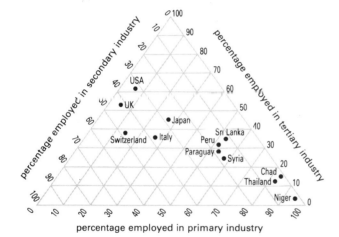

a) Complete the following table.

	USA	Sri Lanka	Thailand
Primary industry	6		82
Secondary industry	32	12	
Tertiary industry	62		

(4)

b) (i) Using Figure 8.10, which country has most of its workers in the tertiary sector?
(ii) Which country has 27% in primary industry, 34% in secondary industry and 39% in tertiary industry? (2)

c) (i) Explain what is meant by the terms: 'primary industry', 'secondary industry' and 'tertiary industry'.
(ii) Give an example of each type. (6)

d) Using Figure 8.10:
(i) Name the two most developed countries. (1)
(ii) Name the two least developed countries. (1)
(iii) Give three differences between the figures of these two sets of countries. (3)
(iv) Give three reasons for these differences. (3)

4 *(Page 64)*

Many of Britain's newer industries are said to be 'footloose' and are located on industrial estates which have been built on the outskirts of urban areas.

a) (i) What is meant by the terms: a footloose industry; an industrial estate? (2)
(ii) Give three reasons why industrial estates are found on the outskirts of urban areas. (3)
(iii) List four factors describing industrial estates. (4)
(iv) Why are footloose industries found on industrial estates? (1)
(v) What types of industry are found on industrial estates? (2)

b) A firm which has a factory in an old inner city area wishes to move to an industrial estate.
(i) Suggest three advantages of the proposed move.
(ii) Suggest two disadvantages of the proposed move. (5)

5 *(Page 66)*

In recent years there has been a rapid growth of high-technology (hi-tech) industries in the area between London and Bristol.

a) (i) What is meant by a 'hi-tech' industry?
(ii) Give two examples of hi-tech industries.
(iii) What is a science park? (3)

b) How have the following encouraged the location of hi-tech industries between London and Bristol?
(i) Accessibility *(ii)* Labour supply *(iii)* Universities *(iv)* Attractive countryside *(v)* Cultural and social attractions. (5)

6 *(Page 68)*

a) Study Figure 8.26 which shows changing employment in Corby since 1926.
(i) Explain how important British Steel has been to Corby's economy. (2)
(ii) What evidence is there to suggest that there has been some success in attracting new employment to Corby since the closure of the steelworks? (4)

b) Study Figure 8.27. This advertisement appeared in several national newspapers in an attempt to attract new industry to Corby following the closure of the steelworks.
(i) If you were an industrialist reading the newspaper, what factors given in the advert would attract you to Corby?
(ii) What factors not given in the advert would you have to consider before deciding whether or not to move to Corby? (6)

c) For any *other* industry that you have studied:
(i) Name an area in which it is located. (1)
(ii) Draw a sketch map to show its location. (3)
(iii) Give three reasons why that industry has *either* grown *or* declined in the area named.
(iv) What effects has this growth *or* decline had on the local economy? (3)

7 *(Page 70)*

a) List four features of a multinational company. (4)

b) Governments of developing countries have encouraged multinationals to open up factories in their countries.
(i) Give three reasons why these governments want multinationals. (3)
(ii) Give three disadvantages of multinationals to the countries in which they have opened factories. (3)

Farming systems and types

Farming is an industry, and like other industries it has inputs into the farm, processes which take place on the farm and outputs. This system can, at its simplest, be shown as

Inputs	→	Processes	→	Outputs
(physical environment e.g. natural inputs, human-economic inputs) Expenditure		(pattern and method of farming e.g. cultivating, rearing and storage)		(products e.g. crops, animals) Profits

(See Figure 10.1)

The farmer as a decision maker

Each individual farmer's decision on what crops to grow or animals to rear and which methods to use to produce the outputs depends on an understanding of the most favourable physical and economic conditions for the farm. Sometimes the farmer may have several choices, and the outputs exceed the inputs to give a profit (commercial). Often, in many parts of the world, the farmer has limited choice, and the outputs may not exceed inputs leaving the family struggling for survival (subsistence).

This system will vary between and within countries. Figure 10.2 shows two farming schemes; (a) is in a developing country and (b) is in a developed country.

▽ **Figure 10.1** Factors affecting the farmer's decisions about which animals to rear or which crops to grow

▽ **Figure 10.2(a)** Transplanting rice in Madras State, India

▽ **Figure 10.2(b)** Mixed farming in the English Midlands

Physical inputs

climate {
amount and season of rain
temperature (summer and winter)
growing season
}

relief
soils and drainage

Human and economic inputs

labour (workforce)
rent
transport costs
machinery
fertilisers and pesticides
government control
seeds – livestock
farm buildings
energy (electricity)

the farmer – the decision maker

in developed countries usually a profit for reinvestment

Processes
growing crops
rearing animals
storage

Outputs
crops
animal products
animals

in developing countries most of the outputs may be consumed by the family

Possible changes to the system

floods
drought
disease
pests
change in demand
change in market price
change in subsidy
improved technology
(beyond the farmer's control)

A Inputs	Processes	Outputs
plenty of rain growing season all year flat land rich soils much labour hand tools 1 ox rice seed	2 hectares of land 10 chickens 2 cows 1 ox rice and wheat	rice some wheat eggs chicken

= no profit

B Inputs		Processes	Outputs
skilled labour electricity seeds rain all year growing season 8 months	machines fertiliser cattle feed barns for storage low undulating relief and deep soils	land 240 hectares animals 40 calves 160 cows 40 pigs crops grass barley potatoes	milk pigs cattle barley hay manure potatoes

= profit

Classification of farming systems

No classification can include all types of farming, but that given in Figures 10.3 and 10.4 has been based on the following criteria:

1 **Arable** (the growing of crops), **pastoral** (the rearing of animals) or **mixed** (crops and animals).

2 **Subsistence** (growing just enough food for the farmer's family) or **commercial** (the growing of crops or rearing of animals for sale).

3 **Extensive** or **intensive** depending upon the ratio between land, labour and capital.
   (a) **Extensive** is where the farm size is very large but either the amount of money spent on it or the numbers working on it are low (e.g. Amazon Basin) or when the numbers working on it are low in comparison with the size of the farm and the capital spent on it (e.g. Prairies).

(b) **Intensive** can be either when the numbers working on the land are very high in proportion to the size of the farms (e.g. Ganges Valley) or when a considerable amount of money is used in comparison with the small numbers employed (e.g. the Netherlands).

4 **Shifting cultivation** (where the farmers move from area to area) or **sedentary** (where there is permanent farming and settlement).

A fifth category may also be used based on land tenure when the farm may be:

Individually owned as in most capitalist, developed countries.

State owned as in the centrally planned, socialist economies.

Rented by a tenant or by a sharecropper as in colonial times and in many less developed countries.

▽ **Figure 10.3** World farming types

▽ **Figure 10.4** Types of farming

Look again at Figures 10.3 and 10.4, and then answer the following questions.

(a) For each type of farming, give a second example using the following ten examples: Bedouin of the Sahara; Bushmen of the Kalahari; cocoa in Ghana; a commune in China; glasshouses in the Netherlands; Indus Valley of Pakistan; maize in the American Mid-West; the Maring of Papua New Guinea; sheep in Australia; fruits and vines in Victoria (Australia).

(b) For the ten types of farming say whether each is:
   (i) arable, pastoral or mixed
   (ii) subsistence or commercial
   (iii) extensive or intensive
   (iv) shifting or sedentary

(c) Which types of farming do not fit into the above classifications?

Key (to Figure 10.3)	Type of farming	Named example
1	nomadic hunting and collecting	Australian Aborigines
2	nomadic herding	Fulani of West Africa
3	shifting cultivation	Amerindians of Amazon Basin
4	intensive subsistence agriculture	rice in the Ganges Valley
5	plantation agriculture	coffee in Brazil
6	livestock ranching (commercial pastoral)	beef on the Pampas
7	cereal cultivation (commercial grain)	Canadian Prairies and Russian Steppes
8	mixed farming	Netherlands
9	Mediterranean agriculture	southern Italy
10/I	irrigation	Nile Valley
11	unsuitable for agriculture	

FARMING
Changes in developed countries

Modern farming or 'agribusiness'

Agribusiness is a new term applied to the increasing 'industrialisation' of farming. Farming is now as organised, financed, mechanised and managed as any successful industry, and it has become increasingly 'commercialised' and 'intensive'.

Effect on the environment

Use of chemicals (Figure 10.5):

(a) **Pesticide** is defined as all chemicals applied to crops to control pests, disease and weeds. The United Nations claimed in the 1960s that 30-35% of the world's crops were lost due to pests, diseases and weeds. In the mid-1980s it is still claimed that without pesticides cereal crops would be reduced by 25% after one year and 45% after three years. In developed countries strict control of existing and new pesticides should make them safe (the risks are greater in developing countries due to lack of instruction, fewer regulations and faulty equipment). In the UK no fatalities have been reported in the last ten years, although there has been concern over the decline in the bee population following spraying. Direct poisonings of wildlife are usually due to careless or deliberate misuse of chemicals.

(b) **Fertiliser** is a mineral compound containing one or more of the main six elements needed for plant growth. The average soil does not contain sufficient of the essential nutrients (especially the three most significant ones, nitrogen, phosphorous and potassium) to provide either a healthy crop or an economic yield. There is concern when the soil produces nitrates which may be washed (leached) through the soil either into rivers, where they might kill fish, or into underground supplies of drinking water. In 1985 a directive from the EEC (European Economic Community) called for a reduction in the desirable nitrate levels in water.

Removal of vegetation cover can increase the erosion (loss) of soil by running water and the wind.

Burning straw due to a falling demand for the product. Ploughing it back into the soil clogs up machinery, increases the costs of labour, and can limit root growth of new plants. By burning the straw, fungal spores and weed seeds are destroyed to give a cleaner soil. However the burning of straw does affect the environment by creating air pollution, reducing visibility for road users, harming wildlife and damaging hedgerows and trees. Restrictions on burning are already in force, and a total ban is possible in the future.

◁ **Figure 10.5** Unformed brussels sprouts are sprayed for pests. Bedfordshire, England

△ **Figure 10.6** The less acceptable face of modern farming. The removal of hedges and trees during the 1950s and 1960s has left prairie-like scenes such as this

hedges reduce wind speed and bind soil together, reducing erosion

trees as a habitat for wildlife and to provide shade

bushes cut and laid almost horizontally – initially unsightly, these soon produce a thick cover

wider base adds to attractiveness as well as providing an environment for wildlife

△ **Figure 10.7** A recent reversal of policy has led to more trimmed hedges with wide bases which encourage wildlife

▽ **Figure 10.8** Increased mechanisation on farms

Removal of hedgerows Between 1945 and 1975 25% of British hedgerows disappeared (over 45% in Norfolk). Farmers removed hedgerows and trees to create larger fields (Figure 10.6) because hedgerows are costly and time-consuming to maintain, they take up space which could be used for crops and they limit the size of machinery. Trees get in the way of the new mechanised hedgetrimmers. Yet the destruction of hedgerows can harm the environment as there are fewer roots to bind the soil together leaving it exposed to running water and, in the flatter areas of Fenland and East Anglia, the wind. Wildlife in the form of plants, insects, birds and animals lose their natural habitat, and many people feel that the landscape becomes less attractive. Figure 10.7 shows the advantages of well maintained hedgerows.

Reclamation of moorlands and draining wetlands has changed the local ecology.

Irrigation is needed when the climate is hot and dry but the resultant high rates of evapo-transpiration bring salts to the surface (salinisation).

▽ **Figure 10.9** Factory farming (USSR)

Economic implications

Larger farms and field size Since 1964 the number of farms under 20 hectares in size in Britain has declined by over a half, with a corresponding increase in the number over 200 hectares. This is partly due to the higher cost of inputs into a modern farm which can only be repaid by the farmer buying up more land and turning it into more economic plots.

Increased mechanisation in the 1950s saw tractors replacing horses, and more recently the introduction of larger combine harvesters and specialised equipment for harvesting crops such as peas and potatoes. Mechanisation adds to the capital outlay of the farmer and has continually reduced the labour force (Figure 10.8).

Factory farming where certain animals rarely see the light of day. While some groups of people question the morality of rearing thousands of chickens in broiler houses, or feeding cattle by using micro-computer systems (Figure 10.9), such 'factory' methods have increased yields and lowered prices to the consumer.

Improved accessibility enabling produce to reach markets more rapidly.

Market pricing systems by which the government assures the farmer of a minimum price for such products as eggs and milk regardless of changes in demand by the consumer.

Government subsidies and grants also help the farmer to build modern specialist buildings, and to purchase the most efficient forms of machinery.

EEC and the Common Agricultural Policy (CAP) The basic concepts for a common farm policy were set out in the 1957 Treaty of Rome as follows:

(a) to increase agricultural productivity

(b) to ensure a fair standard of living for farmers

(c) to stabilise markets

(d) to ensure reasonable consumer prices.

These aims have replaced all existing national policies and often cause conflict between members. Figure 10.10 tries to show some of the arguments used by the 'pro' and 'anti' groups.

Conflict with other land users

The competition for land has increased in recent years, e.g.

☐ The growing demand for more houses and factories built on the edges of urban areas (urban sprawl) and the desire of some people to live in the countryside and to commute to work.

☐ The conflicting demands of the forestry commission, water authorities and tourists.

Some achievements of CAP

Achieved a larger measure of self sufficiency. This reduces the costs and dependence on unreliable imports

Created higher yields due to input of capital for machinery and fertiliser

In NW Europe the average farm size has increased almost to the recommended level

Amalgamation of fields – in parts of France the number of fields has been reduced to one-eighth of the 1950 total

Production has changed according to demands, e.g., less wheat and potatoes and more sugar beet and animal products

Subsidies to hill farmers have reduced rural depopulation

Poorer farmers gain an opportunity to receive a second income by working in nearby factories ('five o'clock farmers') or from tourism

Higher income for farmers

Subsidies have reduced the risk of even higher unemployment in such rural areas as the Mezzogiorno

Reduced reliance on crops imported from developing countries who themselves have a food shortage

A surplus one year can offset a possible crop failure in another year

Some problems still facing CAP

An increase in food prices, especially in the net importing EEC countries of West Germany and the UK

Creation of food surpluses – the so called 'mountains and lakes'

Selling of surplus products at reduced prices to Eastern European countries (causes both political and economic opposition)

Increased gap between the favoured 'core' agriculture regions and the periphery

Peripheral farm units still very small and often uneconomic

High costs of subsidies. 'Industrial' countries such as the UK object to 70% of the EEC budget being spent on agriculture

'Five o'clock farmers' spend insufficient time on their farms. In France 15%, and in West Germany 30%, of farmers have a second income

Destruction of hedges to create larger fields destroys wild life and increases the risk of soil erosion

By reducing imports from developing countries the latter's main source of income is lost thus increasing the trade gap between the two areas

◁ **Figure 10.10** A balance sheet showing some of the EEC's achievements and problems. How successful has the Common Agricultural Policy been? In all EEC member countries there are 'pro-marketeers' and 'anti-marketeers.' Trying to get a balanced interpretation is difficult

83

FARMING
Intensive farming

Japan

Only 15% of Japan is classed as flat land – the remainder is highland with very steep sides, which hinders economic development. With so little flat land there is great competition for space for housing, industry, communications and farming. Even away from the large cities, such areas as the Obitsu Valley (Figure 10.11) are half urban and half rural. The small, rectangular fields are surrounded by large villages. The average Japanese farm is 1.1 hectares, the equivalent of two football pitches, and so has to be carefully looked after and intensively used by the farmer and his family. Just as Japan has become a major industrial country, so too has farming changed rapidly.

△ **Figure 10.12** Intensive farming in Japan using vinyl sheets. Most vegetables are grown in vinyl-lined tunnels or under sheets such as these to encourage rapid growth

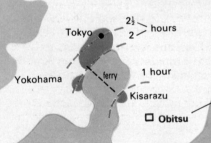

Kanuma   □ **Ochiai**

Old Mr and Mrs Maeda still farm. Their eldest son runs the family lumber business. Their grandson is a construction worker and his wife works in an electrical components factory in Kanuma.

N

Tokyo   2½ ⟩ hours   2

Yokohama   ferry   1 hour

Kisarazu

□ **Obitsu**

Mr and Mrs Ito both work full time on their two hectare farm. Their two daughters are at school and help on the farm. They want office jobs and do not want to marry farmers. Their son is a lorry driver delivering eggs.

0   25 km

◁ **Figure 10.11** The location of two farming families in Japan

▽ **Figure 10.13** Mechanisation on a Japanese farm – a labour-saving machine for harvesting rice

Obitsu means 'little rice box', and in this valley, as in most of Japan, rice has been the major crop. The southern parts of Japan have mild winters, hot and very wet summers and rich soils either from volcanoes or from alluvium brought down from the mountains by fast flowing rivers. However, rice is now being overproduced and the Japanese government, faced with a rice mountain, is trying to limit production and to diversify farming. Reasons for this overproduction include:

□ Bumper yields following a succession of favourable harvests.

□ The increasing use of labour-saving machines designed for small farms (Figure 10.13). Most farms now have a power cultivator (fields are unsuitable for tractors), a rice planter, autothreshers and sprayers. The time saved may be sufficient to grow a second crop.

□ The increasing use of fertilisers (Japan uses more fertiliser per hectare than any country in the world) and pesticides.

□ The climate enabling two, and sometimes three, crops a year to be grown on the same plot.

□ A fall in demand for rice as the Japanese are turning increasingly to western foods.

□ The long hours (usually in excess of ten hours a day) worked by the farmer *and* his wife. In Japan the farmer's wife does at least as much work on the farm as her husband – and she still has a home and family to look after.

Rice is planted in April in readiness for the monsoon rains of summer which flood the padi-fields. In winter a second crop is grown. This is usually either a cereal (wheat or barley) or a vegetable (peas or beans).

Recently there has been a rapid increase in part-time farmers, and by 1985 88% of farm families had one or more members in non-farm work. This non-farm work accounted for, on average, 67% of the total income. The relative ease of being able to commute to the cities is due to the short distances between rural to urban areas, and Japan's modern transport system. Figure 10.11 shows the home areas of two Japanese families, and the labelling suggests that some members of the family, mainly the younger generation, are preferring jobs in the city.

Central Valley of California

This region is noted for long hours of sunshine, its hot, dry summers and mild, wet winters (a Mediterranean climate) and its rich alluvial soils deposited by the Sacramento and San Joaquin rivers. However before the commercial growing of fruit and vegetables could begin, an elaborate irrigation system had to be built to overcome the water shortage problem. The problem was that three-quarters of California's water supply is found in the north of the state, yet three-quarters of the demand comes from the agricultural Central Valley and the coastal cities of San Francisco and Los Angeles. Dams, such as that at Shasta, hold back water which is later pumped via the Delta-Mendota Canal to those areas with water deficiency. To justify such expensive water transfer schemes, the maximum use must be made of the land. The major crops in the Central Valley are:

1 Fruit – peaches, apricots, grapes and citrus fruits.

2 Vegetables – lettuce, tomatoes and other 'early vegetables' so called because due to the mild winters, they are ready before similar crops in many other parts of America.

3 Specialist crops such as rice and cotton.

△ **Figure 10.14** Tomato picking in central California using Mexican migrant labour

▽ **Figure 10.15** Landsat photograph of part of the Central Valley of California

These crops are also grown in the area because of:

☐ Its nearness to large urban markets.

☐ Its access to these well-off markets by fast roads and railways.

☐ The availability of cheap and seasonal labour at harvest time. Much of this labour is provided by illegal Mexican migrant workers (page 30).

☐ The high level of mechanisation. One example of a common harvester is a lettuce packer. As the machine crawls at 2km per hour, men follow on foot cutting ripe heads. Women riding the harvester cut off outer leaves and wrap each head in transparent plastic, which is then tightened by a heated 'shrink tunnel'. Men at the centre pack 200 cartons per hour and leave them for trucks to rush them to urban markets. After harvest the machine folds its 'wings' and sets off at 70km per hour down the freeway to the next crop.

Satellite geography Figure 10.15 is a landsat photograph taken by satellite, using false colours.

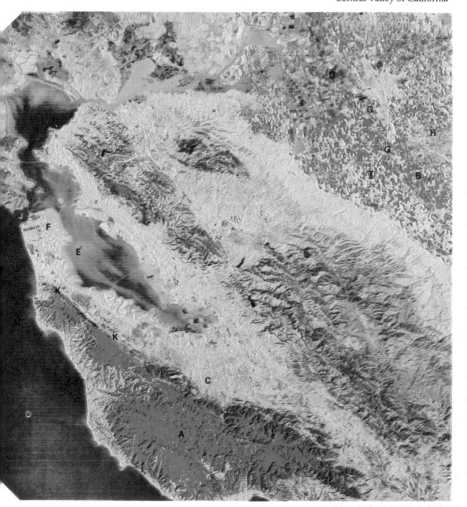

Colour	Land use	Letter on Figure 10.15
Red magenta	Dense vegetation (forest) or crops ready for harvesting	A B
Pink	Less dense vegetation or farmland in early stages of growth	C
Dark blue to black	Water surfaces	D
Grey or steel blue	Heavily sedimented or polluted water	E
Light blue	Urban areas	F

The San Joaquin River meanders through the Central Valley (G). Notice the reds of the San Joaquin Valley (B) indicating its intensive 'industrial' farming techniques. To the east of the river (H) are smaller fields, and to the west (I) the larger fields resulting from the building of the Delta-Mendota Canal. With good eyes you may be able to recognise the city of San Francisco (F) and the Golden Gate Bridge (J). The San Andreas Fault (K) is recognised by the sharp contrast in colour to either side of it.

Extensive farming

Commercial grain – Canadian Prairies

Using the systems approach described on page 80, the inputs on a Prairie farm can be summarised as:

Temperatures Long, sunny days in summer; winter frosts break up the soil.

Precipitation Relatively low with a maximum in summer when wheat is growing; winter snow insulates the ground.

Winds Chinook melts winter snow.

Relief Flat or gently rolling landscape helps machinery and building of roads and railways.

Soils Deep and full of humus giving it a black or dark brown colour (chernozem).

Mechanisation High input of capital in relation to labour force, e.g. fleets of combine harvesters.

Communications Straight, fast road and rail routes essential as most of wheat is exported.

Seeds Improved quality, e.g. disease resistant, drought resistant, quicker growing (within 90 days).

Buildings Include large elevators in which to store the wheat, and built next to railways.

Fertiliser and pesticides Both used increasingly.

△ **Figure 10.16** A prairie landscape in Alberta, Canada

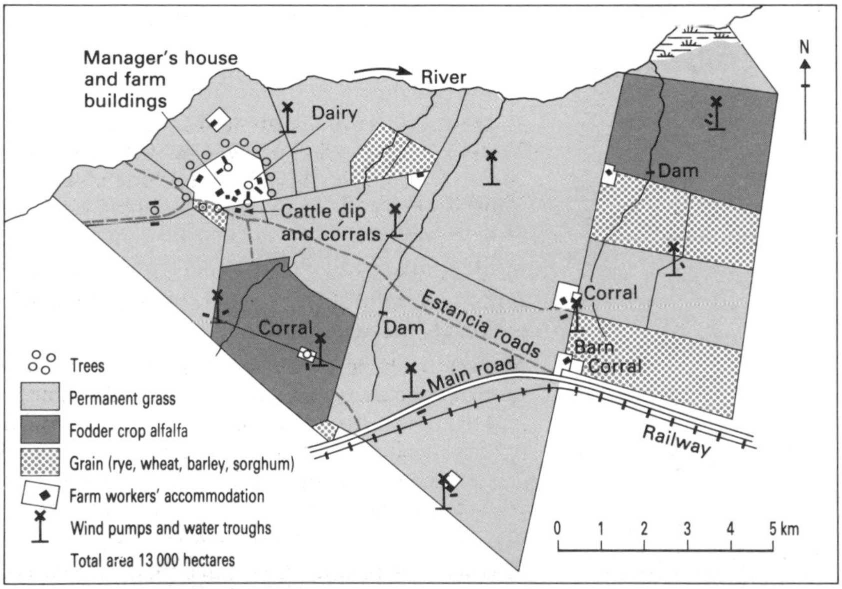

▽ **Figure 10.17** Land use on a typical estancia (cattle ranch) in Argentina (map, left)

▽ **Figure 10.18** A South American cowboy or gaucho tending his herd as it feeds on pampa grasses (photo, below left)

Map (Figure 10.17)

Manager's house and farm buildings
River
Dairy
Dam
Cattle dip and corrals
Corral
Estancia roads
Corral
Dam
Barn
Main road
Corral
Railway

Key:
- ° ° Trees
- Permanent grass
- Fodder crop alfalfa
- Grain (rye, wheat, barley, sorghum)
- ◆ Farm workers' accommodation
- ⬥ Wind pumps and water troughs

Total area 13 000 hectares

0 1 2 3 4 5 km

Commercial livestock – the Pampas

The Pampas is a very flat area in Uruguay and northern Argentina. The early settlers found the deep, alluvial soils covered in grass ideally suited to rearing cattle. The land was divided into large ranches called estancias, and each estancia was then divided into large paddocks. Today some estancias exceed 100km² and keep 20 000 head of cattle. Most are owned by businessmen or large companies based in the large cities, and run by a manager with the help of cowboys called gauchos (Figure 10.18). In the last 100 years, several improvements have been made, including:

- Improved breeds of cattle mainly by crossing British Herefords with Asian Brahman bulls to give a good beef cow able to live in a hot, dry climate.

- Improved quality of grass, for although half of the estancia may still be under permanent pasture much of this dies off in winter, and so large amounts of alfalfa (a leguminous, moisture retaining crop) and cereal crops, as shown in Figure 10.17 are grown.

- The construction of a dense network of roads and railways linking the estancias to the stockyards (frigorificos) – where the cattle are slaughtered and refrigerated – at the ports of Rosario, Buenos Aires, La Plata and Montevideo on the Rio de la Plata (River Plate).

- The invention of barbed wire for fences (the land away from rivers is too dry for hedges and trees), the refrigerator (to take frozen meat to North America and western Europe) and the tin can (for corned beef).

Mixed farming

A Danish co-operative

Before 1960

Denmark had been a major producer of wheat during the 19th century until, in the 1870s, the building of railways across Canada opened up the Prairies. Denmark could not compete with the flood of cheap wheat but realised that there was a demand for dairy products in the rapidly industrialising countries of Britain and West Germany. By 1960 most farms had large numbers of dairy cows (butter and cheese), pigs (the Landrace breed gives bacon and pork) and hens (eggs).

Since 1960

Denmark's climate has always been more suitable for the growing of cereals than for grass. Also the reliance upon one type of farming is more vulnerable to adverse climatic conditions, changes in market demand and price, and to disease and pests than is mixed farming where the farmers can earn their income from several sources and alternatives. Figure 10.20 shows a modern farming

	1960	1982
Land use		
% under cereals	47	75
% under roots	18	8
% under grass	32	9
% non-agricultural land	3	8
Animals		
cows (1000s)	1438	1063
pigs (1000s)	6147	9348
Mechanisation		
number of horses	171	42
number of tractors	111 300	176 300
number of combine harvesters	8900	38 400
% in agriculture	16	6.1
average size of farm (hectares)	15.8	26.7

landscape in Denmark. Fields are still relatively small and bordered by hedges. Dairy cattle remain important (they also provide the skimmed milk for the pigs), but in winter they are kept indoors, as the pigs and poultry are for the whole year. Many farmers have adopted an eight year rotation system which may be wheat–root crops–barley–sugar beet–barley–grass–mixed barley and oats–sugar beet.

The cereals are often cut green for silage, while root crops and sugar beet are not only valuable crops in their own right, but help to replace nitrogen in the soil previously used by the cereal crops.

Figure 10.19 summarises the major recent changes.

Co-operatives

Most Danish farms are owner-occupied, but the farmers work together to try to get the maximum benefit from buying in bulk and selling on a collective basis. Co-operatives can help individual farmers by:

Bulk buying Co-operatives buy such items as cattle feed, fertilisers and seed in bulk, so reducing the cost to farmers.

Market products 200 or 300 farmers may, between them, own a dairy. The milk is sent to this dairy and the dairy does the processing and selling. The profits are shared according to the amount of milk that each farmer supplies. The dairy will also provide the transport, which is a more efficient method than each individual having to do so.

Finance The co-operatives have their own banks which allow cheaper loans for machinery and buildings.

Quality Each farmer is expected to produce goods of the highest quality, and the co-operatives help to ensure that goods, such as those branded Lurpack, are equated with top quality.

Back up services These include a veterinary service (Figure 10.21); free advice on new methods of farming and quality control; research into new techniques; colleges to train young people and to retrain practising farmers; and links with associated agricultural industries (e.g. bacon curing, brewing, milling, the production of butter and cheese, and the manufacture of farm machinery).

△ **Figure 10.19** Recent changes in Danish agriculture (top right)

△ **Figure 10.20** Mixed farming in Denmark. Dairy cows and cereal crops are found in adjacent small fields surrounding a typical Jutland farm

◁ **Figure 10.21** Danish farming has tight controls to ensure that only the highest quality is produced. This shows a young pig being injected.

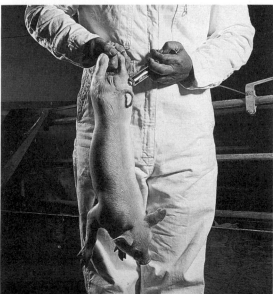

FARMING
In developing countries

Shifting cultivation

Shifting cultivation is a form of subsistence farming, and is a traditional form of agriculture found in many areas of the tropical rainforests. It tends now to be found in only the most inaccessible and least 'exploited' areas. The Indians use stone axes and machetes to fell about one hectare of forest, and any undergrowth has to be cleared immediately to prevent it growing rapidly in the hot, wet climate. After a time the felled trees, having been given time to dry, are burned. This burning helps to provide nutrients for the soil as the ash is spread over the ground as a fertiliser. This is also known as 'slash and burn'.

Within the clearings are built the tribal homes or 'maloca'. These usually consist of tree trunks lashed together with lianas, and thatched with leaves. Nearer the rivers the houses are built on stilts (Figure 10.24) as the water level can rise by 15m after the rainy reason.

The clearings, or gardens, are called chagras. Here the women grow virtually all of the tribe's carbohydrate needs. The main crop is manioc, the 'bread of the tropics', which is crushed to produce a flour called cassava (Figure 10.23). It can also provide sugar and a local beer. Other crops are yams (though these need a richer soil), beans and pumpkins. The men have to supplement this diet by hunting, mainly for tapirs and monkeys, fishing and collecting fruit. The blow pipe and bow and arrow are still used.

Unfortunately the balance between plants and soil is very delicate. Once the canopy of trees has been removed, the heavy rains associated with afternoon storms can hit the now bare soil. This not only causes soil erosion, but it leaches any minerals in the soil downwards. As the source of humus, the trees, has been removed, and as there is a lack of fertiliser and animal manure, the soil rapidly loses its fertility. Within four or five years yields decline, and the tribe will 'shift' to another part of the forest to begin the cycle all over again.

Shifting cultivation needs a high labour input, and large areas of land to provide enough food for a few people. Although it is a wasteful method of farming, it causes less harm to the environment than permanent agriculture would.

Recently the Amerindians of the Amazon rainforest have been forced to move further into the forest or to live on reservations (pages 128–129). Large numbers have died, mainly because they lack immunity to 'western' diseases, and those surviving have the difficult choice of either trying to live in increasingly difficult surroundings, or joining the other homeless and jobless in favelas in the larger urban areas (page 25).

▷ **Figure 10.22** A clearing in the Amazon forest (top)

▷ **Figure 10.24** A maloca, or Indian house, built from materials from the tropical rainforests (near Manaus, Brazil) (bottom left)

▷ **Figure 10.23** Cassava flour being prepared from manioc (middle left)

▷ **Figure 10.25** Rice growing in India (map)

▷ **Figure 10.26** Traditional methods of rice farming. A water buffalo with its wooden plough is used to plough the padi-fields (ready for planting), in Malaysia (inset photo, right)

▷ **Figure 10.27** Traditional methods of rice farming. The back-breaking job of planting young rice plants in the flooded padi-fields, India (main photo, right)

Intensive subsistence farming

Rice growing in India

Mainly because it gives the highest yield per hectare and is suited to the climate, rice is the staple food in India. It is labour-intensive, needing a large number of workers on a relatively small area of land and with little capital involved.

Rice grows in three very contrasting environments in India (Figure 10.25). Describe these three areas, explain how a crop so demanding on the soil can be continually grown in India, and explain the difference between the two main types of rice.

The growing of rice is hard work, involves the whole family, and, due to the climate, can be grown twice a year in the same field.

1 River Ganges floods fields allowing 'wet' rice to grow in the thick, fertile silt left by the floods

2 Assam – 'dry' or hill rice grown on terraces on steep hillsides

too dry

1(a) flood plain
1
1(b) delta

rice needs minimum 10°C to germinate
traditionally a growing season of 150 days – now reduced to 100 days can grow any time in India
much moisture – heavy monsoon rain in summer

3 Deccan Plateau and other drier areas where 'dry rice' grows under irrigation on fertile soil from lava flows

The Farmer's Year

May Nursery beds, above the flood level, are prepared and manured.

June As soon as the rains come the rice seeds are planted in the nurseries, and the padi-fields are manured (using compost or animal dung) and then ploughed into a thick mud. The ploughing is still usually done by a wooden plough drawn by two water buffalo. The mud is then levelled. Most of the work so far has been done by the males (Figure 10.26).

July and August The rice seedlings are transplanted into the flooded padi-fields – a back breaking job done by the women and children (Figure 10.27). Each seedling has to be pushed individually into the mud. The plant grows rapidly – as do weeds.

September/October Constant weeding.

November/December Water is either drained from the fields or has evaporated, and the rice is cut by hand just above ground level, dried in the sun, threshed to remove the grain, winnowed and dried again in the sun before being stored.

Although these jobs involve most of the family, the men tend to do the cutting and threshing, and the women the winnowing.

January The fields are ploughed again, and a second crop is planted. This could be rice if there is water for irrigation, but usually it is peas, beans, lentils, wheat or barley.

March-April The second crop is harvested.

The Green Revolution

In the 1960s in India most farmers were either landless or tenants. The government realised that more food was needed both in terms of quantity and quality, and that the standard of living of the farmers had to be raised. Should the government go for land reform and redistribute the land or go for technological change? For many reasons, political as well as social and economic, technological change was chosen. As a result:

- 18 000 tonnes of Mexican wheat seed (drought resistant) was given to Indian farmers. These HYV (high-yielding varieties) seeds grew more rapidly (ensuring a second crop could be grown each year) and the plant had a short stiff stem that was more resistant to wind and rain.

- More fertiliser was needed as the HYV were even more demanding than the traditional seeds.

- Tractors began to replace water buffalo (oxen).

- Communications improved and facilities for farmers to borrow money were extended.

Success!

Farmers who could afford the HYV and fertiliser increased their yields three times. By using rice, maize and wheat seeds they widened their output, and the faster growing plants meant multiple cropping each year. As output increased more was available to sell to the cities, and so more fertiliser and even a tractor could be bought, and the standard of living rose.

Failure!

Many landless and poor farmers could *not* afford to buy HYV and fertiliser and so their yields remained the same. If they tried to borrow they rarely managed to repay the money and they got further into debt. These farmers could either go on farming in the traditional way, having nothing to sell, and seeing their relative standard of living decline, or they could migrate to the large cities.

In developing countries

Plantation agriculture

What is a plantation?

Plantations were developed in tropical parts of the world in the 18th and 19th centuries mainly by European and North American merchants. The natural forest was cleared and a single crop (usually a bush or tree) was planted in rows. This so-called 'cash-crop' was grown for export, and was not used or consumed locally. Plantations needed a high capital investment to clear, drain and irrigate the land, to build estate roads, schools and hospitals, and to bridge the several years before the first crop could be harvested. Much manual labour was also needed so although the managers were white, black and Asian labourers, obtained locally or often brought in from other countries, were used because they were cheap and were able to work in the hot, humid climate. The almost continuous growing season meant that the crop could be harvested virtually throughout the year. Today most plantations are still owned by 'multinational' companies. Most of the world's rubber, bananas, palm oil, tea, coffee, cocoa, sugar cane, cotton, and tobacco are produced in this way.

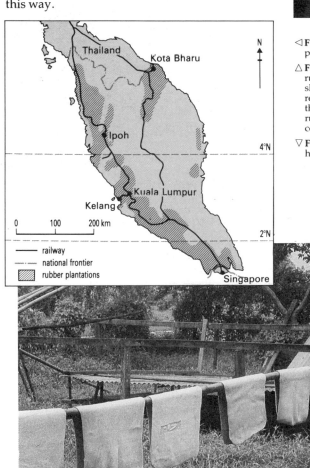

◁ **Figure 10.28** Major rubber producing areas in Malaysia

△ **Figure 10.29** Tapping a rubber tree (Malaysia). This shows how strips of bark are removed from a tree so that the latex (a white liquid) may run down the trunk and be collected in small cups.

▽ **Figure 10.30** Sheets of rubber hanging to dry

Rubber in Malaysia

Over half of the world's natural rubber comes from Malaysia (Figure 10.28). The tree came from the Amazon forest but seeds were smuggled out of that area in 1877, germinated in Kew Gardens (London) and taken out to Malaysia. The trees thrive in the hot, wet conditions, and grow best on the gentle lower slopes of the mountains running through the centre of the country. As Figure 10.28 shows, rubber tends not to be grown on the coasts where the land is often swampy, but is grown near to the relatively few railway lines and the main ports. The 'cheap' labour needed to clear the forest, plant new trees (trees only produce for 25 years) and tap the mature trees is provided by Chinese, Indians and poorer Malays.

Rubber comes from latex which is a white liquid found in the trunk of the tree. Tappers go out early in the morning, often with lamps fitted to their heads as it may still be dark. A curved knife is used to remove a thin strip of bark (Figure 10.29). There are usually several cuts, and the latex runs down these to be collected in a cup. An experienced tapper can cover about two hectares and cut 500 trees in a day. The latex is then sent to the local processing factory where it is poured into large pans along with water and acid. The rubber particles cling together to make a 'sheet' which is then washed, rolled and hung on lines to dry (Figure 10.30).

Today there are more rubber trees on small, privately owned smallholdings of about two hectares, although over half the rubber produced still comes from the large plantations. Rubber suffers from rapidly fluctuating world prices, and from competition with synthetic rubber.

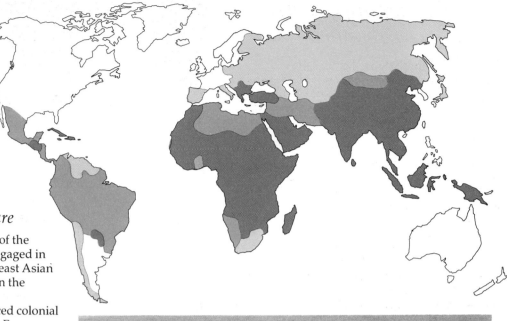

▷**Figure 10.31** Percentage
employed in agriculture

Problems in developing agriculture

As shown in Figure 10.31, the majority of the
workforce in developing countries is engaged in
agriculture. In most African and south-east Asian
countries the figure exceeds 60%, and in the
Himalayan country of Nepal, it is 93%.
Many of these countries have experienced colonial
rule, and a legacy of this domination by European
countries has been the development of plantations
and cash crops. While this, today, gives several
countries a source of wealth, it is often at the
expense of growing crops for their own use. Two
main problems may result:

1 A reliance on one or possibly two cash crops,
such as coffee, cocoa or tea, which may be
vulnerable to disease, climate and to changes in
world demand and prices. These crops are
usually exported in a non-processed form.

2 The land given over to such crops often means
that the local labourers will have insufficient
food, both in terms of amount and balanced
diet.

One example is in North East Brazil where large
landowners are growing an increasing amount of
sugar cane. The cane is used to produce alcohol to
drive cars and so to help reduce Brazil's large oil
debt (page 53) but to these labourers it means
there is less land on which to grow their own
subsistence crops.

What is needed?

A change in land ownership and farm size
Throughout most of Asia, Africa and Latin
America farms are remarkably small – a few
hectares at the most. They are highly fragmented,
being made up of fields scattered at some distance
from one another. Farmers waste time moving
between plots, and the layout increases the
difficulties of irrigation, moving fertilisers and
controlling plant diseases. Farms are in many
cases so small that they cannot provide an
adequate income to sustain the family, let alone
allow investment in the new inputs such as
fertilisers, new seeds and better implements that
are essential for change. In spite of land reform
campaigns in many developing countries, most
farmers still have to rent land from landlords at
high rates. Of course if farm sizes increased, it
would probably mean that fewer farmers would be
needed.

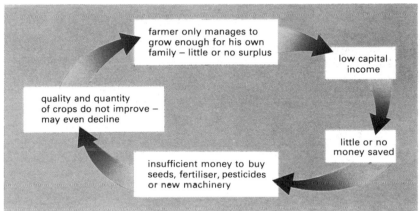

farmer only manages to
grow enough for his own
family – little or no surplus

low capital
income

little or no
money saved

insufficient money to buy
seeds, fertiliser, pesticides
or new machinery

quality and quantity
of crops do not improve –
may even decline

△ **Figure 10.32** The vicious
circle of poverty in agriculture

Capital Most farmers are unable to save to
improve their farms and by borrowing money at
high interest rates, they are soon caught in a spiral
of debt, a vicious circle out of which they cannot
escape (Figure 10.32). Capital that is being used at
present for some large prestigious scheme could
more usefully be given to:

☐ Appropriate technology for farming the small
plots and not large tractors and combine
harvesters – third world countries have a large
labour force.

☐ Fertiliser and pesticides so that yields can be
improved.

☐ The development of projects to help
agriculture rather than to have to receive world
aid at times of crisis.

Transport This also needs to be improved so that
farmers can get any surplus crop to market before
it perishes (even more important if it is for export).
Transport tends to be worst in areas where food
shortages are greatest. Even when Live Aid got
food to Ethiopia, there were neither roads nor
lorries to take it to the refugee camps.

Education Even if labourers are given land, will
they have the knowledge and ability to use it?
They need to be taught how to conserve soil, and
to use fertiliser and pesticides correctly.

In centrally planned economies

Collective farming in the USSR

After the Russian Revolution the communists believed that large scale farms were preferable to inefficient smallholdings, and that cooperative enterprises were better than those run by individuals. Instead of a farmer making a profit, the government should use this money to improve farming techniques and output.

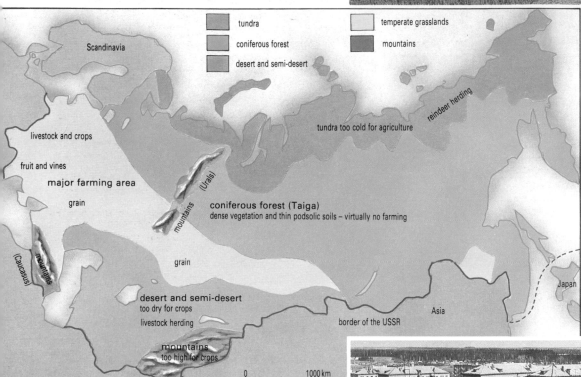

◁ **Figure 10.33** The limits of agricultural land in the USSR

△ **Figure 10.34** Mechanisation on a state farm – harvesting wheat in Kazakhstan, a recently developed farming area in southern USSR

	% of farmland	size of community	average size (hectares)
sovkhoz	61	20 000 to 40 000	1500
kolkhoz	38	400	500
privately owned	1	4	5

Kolkhoz system

In the late 1920s, in order to produce the food needed for the rapidly growing cities, Stalin decided to enforce collectivisation, and farms were forced to join together with neighbouring farms to form larger units. A Kolkhoz is a collective farm managed by an elected chairperson and committee with the farmers becoming members of the collective. Despite strong resistance by the peasants the number of individual farms fell from 25 million in 1928 to only 0.2 million in 1940.

The Second World War again saw a major food shortage in the Soviet Union. Despite its size, as shown in Figure 10.33, only about 25% of the Soviet Union is suitable for agriculture and only 10% for arable farming. Because many Kolkhozs were not meeting the production targets set by the national government, they began to be replaced by the Sovkhoz system.

Sovkhoz system

A Sovkhoz is a state-owned farm where the workers are paid a weekly wage. Initially set up to grow grain in areas not previously farmed, they also produce milk, vegetables and eggs if near large cities and cotton if irrigation is possible. The Soviet government favours this system as it can control and set production targets which the farm must meet. (The individual farmer as a decision maker does not exist in the USSR.) The state provides machinery (Figure 10.34) and fertiliser. The state is also encouraging Kolkhoz farms to become Sovkhoz units with the result that state farms are growing at the expense of the collectives.

In both systems, workers may be given their own plot of land, about half a hectare, in which to grow their own vegetables and to keep some animals. In return for using state machinery, some produce must be given to the state, but then any surplus can be sold privately.

△ **Figure 10.35** Flats on a sovkhoz, a state-owned farm in the USSR. A modern sovkhoz is so large that workers are divided into 'brigades' which each specialise in a job, e.g. mechanic, accountant, tractor driver, livestock rearer. The farms have their own schools, shops, cinemas and libraries.

Communes in China

1948 saw the communists finally taking over in China. One of their first acts was to take land from the large landowners and to redistribute it among the peasants. Various schemes, including the setting up of co-operatives were tried, unsuccessfully, until 1958.

People's Communes

The aim was to combine the various co-operatives to try to create self-sufficient communes. These communes were organised into a three tier hierarchy (Figure 10.36) with production teams forming the lower tier, brigades the middle tier and the commune the upper tier. The team was responsible for its own finances and when various taxes for welfare services had been paid it could distribute the surplus income. The brigade was in charge of overall planning, but left the actual details of farming to the team. The communes ran small scale industry, organised housing and services and were responsible for flood control and irrigation. The layout of a typical commune is shown in Figure 10.37. Notice the attempts to make it self-sufficient by having adequate food supply (crops, livestock, fruit and fish), water control, industry, housing and services. Members of the commune elected a people's council, who in turn elected a committee to ensure that production targets were met, and that machinery, fertiliser and new strains of seed were used correctly.

Production Responsibility Scheme 1978

In the countryside, emphasis is now on rewarding the efforts of individuals and small units such as households instead of the larger units – communes, brigades and teams. In the towns, enterprises are being given much more responsibility for their own affairs. These changes have excited much comment, as they seem to be a move away from socialist equality towards capitalist inequality.

The process of dismantling the communes and replacing them by administrative districts and townships is still in progress (1985), but the production team is now the largest unit and smaller units – the work group, the household and the individual – are now responsible for the decisions once made at commune level.

Under the commune system, land was collectively farmed, with peasant households assigned to tasks for which they received the distributed collective income. Under the responsibility system, individual households may contract with the state to supply a fixed quota of crops in return for the use of a plot of land; they may also retain any surplus produced for their own use, or for sale in local free markets. Thus the responsibility or contract system pays households on completion of the work, not while work is in progress; the method of production and the time and effort put into it is left to the household. In these circumstances, some peasants are prepared to work hard and maximise their production; others are not (it has been estimated that collective agriculture could well have operated with half the labour force actually employed).

(*Geographical Magazine*, 1985)

50 families	=1 production team	(300 people, 20 hectares)
10 production teams	=1 brigade	(3000 people, 200 hectares)
5 brigades	=1 commune	(15 000 people, 1000 hectares)

△ **Figure 10.36** The structure of a Chinese commune

▽ **Figure 10.37** Land use on a Chinese commune

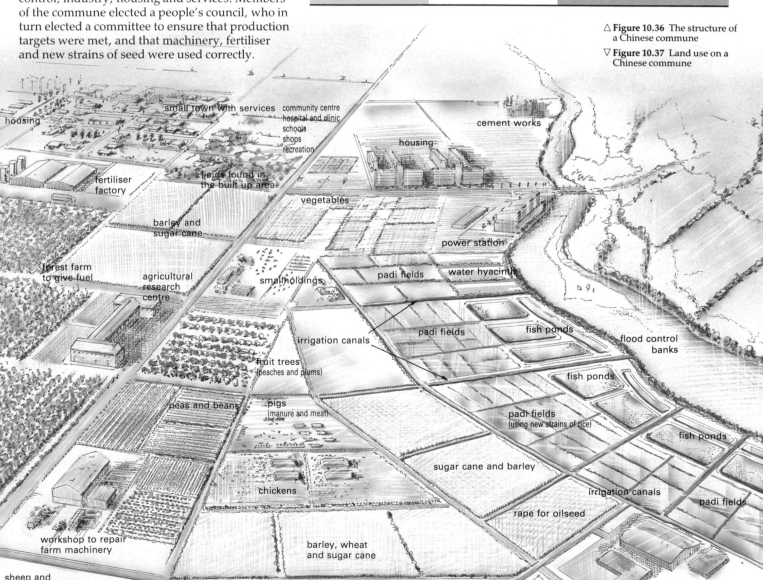

Food supply

The Food and Agriculture Organisation (FAO) claimed that 1985 saw a satisfactory global cereal harvest. Food production grew faster in all areas, other than in parts of Africa, than the increase in population. In most parts of the world nutritional levels improved, although certain areas still remained critically low. In 1985, 45 nations south of the Sahara had record harvests, and the food emergency crisis was over in 16 of the worst affected 21 countries – although several areas will need food relief for several years.

Even so...

Each year 40 million people, almost half of whom are children, die from hunger and hunger-related diseases. An energy intake of less than 1600 Calories per day is likely to cause severe malnutrition. Even if malnutrition does not kill, it reduces the capacity to work and increases susceptibility to disease. Among children, a lack of protein can cause a slow mental and physical development. In 1975 there were 435 million people suffering from malnutrition, in 1985 almost 500 million and by 2000 an estimated 600 million.

Yet at the same time

In the developed countries many people suffer from overeating. Over one-third of Americans are considerably overweight, and are likely to suffer from heart disease and diabetes. In 1982 the UK spent seven times more on slimming aids than it spent on donating hunger relief to such agencies as Oxfam. How much food does the average family in the developed world leave or waste each day?

Trends in food supply

Figure 10.38 shows the relative increase in grain output and population between 1970 and 1982. Figure 10.38(a) shows that on a world scale, the increase in cereal production was greater, suggesting that more people should be better fed. Surprisingly, perhaps, this improvement was greater in the developing countries than in the developed. However this graph disguises regional differences. Figures 10.38(b) and 10.39 show that while steady improvements have occurred in Latin America and in Asia, much of Africa has experienced a decline. Also those countries experiencing a gain in Africa were so poorly off to begin with that a small increase will have only a minimal effect.

1 Why do you think eastern Asia (China, Japan and Malaysia) has seen the biggest improvement in yields? And why a smaller growth in population?

2 Which two areas have seen a greater population growth than cereal growth? Which area in particular was Live Aid set up to help?

The FAO also announced that in 1986, contrary to belief, there was sufficient food grown in the world to feed everyone – the problem was its uneven distribution and its increasing cost to buy.

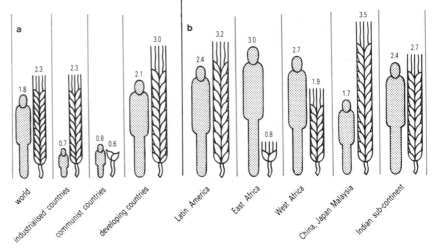

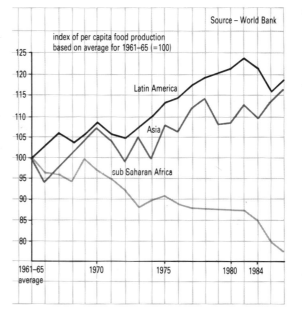

△ **Figure 10.38** The annual population growth and increase in cereal production (%), 1970–82. (Cereals = wheat, rice, maize, rye, sorghum, millet, barley and oats.)

◁ **Figure 10.39** Areas of increased and decreased food production

▽ **Figure 10.40** Food surpluses in the EEC – 'mountains and lakes'

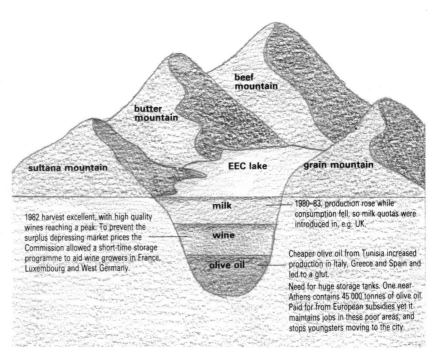

North America, the EEC and Argentina already produce much surplus wheat. The EEC has a 'grain mountain' (Figure 10.40) and England alone (*not* the UK!) has over 140 warehouses full of stored grain. Even within countries some regions may experience a shortage while others have a surplus (compare the north east of Brazil with the south east). In 1985 India had stocks of grain amounting to 30 million tonnes, and yet up to 350 million Indians were underfed because they could not afford to buy that grain. The 'green revolution' has made food production expensive. Hybrid high-yielding varieties need costly fertilisers and pesticides. Even in the developed countries the increased cost of the inputs into a modern farm do not make many farmers very well off.

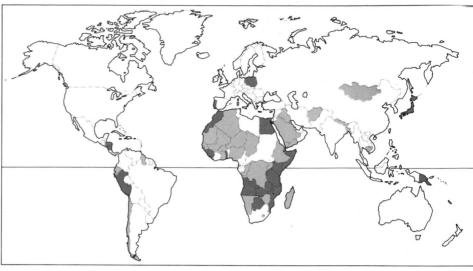

Conclusions

- World food output has increased more rapidly than population since the early 1950s.
- Food output is increasing more rapidly in the developing world than in the developed. The greater population increase in the developing world has led to a lower increase in the amount of food per person than in the developed world.
- Food output per person has actually declined in several countries, mainly in Africa, since 1961 (Figure 10.41), and in an increasing number of countries since 1971.
- There is sufficient food available in the world but it is not evenly distributed, and is becoming increasingly expensive to buy.
- There are still many areas in the world, mainly in Africa and within the tropics, that suffer from malnutrition (Figure 10.42).
- Locust plagues in Africa (1986) destroyed many crops.

Why do parts of Africa suffer from malnutrition?

- The people do not have the money to buy high yielding seeds, fertiliser or pesticides. The seeds they do have are often low yielding.

- The land has been overused in the past and most of the nutrients have been used up.
- When food is scarce, these poorer countries cannot buy the surplus, due to high prices.
- Many areas suffer from drought. The Sahel (the countries bordering the southern fringes of the Sahara) receives less than 500mm of rain a year, and amounts vary from year to year.
- Other areas, where the natural vegetation has been cleared, suffer from soil erosion. Once exposed to water and the wind, the soil is rapidly removed.
- Pests such as the locust, tse-tse fly and caterpillar.
- Due to bad storage much of the crop may be eaten by rats or affected by fungus.
- Governments encourage foreign firms to take over the food-producing land by giving them tax concessions. These multinationals, as in colonial times, grow cash crops for export.
- Lack of protein in the diet.
- Civil war in several countries.

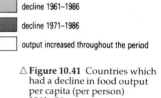

decline 1961–1986
decline 1971–1986
output increased throughout the period

△ **Figure 10.41** Countries which had a decline in food output per capita (per person) 1961–86

▽ **Figure 10.42** Diet and Calorie intake – overeating and hunger

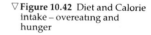
over 100% of requirement

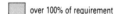
85–99% of requirement

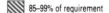
less than 85% of requirement

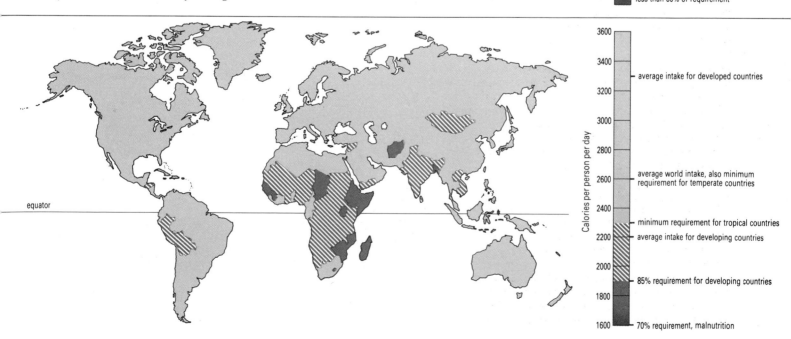

equator

Calories per person per day

- 3600 — average intake for developed countries
- 3400
- 3200
- 3000
- 2800
- 2600 — average world intake, also minimum requirement for temperate countries
- 2400 — minimum requirement for tropical countries
- 2200 — average intake for developing countries
- 2000
- 1800 — 85% requirement for developing countries
- 1600 — 70% requirement, malnutrition

Markets and partners

British trade

The changes in Britain's trade and trading partners between 1973 and 1983 are shown in Figure 11.1. These graphs are typical of most industrialised European countries.

☐ The biggest increase has been with our major trading partners in the EEC. Whether we like being in the EEC or not, the graph shows how important it is for our trade.

☐ 77% of Britain's trade was with developed countries (North America, Europe and Japan).

☐ There is relatively little trade with the developing countries. Most imports are primary goods (i.e. raw materials and agricultural products) which were mainly developed during colonial times, e.g. cocoa from Ghana, tea from Sri Lanka and bananas from Jamaica. In return Britain still tries to export processed and manufactured goods. The result is a favourable trade balance (surplus) in Britain's favour.

☐ Britain does have links with one group of developing countries – the oil producing or OPEC countries (Figure 11.2).

☐ There is minimal trade with the communist bloc (the centrally planned economies of Figure 11.2).

Centrally Planned Economies

Japan

△ **Figure 11.2** Major world trading groups

- European Economic Community (EEC)
- European Free Trade Association (EFTA)
- Organisation of Petroleum Exporting Countries (OPEC)
- Latin American Free Trade Association (LAFTA)
- Comecon (Centrally Planned Economies)

▽ **Figure 11.1** British trading partners by value of goods exchanged

▽ **Figure 11.3** Countries in debt – foreign debts in billions of US dollars, 1985

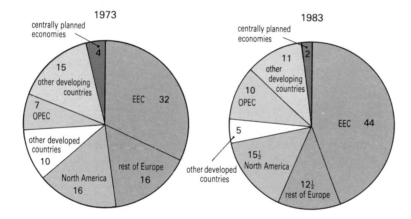

1973

1983

World trade

Many countries have grouped together for the purposes of defence or trade. Figure 11.2 shows the major trading partners. It is only possible here to make several generalisations about trends in world trade.

☐ Most of the world's trade is between the advanced industrialised countries. The growing problem here is that the older industrialised countries in North America and Europe are facing strong competition from the newer ones in Eastern Asia (South Korea and Japan).

☐ Most trade is with neighbouring states, and least with countries furthest away.

☐ Trade is slowly increasing between developing countries. However in 1986 eight developing countries (those who have been more successful in trying to industrialise) accounted for over half of the 'south-south' trade, e.g. Brazil, Mexico and Sri Lanka.

☐ Trade slumped after 1980 (although there have been signs of a small recovery since 1984) with the exports from developing countries to the industrialised countries most affected.

☐ Developing countries export primary goods and import manufactured goods resulting in a trade gap (loss). Developing countries tend to get deeper into debt, and those spending money on new factories and energy schemes incur the biggest debts (Figure 11.3).

☐ The goods (primary products) exported by the developing countries are more vulnerable to changes in market prices and market demand than goods produced in the developed countries.

☐ Many developing countries rely on only one major export as their source of income, e.g. Zambia 90% from copper, Nigeria 89% from oil, Uganda 86% from coffee and Mauritius 90% from sugar-cane.

☐ World trade is becoming increasingly dominated by the multinational companies (page 70).

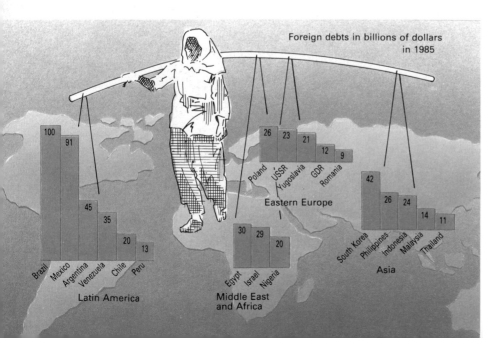

Future trade and the developing countries

Developing countries are making demands for a fairer trading system. These demands include:

☐ Higher and fixed prices for primary products. Prices of coffee, cocoa and copper have fluctuated considerably over the last few years, whereas the price of manufactured goods has risen steadily. This also means the gap between primary products and manufactured goods continues to widen. In 1970 Honduras had to produce three tonnes of bananas to buy one tractor. By 1980 she had to produce 11 tonnes.

☐ Improved access to markets in the industrialised countries. At present, however, if there is a recession or if a developing country begins to increase its trade too much with these industrialised countries, the latter will impose quotas to limit the number of goods imported, or add tariffs so that the price of imported goods will increase and become less competitive. In Britain we complain about losing jobs due to cheap imports from overseas, yet how else can those countries earn money to buy our goods?

☐ Changes in the international money system to eliminate fluctuations in currencies.

☐ Encouraging the industrialised countries to share their technology and stopping the industrialised countries 'dumping' unwanted and sometimes untested and banned products in developing countries.

☐ Releasing the developing countries from 'economic slavery' which has replaced the 19th century 'colonial slavery'.

☐ A reduction in interest rates (to help the country's debt) and an increase in aid. Aid is a complex 'solution' – for it does not necessarily help the receiving country to develop or to solve its problems. Until recently there have been three main sources. *Bilateral* aid is when a government gives money, but often imposes conditions. *Multinational* aid is funded by international agencies such as FAO, Unesco and the World Bank, but often at high interest rates. *Charities* (Oxfam, Christian Aid) have insufficient funds. However the most successful form of aid has come from a new source – Live Aid (1985)'.

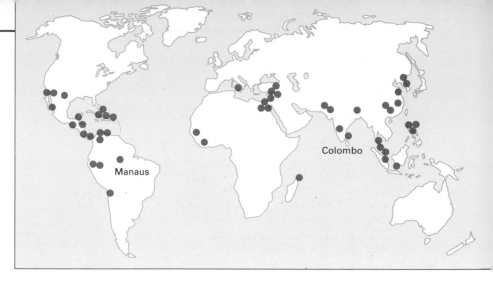

△ **Figure 11.5** The world's free trade zones in 1985

Free trade zones

These are areas within developing cities where goods can be made or assembled without payment of import or export duties, and where profits can be sent back to the parent company without being taxed (Figure 11.5).

Two contrasting views:

1 Manaus (Brazil) grew rapidly during the rubber boom at the turn of this century (see Figure 11.6(a)), but after rubber seeds were smuggled to Malaysia the city rapidly declined. The free trade zone has totally revived the city. There are now over 250 enterprises which have generated thousands of skilled jobs and improved the living conditions of the local population. Firms such as Sanyo, Philips, Telefunken, Honda and Omega have set up assembly plants to produce computers, calculators, TV sets, videos, watches, jewellery, motorcycles and cycles. These are sold in modern free zone shopping centres (one of which has 76 shops). Hotels and large office blocks have also been built (Figure 11.6(b)) as well as a modern airport. Several flights a day see passengers from the south east of Brazil leaving armed with the latest electrical and hi-tech equipment.

2 Colombo (Sri Lanka). By 1984 this had attracted 75 multinational companies and created 30 000 local jobs. However, none of these firms has to pay taxes on its goods or profits and so the local community does not benefit financially. Even skilled assembly workers only receive £30 a month, and three-quarters of the workforce are women. This exploitation of female workers, most of whom are between 15 and 25 years old, is because women are seen to be more patient and passive, ready to do repetitive and low skilled assembly work, less likely to go on strike, and to work for lower wages – differences caused not by biology but by society. The women are expected to work eight hour shifts six days a week, to do compulsory overtime and to live in unhealthy conditions to be near to their work.

◁ **Figure 11.4** Bob Geldof with refugee children who had received food from his Live Aid project

▷ **Figure 11.6(a)** The Opera House in Manaus, Brazil, built by rubber barons (inset)

▷ **Figure 11.6(b)** The modern free port of Manaus showing new office buildings towering over the older customs house

Different economies

One of the features of the present day world is its subdivision into areas with similar political and economic systems.

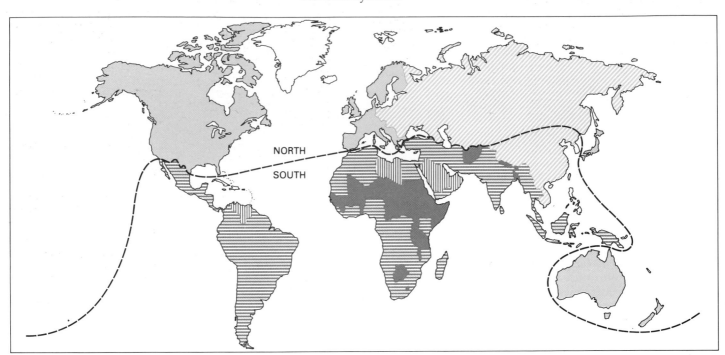

	Country	GNP $US per cap	Birth rate per 1000	% urban dwellers	Life expectancy	Calories per day	% in agriculture
Market (capitalist) economies	Sweden	14 881	11	83	75	2849	6
	USA	11 363	16	76	74	3580	4
	Japan	9352	16	76	76	2552	10
	UK	8873	12	76	73	3340	3
Centrally planned (socialist) economies	USSR	2086	18	65	70	3460	17
	Poland	1876	21	62	70	2880	44
High income (oil producing) countries	Kuwait	18 086	36	58	69	2728	17
	Libya	7289	50	41	56	2690	21
Middle income (developing) countries	Costa Rica	1860	31	43	70	2329	38
	Bolivia	757	47	33	51	1970	65
	Philippines	733	40	36	59	2241	69
Low income (developing) countries	Uganda	222	46	17	54	2146	68
	Bangladesh	145	40	11	47	2113	71
	Ethiopia	97	49	13	40	1826	76

△ **Figure 12.1** Different world economies

△ **Figure 12.2** Poverty/wealth index

Capitalist

Capitalist countries correspond to the industrialised countries of the developed world (Figure 12.1). They are said to have 'market economies'. Private enterprise has been allowed to develop and today, although some nationalisation (state ownership) has occurred, most units of production are still privately owned. The aim of the entrepreneur (the person in control of the unit and who may have financed it) is to make as large a profit as possible. The owner or manager of the unit, whether a farmer, industrialist or shopkeeper, will have to be his or her own decision maker. Capitalist countries tend to have the highest standards of living (Figure 12.2) although the gap between the rich and poor within these countries may be large.

Communist

Communist countries have a socialist or a centrally planned economy. The units of production (farms, mines, factories, shops and banks) are owned by the state, and it is the state which is responsible for planning and for making all decisions. Targets will be set for the individual units (page 92). The individual is neither a decision maker nor a profit maker, but is expected to work for the benefit of the state, just as state decisions and policy are meant to serve the interests of the country. Socialist countries have moderately high incomes, and there is little gap in wealth between the members of that country.

Developing countries

These are almost all former European colonies, and apart from the oil rich countries (Figures 12.1 and 12.2) they all have low levels of income, industrialisation, technology, literacy, energy production, service provision and life expectancy. They also have high birth rates, population growth, and numbers employed (or often underemployed) in agriculture. In 1968, the term 'least developed countries' (LDC) was introduced by the United Nations. LDCs have:

1 A GNP per capita of under 2000 US$ (and 19 of them had a lower GNP in 1983 than they had in 1979)

2 Manufacturing accounting for less than 10% of their GNP.

3 An adult literacy rate of 20% or less.

In 1981 there were 31 LDCs, in 1986 there were 36. All are vulnerable to disasters (drought, floods, cyclones, earthquakes and armed conflict). In all developing countries there is a big gap between the rich and poor.

	developed countries	developing countries
Gross National Product	majority over 5000 US$ per person per year; 80% of world's total income	majority under 2000 US$ per person per year; 20% of world's total income
population growth	relatively slow partly due to family planning; 25% of world's population; population doubles in 80 years	extremely fast, little or no family planning; 75% of world's population; population doubles in 30 years
housing	high standard of permanent housing; indoor amenities e.g. electricity, water supply and sewerage	low standard, mainly temporary housing; very rarely any amenities
types of jobs	manufacturing and service industries, (90% of world's manufacturing industry)	mainly in primary industries
levels of mechanisation	highly mechanised with new techniques, 96% of world spending on development projects and research	mainly hand labour or the use of animals
exports	manufactured goods	unprocessed raw materials
energy	high level of consumption; main sources are coal, oil, HEP and nuclear power	low level of consumption; wood still a major source
communications	motorways, railways and airports	road, rail and airports only near main cities, rural areas have little development
diet	balanced diet; several meals per day; high protein intake	unbalanced diet; 20% of population suffers from malnutrition; low protein intake
life expectancy	over 70 years	under 50 years
health service	very good, large numbers of doctors and good hospital facilities	very poor, few doctors and inadequate hospital facilities
education	majority have full time secondary education (16+)	very few have any formal education

△ **Figure 12.3** Differences between developed and developing countries

As in all classifications, there are countries that can fit into more than one category – e.g. China, Cuba. Throughout this book reference has been made to differences between developed and developing countries. Some of these differences have been summarised in Figure 12.3.

Using mainly Figure 12.2, and your own knowledge:

1 (a) Which country has the highest GNP? Give a reason for your answer.

2 (a) What does GNP (per capita) stand for?
  (b) What is the GNP (per capita) for the UK?

3 (a) In which continents are (i) the capitalist countries (ii) the centrally planned economies (iii) the low income developing countries?

4 What evidence is there in Figure 12.2 to confirm that 'most workers in a developing country are employed in agriculture'?

5 Why is life expectancy much higher in the capitalist (developed) and socialist countries than in the developing countries?

6 (a) Can you think of any measure of wealth not listed in Figure 12.2?
  (b) Do you consider wealth to be the only method of defining the stage of development of a country?

7 On page 54 a scattergraph was drawn to try to see if there was a correlation between wealth (GNP) and energy consumption.
  (a) Using the figures in Figure 12.2, draw a scattergraph to show any possible correlation between GNP and birth rates for the 14 countries. Sweden has been plotted for you.
  (b) Is the correlation negative or positive?

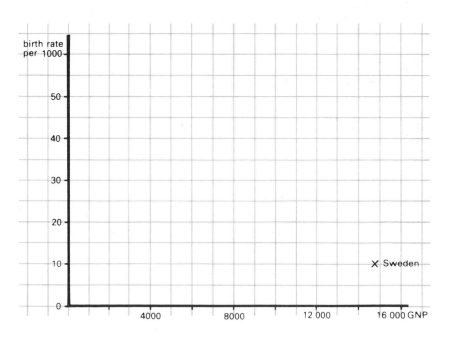

13
WATER SUPPLY
Uneven distribution

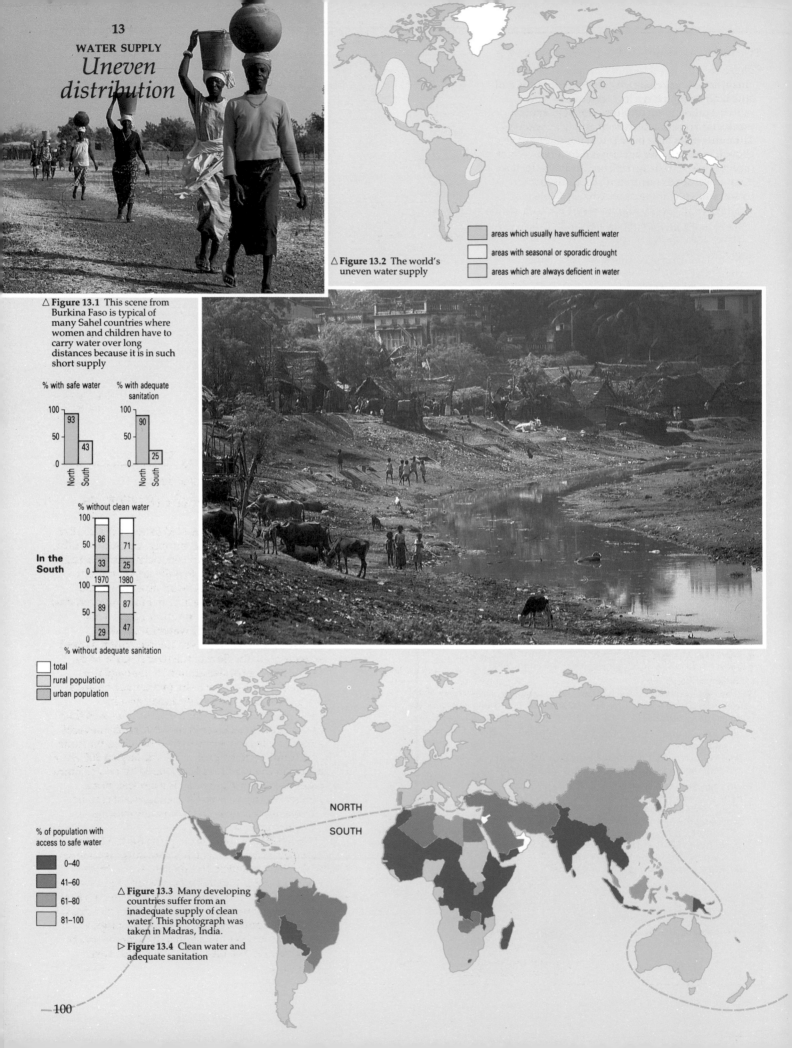

△ **Figure 13.1** This scene from Burkina Faso is typical of many Sahel countries where women and children have to carry water over long distances because it is in such short supply

△ **Figure 13.2** The world's uneven water supply

areas which usually have sufficient water

areas with seasonal or sporadic drought

areas which are always deficient in water

% with safe water

100
93
50
43
0
North South

% with adequate sanitation

100
90
50
25
0
North South

% without clean water

In the South

100
86
50
33
0
1970

100
71
50
25
0
1980

100
89
50
29
0

100
87
50
47
0

% without adequate sanitation

total
rural population
urban population

△ **Figure 13.3** Many developing countries suffer from an inadequate supply of clean water. This photograph was taken in Madras, India.

▷ **Figure 13.4** Clean water and adequate sanitation

NORTH

SOUTH

% of population with access to safe water

0–40
41–60
61–80
81–100

Two major problems associated with water supply are:

1 Insufficient, unreliable rainfall with one-third of the land being too dry for agriculture, and several other areas suffering from either a seasonal drought, or from variations in rainfall amounts from year to year (Figure 13.2). Notice how it is mainly the developing countries which seem to have the least reliable amounts. (Is it a lack of adequate water that has hindered development?) In parts of Africa, people may have to walk several kilometres a day to obtain water – a tiring, time consuming job which usually falls upon the women and children (Figure 13.1).

2 Even those countries in the developing world which do have water may well find that it is not clean. To add to this, even fewer areas have adequate safe methods of disposing of human waste (Figure 13.3).

In the 'north' (Figure 13.4) most people have sufficient clean, piped water and mains sanitation. In the 'south' only two out of five people have access to safe water and only one in four has adequate sanitation. Figure 13.4 also shows:

(a) Rural areas are far less likely to have clean water and sanitation than urban areas.

(b) Whereas the percentage without clean water fell between 1970 and 1980, the numbers without adequate sanitation, especially in the urban areas, actually increased – a result of the growth of shanty towns (pages 24-25).

In the developing countries drinking water is often drawn from the same source as that where bathing and laundering is done and where human waste is deposited. Dirty water is believed to account for 80% of the diseases affecting the developing world.

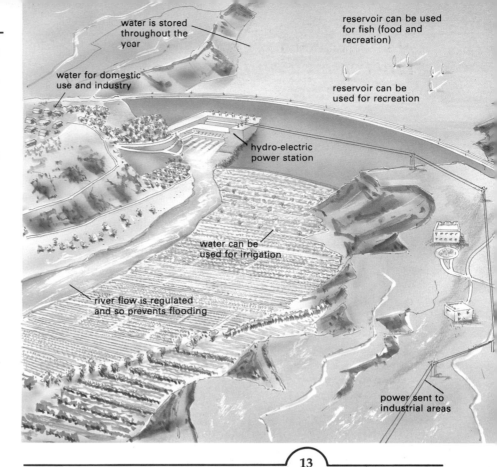

△ **Figure 13.5** A multipurpose water management scheme

▽ **Figure 13.6** Water supply and demand in the UK

supply exceeds demand	demand exceeds supply
heavy rainfall throughout the year	less rain
lower temperatures means less evapotranspiration	higher temperatures in summer means higher evapotranspiration
natural lakes	more and larger cities
relatively few large cities or industries	greater demand from agriculture

→ transfer schemes

N

(evapotranspiration means water lost by evaporation and transpiration)

In developed countries

Water management is needed to boost the quality and quantity of the water supply. Countries in the developed world have the financial reserves and technological resources to build large projects. However the expense of building a dam is too great for just the storage of water for drinking, and so modern schemes are 'multipurpose'. This means the dams provide water for drinking, industry, irrigation, power and recreation as well as regulating the flow of the river (Figure 13.5). Modern schemes also attempt to manage the whole of the drainage basin (a drainage basin is the area of land drained by a river and its tributaries). The first scheme of this size was that of the Tennessee River in the USA where several states had to co-operate in the financing, building and running of the project. Of the largest 200 river basins in the world, 148 are shared by two or more countries (a drainage basin is a natural, not a political, unit), so if water management is to be successful, it is essential that neighbouring countries co-operate.

Even more ambitious are plans for the transfer of water from areas which have a surplus to those which have a deficit. In England, water from the Kielder Dam is transferred eastwards to Tyneside, Wearside and Tees-side. In North America, plans have been drawn up to transfer water from Alaska to the dry south west of the USA, although at present it seems unlikely that the scheme will be implemented because of the enormous cost involved.

In developing countries

Prestige schemes

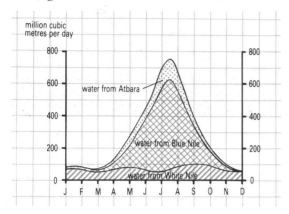

million cubic
metres per day

The Aswan Dam and the environment

Egypt is the gift of the Nile, for without this river the land would be desert and Egypt's 6000 year old civilisation could never have flourished.

The White Nile rises near the equator where it rains throughout the year, giving the river a constant flow (Figure 13.7). As the river flows northwards it receives two large tributaries, the Blue Nile and Atbara, which rise in Ethiopia. Here it rains heavily for nearly six months only to be followed by a drought. It is these two rivers which used to cause the annual flood and which spread fertile silt over the flood plain. For centuries Egyptians have dreamt of controlling the flow of the river to ensure a constant supply of water for irrigating the land. A dam had already been built at Aswan, and twice enlarged during the early 20th century, but it was the High Dam begun in the mid-1960s that was to transform the life of Egypt (Figure 13.8). Aided by Russian money, the dam was completed in 1971. It created a lake measuring the length of England. Figure 13.9 shows how the dam has benefited the Egyptian economy, but it has also had adverse effects upon the environment, which were not fully anticipated.

1 Figure 13.7
  (*a*) What do you notice about the flow of the White Nile throughout the year? Give a reason for your answer.
  (*b*) How much water do the Blue Nile and Atbara contribute during December? Why is this?
  (*c*) In which months was the Nile likely to flood?

2 Figure 13.8
  (*a*) What advantages did the Nile provide to the (i) economy (ii) environment of Egypt before the dam was built?
  (*b*) Why was the Aswan High Dam needed?

3 Figure 13.9
  (*a*) Which two countries co-operated to benefit from the control of the River Nile?
  (*b*) List as many ways as possible in which the Aswan High Dam has benefited the Egyptians.
  (*c*) What problems has the High Dam created? Divide your answer into the following categories· (i) economic (ii) environmental (iii) social.

◁ **Figure 13.7** The regime (annual flow) of the River Nile

▽ **Figure 13.8** The Nile Valley before 1964

▽ **Figure 13.9** The Nile Valley since the building of the Aswan High Dam in 1964

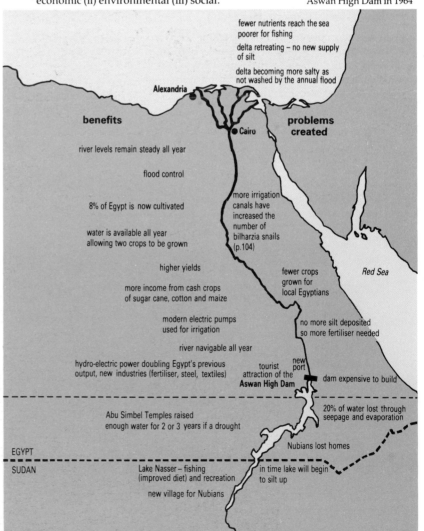

Appropriate technology

Schemes such as that at Aswan are extremely expensive to build, and can cause as many problems as they solve. How can the poorer countries in the world provide a clean and adequate water supply for their population? The need is, again, for appropriate technology.

☐ Water can be applied more efficiently by sprays and sprinklers than by allowing water to flow through channels. For rows of crops (Figure 13.10) drip irrigation is being used increasingly. Here pipes, with small holes in them, are laid over the ground, and water 'drips' at regular intervals onto the crops. No water is wasted.

☐ Village self-help schemes use limited funds to dig holes to try to reach underground supplies. Modern pumps are then used to obtain the water (Figure 13.12).

△ **Figure 13.10** Drip irrigation on a kibbutz in Israel. Small pipes are laid over the ground. Holes in these pipes allow water to drip out at regular intervals where it is needed so that none is wasted.

☐ Many wells and surface reservoirs in hot tropical areas lose much water through evaporation and seepage. New wells have concrete sides and a cover to try to reduce these two problems. Concrete also prevents possible seepage of sewage into the well.

☐ Educating local communities to use their supply wisely, to keep their supply clean and to improve sanitation. Health education is playing an increasingly important role since the World Health Organisation (WHO) suggested that 80% of the world's diseases are caused by dirty water and inadequate sanitation (e.g. cholera, typhoid, malaria, bilharzia and river blindness) (Chapter 14).

Clean water for all

The ten years 1981-1990 were designated, by the United Nations, the 'Clean Water and Sanitation Decade'. By 1983 many developing countries had drawn up short and long term plans to try to provide more and permanent clean water supplies, and to give adequate sanitation. The biggest obstacles to success are not only limited financial and technical resources, but also the rapidly growing populations of many of these countries and the expansion of shanty settlements within urban areas.

△ **Figure 13.11** Blasting a new concrete-lined well in Mali (Sahel)

▷ **Figure 13.12** A clean water stand pump is provided after severe drought in the Sahel

103

HEALTH AND DISEASE
Water-borne diseases

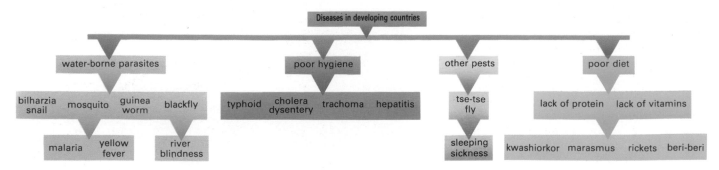

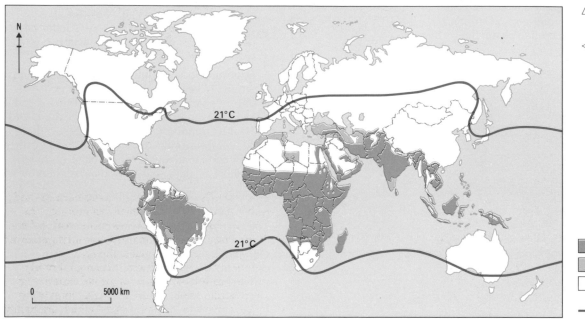

△ **Figure 14.1** Some important diseases found in developing countries

◁ **Figure 14.2** Areas of the world in which malaria may occur

risk of malaria

- occurs or might occur
- limited
- disappeared, eradicated or never existed
- summer isotherms

Mosquito – malaria and yellow fever

Mosquitoes breed in stagnant water in areas with a summer temperature of over 21°C. The female anopheles mosquito, one of 60 species of mosquito, carries a small parasite. If the mosquito bites a person who has malaria, it picks up the parasite as it sucks the human blood. The parasite matures inside the mosquito and is passed on to another human when the mosquito bites again. Malaria causes fever and shivering fits. It is not necessarily a killer in itself, but it weakens the infected people so that they cannot work very hard (which in a developing country usually means less food will be produced). They gradually become weaker and are more likely to fall victim to other diseases.

Malaria used to occur in parts of Europe (e.g. Mezzogiorno) but was eliminated by draining marshes and stagnant pools. Little progress was made in the tropics until DDT was first used in the 1940s. However it was later realised that DDT also polluted the environment. Although then banned in North America and Europe, it remains another example of an insecticide still used, despite its dangers, in the developing countries. By the 1960s large areas of malaria had been eliminated, but in the 1980s there has been a rapid increase in the number of reported cases. Estimates claim one in

four of African children under the age of five are infected every year, and that India now has over 10 million patients when only a few years ago it was thought that the disease had been beaten (see Figure 14.2).

A different species of mosquito is the cause of yellow fever, a disease so called as the victim, once bitten by an infected mosquito, turns yellow. It is now controlled by a vaccine though many tropical countries are too poor to conduct a full vaccination programme.

Guinea worm

This is found mainly in western India and West Africa. The worm infection is caught by drinking water which contains cyclops, tiny water fleas, which in turn contain Guinea worm larvae. The disease is spread by a person with an open sore through which a worm of up to 30cm in length protrudes. From the sore, larvae may be injected into ponds, and eventually caught by other people. The incubation period may be up to a year. The infection rarely results in death but it can cause severe swellings and arthritis in ankle and knee joints and can cause tetanus. At present there is no cure – other than by preventing those people with worms from stepping into water and releasing more larvae.

Bilharzia snail

The bilharzia snail lives in still, shallow waters of tropical areas, and causes the deaths of up to 20 million people a year. The disease is caught by people working in polluted water (e.g. farmers, fishermen). Figure 14.3 shows how the worms living in the snails enter humans (often through the soles of people's feet). The patient usually becomes gradually weaker and suffers from anaemia, and bladder and kidney infection. As in the case of malaria, the disease itself may not be fatal, but it reduces the patients' strength, and their resistance to other diseases. The problem is being tackled by draining stragnant water (but how is this to be achieved in padi-fields?) and by educating the local population.

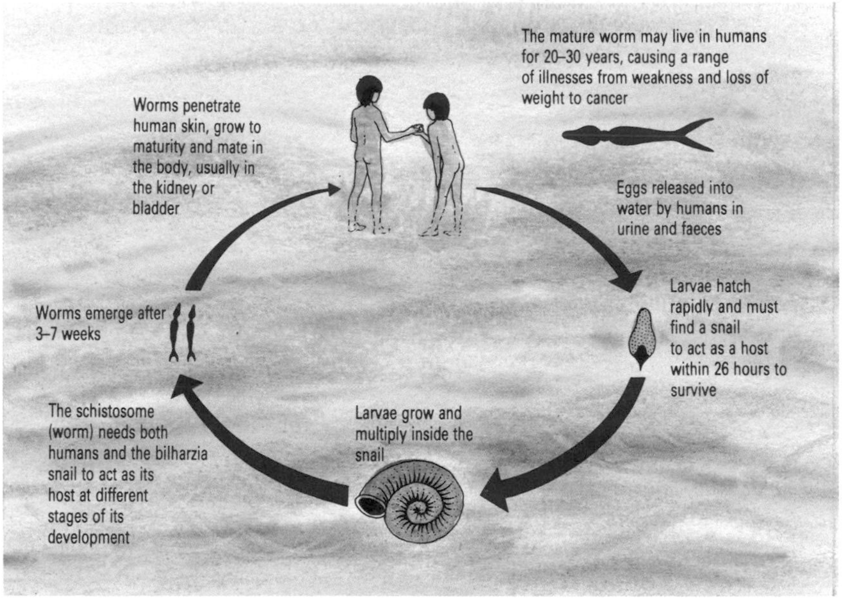

The mature worm may live in humans for 20–30 years, causing a range of illnesses from weakness and loss of weight to cancer

Worms penetrate human skin, grow to maturity and mate in the body, usually in the kidney or bladder

Eggs released into water by humans in urine and faeces

Larvae hatch rapidly and must find a snail to act as a host within 26 hours to survive

Worms emerge after 3–7 weeks

The schistosome (worm) needs both humans and the bilharzia snail to act as its host at different stages of its development

Larvae grow and multiply inside the snail

△ **Figure 14.3** Bilharzia

◁ **Figure 14.4** A Nigerian from near Kano suffering from river blindness

▽ **Figure 14.5** The distribution of tse-tse fly in Africa

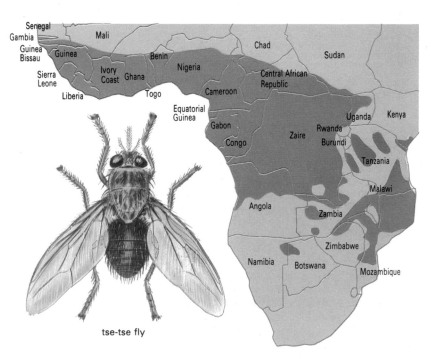

tse-tse fly

Blackfly – river blindness

This small fly, 4mm in length, bites humans and leaves parasitic worms which can produce one million offspring in a year. As these worms die they cause intense itching. If the worms get under the eyelids they can damage the eye and eventually cause blindness. Although it rarely causes death it reduces both the life expectancy and usefulness of the victim. The fly lives in fast flowing rivers (usually in rapids) which are highly oxygenated. These rapids are used by villagers for washing, collecting water and swimming. Most of the world's cases of river blindness are found in the savannas of West Africa with the highest concentrations in Ghana and Nigeria. The patients have a premature old-look and, once blind, can be seen walking about linked to each other by sticks, and led by a sighted guide (Figure 14.4). At present the World Bank is funding a campaign to spray the waters of these areas in the hope of exterminating the fly.

Other pests – tse-tse fly and sleeping sickness

Africa is the only continent in which the tse-tse fly lives. This insect infests areas where the vegetation is tall and bushy as it likes to rest in the shade to digest its food. It is not found in areas which are very hot and dry (Figure 14.5). Over 20 known species of tse-tse fly can infect domestic cattle (reducing their quality and quantity) of which five can affect humans.

The disease is spread by the tse-tse fly biting a human or an animal. In humans the disease is known as sleeping sickness. Initially it causes a loss of energy which, over a lengthy period of time, makes the human body increasingly weak. Ultimately, perhaps after several years, it can result in death. As yet there is no known cure.

Diet deficiency diseases

While many people in developing countries do not get enough to eat, even more suffer from malnutrition. Malnutrition means that people do not get the right diet, which usually means a lack of proteins and vitamins. Figure 14.6 shows the differences in diet between Britain and Tanzania. Notice that most of Tanzania's diet is made up with cereals, whereas in Britain it is mainly protein, fats and vitamins. Christian Aid have given comparative diets for two workers, one in Britain and one in Tanzania (Figure 14.7).

	United Kingdom Factory worker in West Midlands, England	**East Africa** Villager working on coffee plantation in Tanzania
Breakfast	breakfast cereal with milk and sugar, boiled egg, toast with butter and marmalade, tea with sugar and milk	children may have ugali with leafy vegetables and flavourings
Lunch	fish and chips, peas, yoghurt or ice cream	ugali (a maize porridge) stewed meat with vegetables, herbs and seasonings
Evening meal	steak and kidney pie, vegetables, apple pie and custard, tea or coffee	ugali, locust beans, vegetables
Extras	sweets, chocolate, fruit, tea, coffee, cake, biscuits, beer, crisps	fruit, nuts, seeds, honey

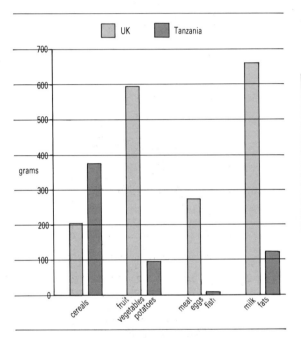

◁ **Figure 14.6** The daily intake of food in the UK and Tanzania

△ **Figure 14.7** The daily diets of two workers, one in the UK and one in Tanzania

▽ **Figure 14.8** Illnesses caused by a poor diet

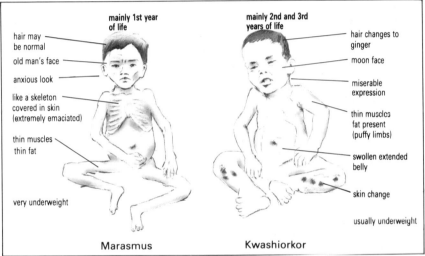

Marasmus   Kwashiorkor

The two major protein deficiency diseases are shown in Figure 14.8. Marasmus is more common in children in their first year of life, while kwashiorkor occurs more frequently in children in their second and third year. Marasmus results from a lack of food over a long period, kwashiorkor from sudden changes in diet and food together with a predominance of cereals and a deficiency of protein in the diet.

Two of several diseases resulting from a lack of vitamins are beri-beri and rickets. Beri-beri, due to a lack of vitamin B, leads to a wasting and paralysis of limbs with possible nerve disorders. Rickets, which is a disease among children who are deficient in vitamin D, causes deformities in bones, legs and the spine.

Figure 14.9 shows how malnutrition begins a cycle which can lead to illness, a reduced ability to work, causing less food to be produced or money earned, which causes a decrease in resistance to disease. This cycle is very hard to break.

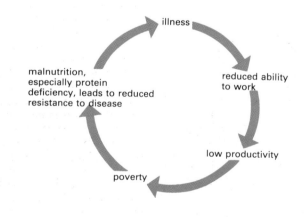

△ **Figure 14.9** The vicious circle of malnutrition

HEALTH AND DISEASE
Health care

Primary Health Care (PHC)

In the world today:

☐ One in two people never see a trained health worker.

☐ One in three people are without clean drinking water.

☐ One in four people have an inadequate diet.

Primary Health Care is an attempt by the World Health Organisation (WHO) to improve the health of young children and poor people. It claims that 'the cost of putting PHC into practice worldwide will be an extra $50 billion a year: less than two-thirds of what the world spends on cigarettes, and only one-fifteenth of world military expenditure.'

Using Figure 14.10:

1 List the eight elements of primary health care (PHC).

2 Describe the problems associated with each of these elements.

3 What solutions does PHC propose? How successful do you think these solutions will be?

▽ **Figure 14.10** Primary Health Care (PHC)

▽ **Figure 14.11** Health education programme in Tanzania

FOOD AND NUTRITION

● Around two-thirds of under-fives in the poor world are malnourished.

PHC means ensuring an adequate, affordable food supply and a balanced diet.

WATER AND SANITATION

● 80% of the world's disease is related to lack of safe water and sanitation.

PHC means providing everyone with clean water and basic sanitation.

DISEASE CONTROL

● Some 5 million children die and another 5 million are disabled yearly from 6 common childhood diseases.

PHC means immunisation against childhood diseases and combatting others like malaria.

MATERNAL AND CHILD HEALTH

● Over half a million mothers die in childbirth and 10% of babies die before their first birthday.

PHC means trained birth attendants, promotion of family planning and monitoring child health.

ESSENTIAL DRUGS

● Up to 50% of health budgets are spent on drugs.

PHC means restricting drugs to 200 essentials, preferably locally manufactured, and made available to everyone at a cost they can afford.

CURATIVE CARE

● 1,000 million cases of acute diarrhoea in under-fives each year.
● 33% of people in the world infested with hookworm.

PHC means training village health workers to diagnose and treat common diseases and injuries.

TRADITIONAL MEDICINE

● Traditional birth attendants deliver 60% – 80% of babies in the developing world.

PHC means enlisting traditional healers, giving additional training and using traditional medicines.

HEALTH EDUCATION

● Preventing ill health depends on changing personal and social habits.

PHC means educating people in understanding the causes of ill health and promoting their own health needs.

A cartoon used in the campaign. "Mtu ni Afya" (Man is health)

1 Take water that comes from a good source.
2 Pour the water into a second jar. Let it settle.
3 Boil some of the water for drinking.
4 The boiled water should be kept in a good place and should be conserved.
5 The remaining water can be used for washing utensils.

Very simple changes in ways of life can help to fight disease. In Tanzania a major mass adult education programme was launched in 1973 aimed at providing information about the symptoms of specific diseases and encouraging groups to take positive action. To back up the Swahili broadcasts, publicity posters, cartoons etc. were used. As well as encouraging greater care over drinking water, over 700 000 new latrines were established. In such health campaigns, people are encouraged to help themselves.

Health education in Tanzania

In 1973 the government of Tanzania introduced a campaign called 'MTU NI AFYA' (man is health – Figure 14.11). The aim was to educate people about diseases – how they were caught and transmitted, and how they could be prevented and, sometimes, cured. The campaign began on the radio (though not everyone in a developing country will have a radio) and was supported by advertisements in newspapers (not readily available to inhabitants of rural areas) and on wall posters. The wall posters were highly visual as a relatively large percentage of Tanzanians were unable to read. In this campaign people were taught to help themselves to improve their health, and to realise that prevention is better than having to find, or finance, a cure. Being a self-help scheme, and because 'leaders' were voluntary workers, the cost of the scheme was relatively cheap. Figure 14.11 lists two successes of the scheme:

1 Safer care and use of drinking water.

2 The building of over 700 000 new latrines.

Farming, trade, economies and wealth, water supply, health and disease

1 *(Page 80 and the diagram below)*

Study the two farming systems. One is a subsistence farm in India, the other is dairy farm in South West England.

a) (i) What is the size of Farm A? (1)
   (ii) How many animals are kept on Farm A? (1)
   (iii) Which two places might use the outputs from Farm A? (2)

b) The boxes labelled 'inputs' and 'outputs' for Farm A have been left empty. From the following list fill in the two boxes to show four likely inputs and four likely outputs: barley, fertiliser, hay, labour, machinery, manure, fattened pigs and milk. (8)

c) (i) What is meant by the term 'subsistence farming'? (1)
   (ii) Explain the differences between the two farms under the following headings: land, labour, machinery, animals and crops. (5)

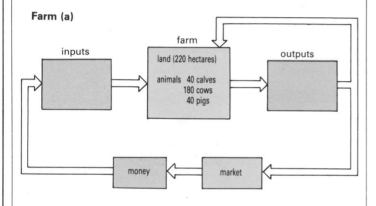

Farm (a)

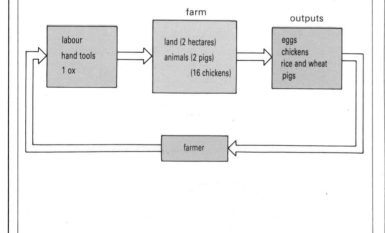

Farm (b)

3 *The Pampas (Figure 10.17, page 86)*

a) (i) What is the size of the estancia in hectares?
   (ii) How wide is the estancia at its widest point? (2)

b) (i) In which direction does the river flow?
   (ii) Why have dams been built?
   (iii) What two facts about the climate are suggested by the presence of wind pumps? (4)

c) (i) Why are fodder crops and cereals grown? (1)
   (ii) What are corrals? Why are there several corrals on the estancia? (2)
   (iii) Why does the manager have to provide accommodation for his workers? (2)
   (iv) Why are the main buildings surrounded by trees? (1)

4 *The green revolution (page 89 and the diagram below)*

a) What is meant by the term 'green revolution'? (1)

b) Name two improvements which have led to increased crop yields. (2)

c) Give two ways by which the farmer may benefit from the larger harvest. (2)

d) In what ways has the green revolution been less successful than had been hoped? (2)

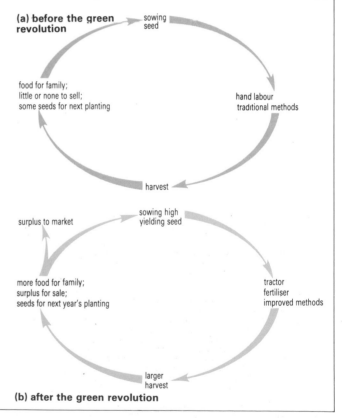

2 *(Page 82)*

a) Why is it an advantage to some farmers to clear hedgerows? (2)

b) Give three ways by which this removal can harm the environment. (3)

c) Describe three other aspects of modern farming which it is claimed might harm the environment. (3)

5 *(Pages 92-93)*

Choose *either* a Russian farm *or* a Chinese farm. How does this farm differ from a British farm in terms of: ownership; accommodation; decision-making; crops grown and animals reared; markets? (5)

6 *(See the figure below)*

Study this advertisement which appeared in many national newspapers in the autumn of 1986.

a) Which parts of Africa were affected by locusts in 1986? (1)

b) (i) What is meant by a 'swarm' of locusts?
(ii) How many locusts can there be in a swarm?
(iii) How many people could survive on the amount of food eaten in a year by one large swarm of locusts? (3)

c) (i) Apart from destroying crops, name two other problems resulting from the locust invasion. (2)
(ii) How is it proposed to use money given as donations? (2)

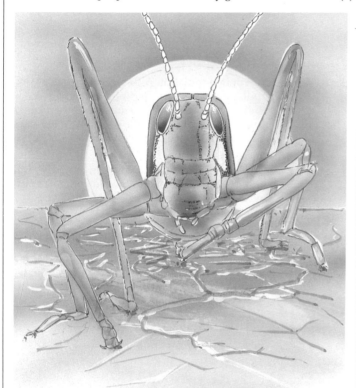

The face of the killer devouring Africa

Plagues of locusts and grasshoppers are swarming across the African continent, destroying precious food crops in their path.

The rains that promised relief from famine have provided ideal breeding conditions. Swarms of up to 40 billion locusts are feared, capable of devouring 80,000 tonnes of crops each day – enough to provide food for almost half a million people for a year.

If the locusts aren't checked *now*, the consequences can be cataclysmic – more crops destroyed . . . widespread famine that could last for years . . . fertile fields turning to desert.

Oxfam has already rushed pesticides and spraying equipment to stricken areas. But much more action must be taken by Oxfam and the wider world community to control the locusts, re-seed for new crops and provide food for the hungry. The need is desperate – please send your donation today.

The areas under threat
Mauritania, Mali, Niger, Chad, Sudan, Ethiopia, Kenya, Tanzania, Zambia, Botswana

Oxfam has made a start
- 6000 litres of pesticide for Chad; cost: £36,624
- 4 Land Rovers & spray equipment for Ethiopia
- 13,000 litres of pesticide spray & protective equipment for the Horn of Africa; cost: £210,131 incl. airfreight

---

7 *Trade*

The two pie charts below show the trade pattern for a typical developing country.

a) (i) Which two items appear as both imports and exports? (1)
(ii) Name, in rank order, the three main exports. (1)
(iii) Are these exports raw materials or manufactured goods? (1)
(iv) Why is this typical for a developing country? (1)

b) (i) Name, in rank order, the three main imports. (1)
(ii) Are these imports raw materials or manufactured goods? (1)
(iii) Why is this typical for a developing country? (1)

c) (i) By how many US dollars do imports exceed exports? (1)
(ii) What problems will this create in the developing country? (2)

d) (i) How might industrialisation help to improve the country's trade balance? (2)
(ii) How might this industrialisation affect countries in the developed world? (2)

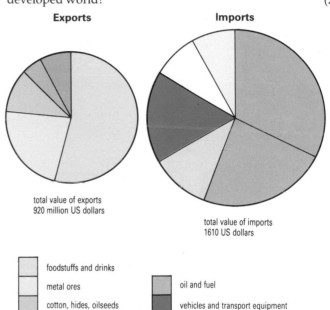

Exports

Imports

total value of exports
920 million US dollars

total value of imports
1610 US dollars

☐ foodstuffs and drinks
☐ metal ores
☐ cotton, hides, oilseeds
☐ manufactured goods
☐ timber

☐ oil and fuel
☐ vehicles and transport equipment
☐ chemicals
☐ processed metals

---

8 *Health and disease (pages 104-106)*

a) (i) What is a parasite?
(ii) Name four water-borne diseases. (2)

b) Choose *one* of these illnesses and then:
(i) Name one country in which it occurs. (1)
(ii) Say why it occurs in this country. (1)
(iii) Describe how it affects the local population. (2)
(iv) Suggest how it might be eliminated. (2)

c) Name two insects that cause illnesses to both humans and animals. (2)

d) (i) Name one diet deficiency disease. (1)
(ii) Describe how you would recognise a person suffering from a diet deficiency disease. (3)

Recent growth

Tourism is one of the fastest growing industries in the world today. It is an important factor in the economy of most developed countries, while it is seen by many developing countries as the one possible way to obtain income and to create jobs (Figure 15.1(a)). In Britain spa towns developed in the 18th century for the wealthy to 'take the waters'. By the late 19th or early 20th centuries, many industrial workers enjoyed a day or even a few days by the seaside. The annual holiday has become part of most families' way of life, with, as seen in Figure 15.1(b), an increasing number of British people now travelling abroad. The British Tourist Authority defines a short-term holiday as being one to three nights away, and a long-term holiday as four nights or more.

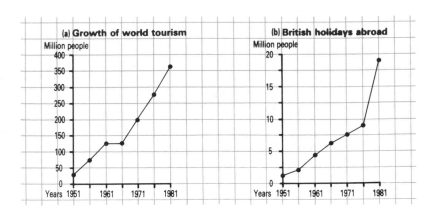

Year	Total population (millions) (including over 65s)	Over 65 years old (millions)
1901	38.2	
1911	42.1	
1921	44.0	
1931	46.0	
1951	50.3	5.5
1961	52.8	6.2
1971	55.9	7.3
1981	56.3	8.5
1991	est. 56.9	9.0
2001	est. 58.0	8.8

△ **Figure 15.1** Trends in world tourism, 1951–81

◁ **Figure 15.2** Population growth in the UK, 1901–2001

▽ **Figure 15.3** Holidays with pay for British employees

▽ **Figure 15.4** Duration of holidays taken by British people

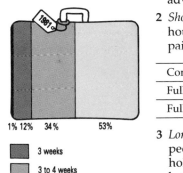

Holidays with pay

- [ ] 2 weeks
- [ ] 2 to 3 weeks
- [ ] 3 weeks
- [ ] 3 to 4 weeks
- [ ] 4 weeks and over

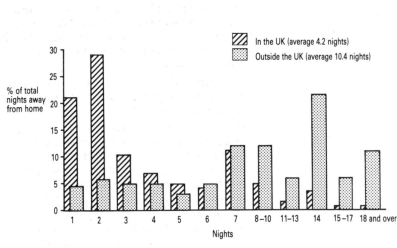

In the UK (average 4.2 nights)
Outside the UK (average 10.4 nights)

Nights

Why the growth in tourism in Britain?

Growth in population Although Britain's rate of population growth has declined in recent years, it is still increasing enough to mean that there are more people wishing to take part in recreational activities and to take holidays (Figure 15.2).

More leisure time

1 *The number of elderly people* is rising rapidly (Figure 15.2), and while some may not be fit or well off enough to take holidays, many are – even if their holiday is spent staying with friends and relations. Also many people are taking early retirement and so are able to take advantage of their greater fitness.

2 *Shorter working week* The number of contractual hours which the average British person works in paid employment has continued to decrease.

Contractual hours	1973	1978	1983
Full-time working woman	37.5	37.5	37.2
Full-time working man	44.7	43.1	41.5

3 *Longer holidays with pay* Figure 15.3 shows how people in employment have gained more holiday in recent years. It does not mention that before the last war those people who did take holidays lost their salary for the time spent away. Many people could not afford this loss of salary and so rarely took a break away from work. In recent years there has been an increase in the numbers able to take more than one holiday a year, sometimes by dividing their main holiday into two, sometimes by taking shorter 'mini-break' holidays at off peak times. Many, however, still prefer the long summer break (Figure 15.4).

Greater affluence Although Britain's unemployment figures have risen throughout the 1980s, the salaries paid to those who have found employment have grown considerably.

	1973	1978	1983
Full-time working woman	£21.2	£55.4	£106.9
Full-time working man	£41.5	£86.9	£163.8

Greater mobility and accessibility The increase in car ownership has given people much greater freedom to choose where and when they go for the day or for a longer period of time. Added to this is the convenience of loading the boot (or roof-rack) with luggage, and being able to drive from door to door. In 1951 only one person in twenty had a car (Figure 15.5(a)) whereas by 1986 over one in three had their own vehicle.

During the same period motorways had increased (Britain had none in 1951), as had the quality of roads and the number of by-passes built to avoid bottlenecks and steep gradients. This has led to a reduction in driving time between places, which has encouraged more people to travel further. Figure 15.6 shows how the reduction in driving time from the Dartmoor National Park, mainly due to the building of the M5, has meant that many more people from London, Birmingham and South Wales are likely to visit the park.

Also in the 1950s, air travel for a holiday was beyond the means of most British families. Since then the use of charter aircraft has reduced fares, and the building of international airports near to large holiday resorts has enabled tourists to travel in larger numbers and greater distances than before. Figure 15.7 shows the dominance of the car for holidays in Britain, and the plane for overseas destinations.

Package holidays This is a holiday for a set period of time in which travel, accommodation and predetermined meals (full board or half board) are all included in the price. Tour operators can charter and make block bookings at holiday resorts at prices more in the range of most British people. In 1984 the major 'package tour' resorts were, in rank order: Benidorm; Corfu; Tenerife; Paris; Ibiza; Majorca and Torremolinos.

(a) Cars on the road (millions)	
1951	2.4
1961	6.1
1971	12.4
1981	20.3
1991 (est.)	26.0
2001 (est.)	30.0

(b) Length of road (km)	1973	1983
motorways	1731	2709
principal roads	32 755	34 587

Figure 15.5 Greater mobility and improved travel in the UK

△ **Figure 15.6** Driving time (in hours) from the Dartmoor National Park, 1971–81

▽ **Figure 15.7** Transport used by British tourists

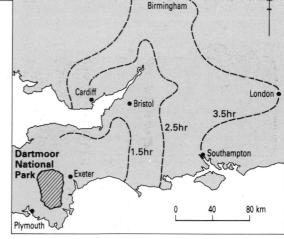

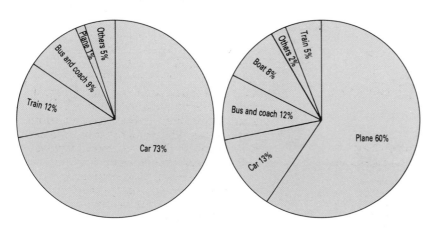

(a) **For holidays in the UK**

(b) **For holidays outside the UK**

Self-catering holidays The increase in camping, caravans and rented holiday flats has further lowered the cost of holidays. This allows families with young children to enjoy a holiday and to stay away from home longer.

Advertising This has made people even more aware of the range of holidays and recreational activities available to them.

Other factors include: the increasing pressure of modern life and, for many, an unattractive local environment which encourages people to 'get away from it all'; the recent advantageous foreign exchange rate which has made overseas holidays cheaper; increased education and a desire to experience other cultures (long haul holidays); and the unreliable British weather and the desire to find places with a hot, dry, sunny climate.

RECREATION & TOURISM
National Parks

These are defined by Act of Parliament (1949) as 'areas of great natural beauty giving opportunity for open-air recreation, established so that natural beauty can be preserved and enhanced, and so that the enjoyment of the scenery by the public can be promoted'.

☐ They contain some of the most diverse and spectacular upland scenery in England and Wales (Pembrokeshire Coast National Park being coastal, is the exception).

☐ They are mainly in private ownership, though bodies such as the National Trust, Forestry Commission and water authorities are important landowners (these parks are not owned by the nation).

☐ Public access is encouraged, but is restricted to footpaths, bridleways, open fells and mountains (with the exceptions of military training areas and grouse moors).

☐ All contain local populations who are dependent on primary (farming, forestry and mining) and tertiary (tourism) forms of employment.

The ten National Parks contain a variety of scenery which in turn provides a wide range of recreational activities. All the parks provide basic opportunities for walking, riding and fishing but some provide specialist attractions, e.g. limestone within the Brecon Beacons and Peak District is used for caving and potholing (Figure 15.8).

Using Figures 15.8 and 15.10:

(a) Which is the only conurbation which is not near to a National Park?

(b) Which park (i) is almost surrounded by motorways (ii) is nearest to most conurbations (iii) is likely to receive most visitors?

(c) Which two parks have been (i) most affected (ii) least affected by the construction of motorways?

(d) Choose one National Park. What impact do you think the motorways have had on (i) the roads leading to the park (ii) the roads within the park (iii) the use of recreation amenities within the park?

△ Figure 15.9(b) The scars of quarrying in the Peak District

Northumberland
▲ moors, forests
● archeology, walking, nature trails

North Yorkshire Moors
▲ moors, coasts
● walking, gliding

Lake District
▲ lakes, mountains, coasts
● water sports, climbing

Yorkshire Dales
▲ moors, valleys
● walking, fishing caving

Peak District
▲ moors, limestone, millstone grit
● grouse, caving, rock climbing

▲ mountains, lakes
● climbing, water sports
Snowdonia

Brecon Beacons
▲ moors, limestone
● walking, caving

Pembroke
▲ coasts
● cliff walking, bird watching

Exmoor
▲ moors, coasts
● riding, beach activities

Dartmoor
▲ moors, tors, valleys
● walking, pony-trekking, fishing, camping

National parks
Motorways
Conurbations
▲ Physical landscape
● Recreational amenities

△ Figure 15.8 National Parks, conurbations and motorways in the UK

◁ Figure 15.9(a) Attempts to reduce further erosion of footpaths

Time and distance to National Parks

The National Parks were located, usually, within easy reach of the major conurbations (Fig. 15.8). This enabled the maximum number of people, including those who lived in large urban areas, to escape to a quieter, pleasant rural environment. Since then the growth of the motorway network has considerably reduced driving times and so in effect has reduced distances between the conurbations and the National Parks.

Who owns the National Parks?

In total, 81% of the land is owned privately, mainly by farmers, with 6% belonging to the Forestry Commission, 5% to the National Trust (a charitable organisation earning revenue from membership, admission fees and souvenirs), 3% to water authorities, 3% to the Ministry of Defence, 1% to county councils and 1% to the national parks themselves.

▽ **Figure 15.10** Numbers of people within a three-hour drive of the National Parks

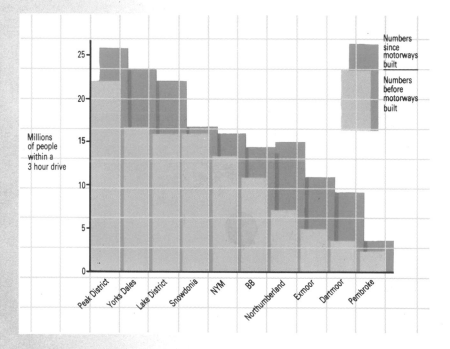

Conflict of users in National Parks

With over two people per hectare, the UK is one of the most densely populated countries in the world, and so there is considerable competition for land. This competition is also seen within the national parks.

- ☐ Town dwellers wish to use the countryside for recreation and relaxation.
- ☐ Farmers wish to protect their land and in areas such as Exmoor are ploughing to a higher altitude by using government grants.
- ☐ The Forestry Commission has planted many hectares of trees in the poorer soils of Northumberland, the North Yorkshire Moors and the Snowdonia Parks.
- ☐ The mining and quarrying of slate (Lake District and Snowdonia) and limestone (Peak District) creates local jobs but ruins the environment (Figure 15.9(b)).
- ☐ Water authorities have created reservoirs in the Lake and Peak Districts.
- ☐ The Ministry of Defence own nearly a quarter of the Northumberland Park.
- ☐ Walkers and climbers wish for free access to all parts of the parks and campers and caravanners seek more sites for accommodation.
- ☐ Despite planning controls, the demand for housing has led to an increased suburbanisation of villages (p. 27) and the use of property as 'second homes' for town dwellers.
- ☐ Nature lovers wish to create nature reserves and to protect birds, animals and plants from the invading tourists.

Honeypots

The National Parks include many of the nation's 'honeypots' – areas of attractive scenery (Malham Cove in the Yorkshire Dales), or of historic interest (the Roman Wall in the Northumberland Park) to which tourists swarm in large numbers. The problem is how can the honeypots' natural beauty, their unspoilt quality (the essence of their appeal) be preserved while providing facilities for the hordes who arrive at peak summer periods? At Malham Cove steps have been cut into the limestone to safeguard paths. It is estimated that £1½ million is needed to repair the six paths leading to the top of Snowdon where, on a summer's day, 2500 people might reach the summit. Parts of the 400km Pennine Way have had to have artifical surfaces laid as in places the tracks of walkers have penetrated over a metre into the peat (Figure 15.9(a)). The footpaths on the Roman Wall are being eroded and, as soil is washed away, the foundations of the wall are being exposed.

◁ **Figure 15.11** How planning in a National Park can help to solve problems such as over-use, congestion and conflicts of use

Problems	Attempted solutions
Footpaths worn away	New routes planned; signposted routes; artificial surfaces laid
Destruction of vegetation	Areas fenced off; education of visitors
Litter, vandalism, trespass	Provision of picnic areas with litter bins; park wardens
Cars parked on grass verges or in narrow lanes	Car parks; one-way systems; park and ride schemes
Congestion on narrow roads	Roads closed to traffic in tourist season/week ends; park and ride; encouraged to use minibuses, cycles or to walk
Heavy lorries, local traffic and tourist traffic	Scenic routes separating local and tourist traffic
'Honeypots' (views, cafés)	Develop alternative honeypots, direct visitors to other attractions
Conflict of users, e.g. a) local farmers/tourists b) between tourists	Restricting tourist access to footpaths and bridlepaths Separating activities e.g. water skiing and angling
New cafés, car parks, and caravan parks	Screened behind trees. Only certain natural colours allowed in paint schemes

Coastal

Ibiza (Spain)

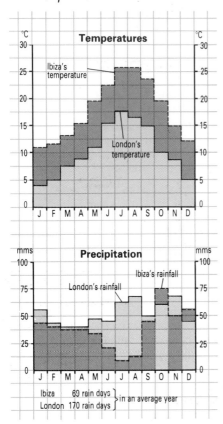

Temperatures

Ibiza's temperature

London's temperature

J F M A M J J A S O N D

Precipitation

Ibiza's rainfall

London's rainfall

J F M A M J J A S O N D

| Ibiza | 60 rain days | } in an average year |
| London | 170 rain days | |

△ **Figure 15.12** Climate graphs for London and Ibiza (Spain)

Roads
Towns/villages

Developments since 1960

Hotel and apartment blocks

Villas and other small scale developments

Electricity supply

New roads

Airport

Hotel Pacific

San Antonio - Ibiza

2 star hotel, situated close to the excitement of San Antonio, the informal, carefree atmosphere appeals to the young, young-at-heart and those seeking a lively time. The beach, ferry boats, town centre and nightlife are all close to hand.

- Well furnished lounge, pleasant bar leading out to the pool.
- Lifts to all floors.
- Dining room with a reputation for good food and service.
- Spacious sun terraces surround the enticing swimming pool.

All our twin bedded rooms have bath, shower, w.c., and balcony.

Playa Bella Apartments

San Antonio - Ibiza

Superb new apartment complex opened in 1985, directly overlooking the beach and small promenade. They are just facing the Hotel Riviera and are furnished in bright polished pine wood with matching fitments.

- Studios can sleep up to 3. One-bedroom apartments up to 4 and two-bedroom units up to 6.
- All units have fridge and electric cooking rings in kitchenette.
- Reception, bar, cafeteria, supermarket, shops.
- Circular swimming pool, children's pool set in spacious sun terraces.
- Cleaning 3 times a week and linen change once.
- Water toboggan (small charge).

All our units have bath, shower, w.c., balcony or patio, sea-view.

		Mar 21 to Mar 31	Apr 01 to Apr 30	May 01 to May 15	May 16 to May 25	May 26 to Jun 05	Jun 06 to Jun 26	Jun 27 to Jul 03	Jul 04 to Jul 17	Jul 18 to Aug 10	Aug 11 to Aug 28	Aug 29 to Sep 07	Sep 08 to Sep 25	Sep 26 to Oct 05	Oct 06 to Oct 16	Oct 17 to Oct 31
HOTEL/APARTMENT	No. of Nights															
Pacific	7	184	179	187	226	212	228	238	260	283	279	272	240	224	196	183
Half Board	14	231	229	239	280	271	291	303	332	361	355	347	306	285	250	233
Playa Bella	7	147	149	145	182	168	178	192	220	232	229	220	198	173	141	134
Self Catering	14	157	159	153	191	179	189	209	245	259	255	245	221	189	149	142

Prices are in £s per person for departures on or between the undernoted dates and include airport taxes and passenger charges.

△ **Figure 15.13** Holiday brochure for Ibiza

◁ **Figure 15.14** Some recent changes in accommodation and services in Ibiza

Portinatx

S Miguel

S Mateo

S Antonio

S Rafael

S Jose

S Eulalia

Ibiza

MEDITERRANEAN SEA

N

0 — 5 km

1 Ibiza is one of Europe's most popular package holiday resorts. What is a package holiday?

2 Using Figure 15.12, explain why Ibiza attracts many tourists in (a) summer (b) winter.

3 Figure 15.13 is from a holiday brochure.
   (a) What are the advantages of staying in a hotel?
   (b) Why do many people, especially families with young children, prefer to stay in apartments?

4 Why do prices vary throughout the year? Why is it almost as expensive to stay for seven nights as it is to stay for 14 nights?

5 What is meant by the following terms?
   (a) half board (b) self catering.

6 (a) Figure 15.14 shows some recent changes in Ibiza as a result of the growth of tourism. Describe, with reasons, the distribution of holiday accommodation.
   (b) As a group, try to decide:
      (i) How the growth in tourism has benefited the local community.
      (ii) How the growth in tourism might harm the environment and local community.

Tourism and Britain's beaches

Britain's beaches and seas are far from clean, although they present less of a health hazard than in the Mediterranean.

In 1975 the EEC set limits for pollution in waters where people bathe. Each government had to name beaches 'where bathing is traditionally carried out by large numbers of people'. These beaches had then to meet EEC requirements by the end of 1985. The UK Government had, even in 1986, named only 27 beaches which it claimed had a minimum of 50 bathers at one time (Figure 15.15). Of these, several had not met the 1985 deadline, and beaches such as at Blackpool, Brighton, Morecambe, Eastbourne and Rhyl were not on the list (presumably as the cost of bringing them up to standard was too great).

Sewage Most of Britain's 690 beaches are affected by untreated domestic sewage. This problem could be cured either by treating the sewage before discharging it into the sea, or by building longer outflow pipes. At present 85% of sewage is discharged within 100 metres of low water mark enabling tides and currents to bring some of it onshore. Normally sunlight, oxygen, salt and bacteria in the sea can soon break down all the effluent deposited in it.

Oil This frequently affects beaches, but it only makes headlines after a serious accident such as the wreck of the Torrey Canyon (1967) and Amaco Cadiz (1978).

Litter Tourists themselves leave broken glass, disused cans and litter.

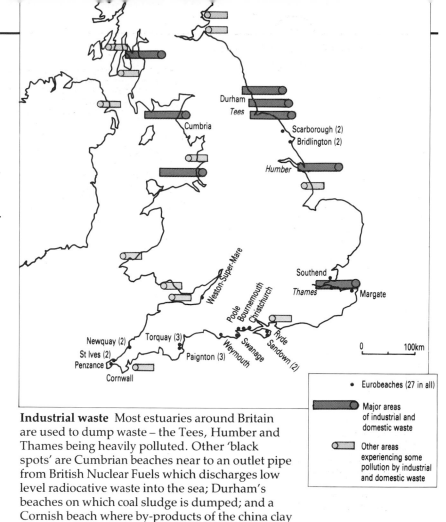

Industrial waste Most estuaries around Britain are used to dump waste – the Tees, Humber and Thames being heavily polluted. Other 'black spots' are Cumbrian beaches near to an outlet pipe from British Nuclear Fuels which discharges low level radioactive waste into the sea; Durham's beaches on which coal sludge is dumped; and a Cornish beach where by-products of the china clay industry are deposited.

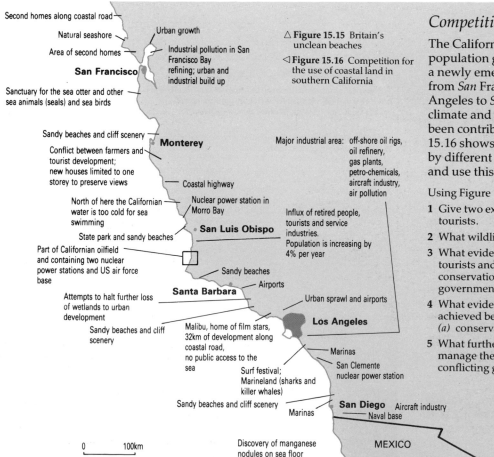

△ **Figure 15.15** Britain's unclean beaches

◁ **Figure 15.16** Competition for the use of coastal land in southern California

Competition for land – California

The Californian coast is experiencing a rapid population growth. 'San San' is the name given to a newly emerging conurbation extending 1000km from *San* Francisco in the north through Los Angeles to *San* Diego in the south. The dry, sunny climate and the spectacular coastal scenery have been contributory factors in this growth. Figure 15.16 shows some of the resultant demands made by different groups of people who wish to settle in and use this coastal area.

Using Figure 15.16:

1 Give two examples of natural scenery which attract tourists.

2 What wildlife can be found on this coast?

3 What evidence is there that there is conflict between tourists and (*a*) farmers (*b*) industrialists (*c*) conservationists (*d*) property developers (*e*) federal government?

4 What evidence is there that some compromise is being achieved between tourists and (*a*) conservationists (*b*) property developers?

5 What further steps do you think should be made to manage the coastal environment so as to satisfy all the conflicting groups who wish to use it?

RECREATION AND TOURISM
Purpose-built resorts

Legend:
- Hotel Ambasador
- Hotel Plat
- Conifers
- Rocky beach
- Shingle beach
- Steps
- Services

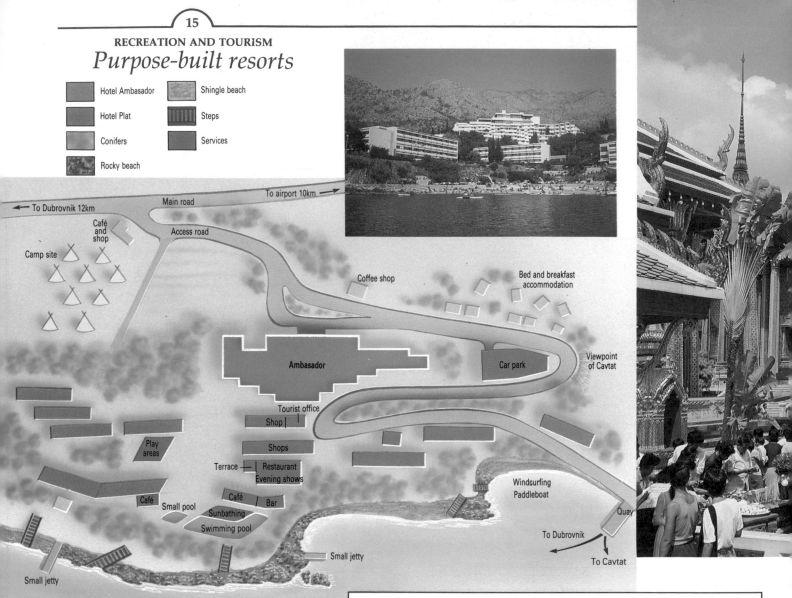

Figure 15.18 map labels: To Dubrovnik 12km · To airport 10km · Main road · Café and shop · Access road · Camp site · Coffee shop · Bed and breakfast accommodation · Ambasador · Car park · Viewpoint of Cavtat · Tourist office · Shop · Shops · Play areas · Terrace · Restaurant · Evening shows · Café · Small pool · Sunbathing · Swimming pool · Café · Bar · Windsurfing · Paddleboat · Quay · To Dubrovnik · To Cavtat · Small jetty · Small jetty · Adriatic Sea

△ **Figure 15.17** The Plat holiday complex near Dubrovnik, Yugoslavia (inset photo)

△ **Figure 15.18** Layout of the Plat complex

▷ **Figure 15.19** Holiday brochure – the Plat complex

▷ **Figure 15.20** The old walled city of Dubrovnik, Yugoslavia (photo, below)

Plat, Yugoslavia

As families have become better off, with more leisure time and increased mobility, the numbers wishing to take holidays and to visit places further from home have increased. The traditional holiday resorts have become too small to cater for this increase in demand, and lack the amenities demanded by the modern tourist. The result has been the building of many purpose-built resorts or holiday complexes. A purpose-built resort caters for all the needs of the tourist, and includes accommodation, set meals and many recreational amenities within one set price. A purpose-built resort like the one at Plat, 12km south of Dubrovnik in Yugoslavia (Figures 15.17, 15.18, and 15.19) caters mainly for visitors from Northern Europe seeking sun and relaxation. Many of these 'new' resorts are still built within easy access of airports and 'older' centres (Figure 15.18).

HOTEL AMBASADOR OFFICIAL RATING A

This hotel is situated 12km from Dubrovnik in an outstanding position amongst cypress trees, low-lying shrubs and brushwood. Not suitable for the elderly or disabled.

Rooms: 302. Floors: 8. Lifts: 3.
Facilities: Bars. Patisserie. Restaurant. Indoor pool (close Jun. to Sept.). Outdoor pool at Hotel Plat below. Sun terrace. TV.
Sport: Bowling, table tennis, billiards, Wind surfing and pedaloes available in the complex.
Special Features: Discotheque: Dancing to band on terrace and fortnightly folklore in hotel complex, June to September.
Beach: Pebbly and rocky – 200 metres below hotel.
Children's Facilities: Play centre in hotel complex. Early meals.
Prices: Prices shown are per person for **half board** in twin-bedded rooms with shower and wc.

HOTEL PLAT OFFICIAL RATING 'B'

Pavilion-type hotel, part of the Plat complex and situated amongst Mediterranean flora with excellent aspects over the blue sea. Not suitable for the elderly or disabled.

Rooms: 494. Floors 2/3.
Facilities: Bar. Restaurant. Terrace. Outdoor pool close by. Hairdresser in complex.

Bangkok and Thailand

Culture, in this sense, means learning about a country's civilisation or, more simply, its way of life. Due to the increase in wealth, package holidays, air flights and travel programmes on TV, people in the more developed countries have become increasingly aware of the more intellectually satisfying holiday of visiting countries and cities with a different lifestyle to their own. Added to this is the appeal of the 'historic' holiday where tourists can gain an insight into the past culture (civilisation) of an area.

One leading long-distance British tour operator claims that 'Thailand has become the most popular destination in our worldwide programme with more people wishing to holiday in Bangkok and the former kingdom of Siam than any other country in the world.' What can a cultural holiday in Thailand offer? Two optional 'cultural' tours are available:

1 The River Kwai which, apart from a visit to the 'death railway' built in the last war, includes a journey through the jungle to a small village.

2 Chiang Mai – Thailand's northern capital. Visitors can see local temples, handicrafts, dances, hill tribe villages and enjoy local food.

△ **Figure 15.21** Thai national dress. Although western dress is becoming more popular, the traditional costumes are more suited to the hot, humid, tropical climate. Visitors may be shown the making of silk and paper umbrellas (inset, top)

◁ **Figure 15.22** Wat Phra Keo (the Emerald Temple). There are over 300 temples, or 'wats', in Bangkok and all are ornately decorated with carvings. The Emerald Temple lies in the grounds of the Grand Palace where the kings of Siam lived until recently. An hour's drive from Bangkok is the largest museum in Thailand with reproductions of 60 Thai palaces, temples and historical monuments

△ **Figure 15.23** Buddhist monks and statues of Buddha in Wat Po, the temple of the reclining Buddha

▷ **Figure 15.24** The floating market, Bangkok. From dawn until mid-morning farmers and traders, many of them women in traditional broad-brimmed straw hats, take their produce to this market in sampans. The sampans are ideally suited to the many local canals or 'klongs'

Switzerland

Mountainous regions also attract tourists. In Switzerland, as in other highland areas of North West Europe, the landscape has been created by ice. Glaciers formed in the mountains and flowed downhill, enlarging and widening valleys, and leaving jagged, spectacular scenery. When the ice melted, lakes were left on the valley floors (Figure 15.25).

Advantages of Switzerland for tourism:

- Warm, sunny summers.
- Cold, bright winters with many sunny days as well as heavy snowfalls.
- Clean air and a healthy environment.
- The extension of main roads into the Alps.
- The opening of tunnels to avoid the previously used high Alpine passes which are blocked by snow for several months every year.
- Spectacular scenery of mountains, lakes and valleys.
- The commercial instinct of the Swiss.

Problems which might reduce tourism:

- Cool, wet summers, or a lack of snow in winter.
- Mild springs causing avalanches.
- Competition from other alpine resorts (there are 600 ski resorts in the Alpine countries)
- Unfavourable foreign exchange rates.
- The high cost of Swiss holidays.

Tourism and its effect on the economy, culture and environment

Read the extract in Figure 15.26 describing recent changes in a Swiss Alpine valley, and answer question 3 on page 123.

A Swiss Alpine valley – the Val d'Anniviers

The Val d'Anniviers was a prosperous valley in the nineteenth century, relying on agriculture (dairying and vines) and forest products. By 1900 a decline in prosperity had led to rural depopulation.

Tourism began in earnest in 1964, when an outside organisation bought two semi-abandoned hotels and turned them, together with an extension, into a 440 bed resort. In 1967 a ski-complex was added, with three ski-lifts and a cable railway. A mountain restaurant, hotel and swimming pool were built but created little employment for locals. A two lane road was opened, a large car park, sewerage and water supply added, although these were partly paid for by the local inhabitants through increased taxes.

Meanwhile, the seasonal migration of farmers had ended. Some vineyards had been sold to property developers, though new ones were established on higher land. Other farmers rented spare rooms and outhouses to visitors, whilst others found seasonal employment as ski-instructors, lift operators, and bed and breakfast proprietors.

The younger members of the community did find more job opportunities and entertainment, and rural depopulation was reversed.

By 1976, 50% of the workforce were employed in tourism in some form or other and the annual number of tourists had risen to 24 000 from 8000. Although greater consideration was given in this valley to traditional buildings and the environment, the new road was affected by landslides; the delicate ecology was harmed; footpaths were eroded, the risk of fires (as well as avalanches) increased. The traditional way of life had been altered.

▽ **Figure 15.26** (Extract)

▽ **Figure 15.25** Landsketch of the Intertaken area of the Swiss Alps

RECREATION AND TOURISM
Seasonal nature of holidays

Few holiday resorts are able to attract tourists throughout the year. Figure 15.27 shows the generalised pattern for four different types of resort.

1 Most British resorts are full during the school summer holidays, but due to an unreliable, often unfavourable climate, their season is very short.

2 Spanish resorts not only have a warmer, drier and much longer summer season, but their winters are mild enough for people to sit out of doors.

3 Alpine resorts have two peak seasons. In winter heavy snowfalls attract skiers, and in summer the lakes and mountains encourage a wider range of visitor.

4 Cultural resorts are less affected by the weather, and can attract tourists (short-stay rather than long-stay) throughout the year.

How do resorts try to extend their season?

British resorts compete with each other:

☐ To host political conferences and exhibitions.

☐ In offering lower out of season prices, minibreaks, free accommodation for young children, and reduced rates for senior citizens.

☐ By providing special attractions such as illuminations, national sporting events and family entertainment.

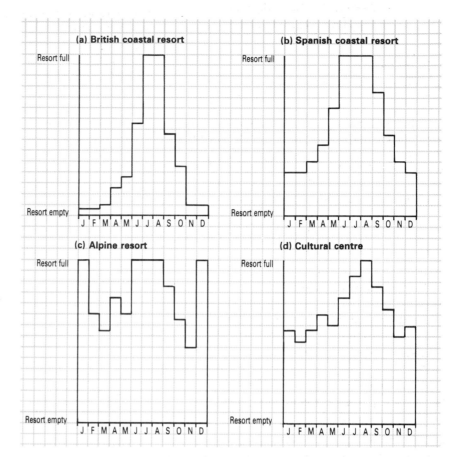

△ **Figure 15.27** The seasonal nature of tourism

▽ **Figure 15.28** Special offers

Spanish resorts, despite their shorter off-peak season still offer:

☐ Reduced rates, sometimes even offering two weeks for the price of one.

☐ Villas to let for several winter months to people from the colder wetter countries to the north.

Alpine and cultural resorts have no real off season yet will still add indoor amenities in case of adverse weather, and services to make the visitor's stay more enjoyable.

Problems caused by the seasonal nature of tourism

During the holiday season:

☐ Traffic congestion in streets, parking problems and delays in reaching and leaving the resort.

☐ Overuse of amenities and services, e.g. queuing for amusements and in cafés.

☐ Pollution in the form of noise and litter.

☐ A rise in crime and vandalism.

☐ The increase in food and other prices will also apply to the local residents.

During the off-peak season:

☐ Loss of income from outside sources.

☐ Loss of trade for shopkeepers, hotel and café owners, and places of entertainment.

☐ Seasonal unemployment.

☐ Local resources will not be used, and will be closed to local residents.

☐ Second homes left empty and smaller resorts will 'die'.

RECREATION AND TOURISM
In developing countries

By the mid-1980s, some 250 million people from western countries had a holiday abroad each year, making tourism the world's largest industry. As holidaymakers tire of Europe's packaged tours so they go further – to Kenya, Tanzania, Sri Lanka, Thailand, Mexico and other favoured developing countries. The attractions of earning money from tourism are considerable to hard-up developing countries, and many see its development as the only way to prosperity. Even so, less than 45 countries take the lion's share of tourists who travel·to developing countries and, as seen on page 121, the damage to the culture and economies of these countries often outweighs the gains.

Kenya and Tanzania – safari holidays

The growth in the numbers of tourists to Kenya and Tanzania is shown in Figure 15.29. Both countries have tried to take advantage of their natural environment by organising safari holidays to game reserves and national parks. One holiday brochure claimed, 'The one element that makes Africa so very different from other holiday destinations is its wildlife – nowhere on earth has remained as nature intended to quite the same extent'. Game reserves and national parks were set up to conserve and protect the environment. 'Safari' means 'hunting trip', but now the only shooting allowed is by camera. Travel is by seven- or nine-seater buses which have roof hatches and sliding windows for improved viewing, and accommodation is in lodges. Yet despite similar advantages, the number of visitors to Kenya far exceeds those to Tanzania.

Tanzania's difficulties

1 A more spartan way of life for the tourist, with more limited menus, and water not always guaranteed.

2 Most of the income from tourists is spent abroad, e.g. buying the types of food demanded by westerners.

3 The government was less keen to support tourism and more keen to promote agriculture.

4 The game reserves and national parks are further from western Europe.

5 There were few roads and no suitable airfield until the 1970s.

Kenya's advantages

1 A more comfortable holiday is available with good menus, swimming pools and, usually, private showers.

2 Most of the income from tourists is retained by the country as it can provide such basic needs as food.

3 The government encouraged tourism at the expense of other sectors of the economy.

4 The game reserves and national parks are nearer western Europe.

5 Nairobi already had an international airport, and local communications were of a reasonable standard.

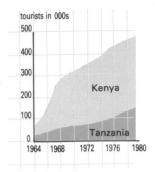

△ **Figure 15.29** Numbers of tourists to Kenya and Tanzania since 1964

▽ **Figure 15.30** Safari parks and game reserves in Kenya and Tanzania

▽ **Figure 15.31** On safari in Kenya and Tanzania (inset)

▷ **Figure 15.32** A holiday village resort in Jamaica (main photo)

Day 1 Ngorongoro
Drive over grasslands to the Ngorongoro crater and then upwards to reach the lip of the extinct crater. After lunch leave by land-rover for the descent into the midst of a breathtaking spectacle — over 250 square km of wildlife paradise. Herds of wilde-beeste and elephant wander over the green carpet, while pelican, ibis and flamingo form a mobile ribbon at the lakeside. This is the country where lion and cheetah rule supreme and dik-dik and warthogs are the jesters. All are here in the grandeur of Ngorongoro.

Day 2 Ngorongoro/Serengeti
Whatever you may have read or heard about the famous park, nothing will adequately prepare you for the impact of the magnificent immensity of Serengeti. Over 15,000 square km of plain and savannah, hills and woodland, provide a beautiful home for what is believed to be the largest concentration of wildlife in the world.
And you will probably see a fascinating selection of big game during your afternoon drive. Overnight at Seronera.

Day 3 Serengeti
Morning game drive. Watch for the magnificently maned lions for which the area is famous — leopard and cheetah, or perhaps the flash of the silver-backed jackal. The list of Serengeti's inhabitants is endless — from the landbound awkwardness of the ostrich to the pink-tinged beauty of flamingo. And, of course, the vast herds of plains game — wildebeeste and zebra.

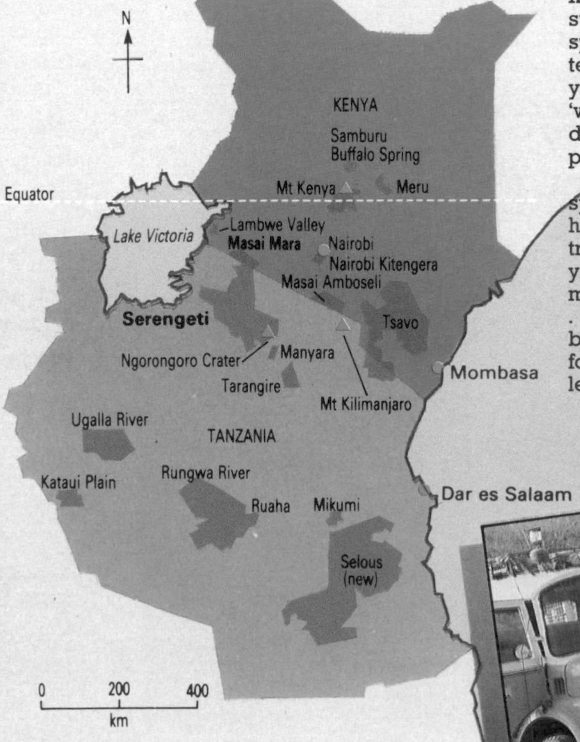

Nairobi/Masai Mara
Today, leave Nairobi by air and fly into the Mara Game Reserve to stay at Keekorok Lodge. The Lodge, constructed in cedar wood and stone offers a spacious dining room and bar. From the terrace overlooking the lawned garden, you are quite likely to be entertained to a 'wildlife show' as you enjoy an after dinner drink. There is also a swimming pool.
The Mara's vast rolling plains interspersed with riverine bush and forested hill are world renowned for their concentration of game. Depending on season, you may well witness the spectacular migration of animals from The Serengeti . . . gazelles, zebra, buffalo and wildebeeste in their thousands, with their avid following of lion, cheetah and the elusive leopard.

KENYA

Samburu
Buffalo Spring

Mt Kenya △   Meru

Equator

Lake Victoria

Lambwe Valley
Nairobi
Masai Mara   Nairobi Kitengera
Masai Amboseli

Serengeti   Tsavo

Ngorongoro Crater △ Manyara
Tarangire
Ugalla River   Mt Kilimanjaro △

Mombasa

TANZANIA
Rungwa River
Kataui Plain   Ruaha   Mikumi

Dar es Salaam

Selous (new)

0   200   400
km

West Indies – a beach village

Attractions of the West Indies

- Winters are much warmer (25°C) than those in North America and Europe. Summers are hot (28°C) but not oppressive.
- Most days have over eight hours of sunshine.
- The scenery is attractive, usually either volcanic mountains covered in forest or coral islands with sandy beaches.
- The warm, clear blue seas are ideal for water sports (sailing, surfing and water skiing).
- There is varied wild life (plants, birds and animals).
- Different customs (calypsos, steel bands, food, festivals and carnivals).
- Cultural and historic resorts.
- Now a relatively short flight time from North America and Europe.

The beach village is a recent attempt to try to disperse accommodation and amenities so that they merge in with the natural environment (Figure 15.32), and to avoid spoiling the advantages which originally attracted tourists to the islands.

Disadvantages of tourism

1 Hotels, airports and roads spoil the visual appearance and create noise, air pollution and litter.

2 Usually only 10% – 20% of the income received from tourists stays in the country. Most hotels are foreign owned and profits go overseas. Tourists spend most of their money in the hotels.

3 Much employment is seasonal. Overseas labour may be brought in to fill the better jobs.

4 Local craft industries may be destroyed in order to provide mass-produced, cheap souvenirs.

5 Farming economy is damaged as land is sold to developers. Much of the food eaten by tourists is imported either because local production is insufficient or to suit the demands for European type foods (but sold at the developing country's prices).

6 Locals cannot afford tourist facilites.

7 Borrowed money increases national debt.

8 Tourists expect unlimited water – up to 500 litres a day or ten times that of the local people. Many areas may be short of water for domestic and farming use.

9 Local cultures and traditions destroyed. New social problems of prostitution, crime, drugs and drunkenness. Lack of respect for local customs and religious beliefs (e.g. semi-naked tourists into mosques and temples).

10 The building of hotels means local people lose their homes, land and traditional means of livelihood (e.g. fishermen, as hotels are built next to beaches) and become dependent on serving wealthy tourists.

. . . Tourism is a form of economic colonialism'

Advantages of tourism

1 The natural environment (sun, sand, sea and scenery) is used to attract tourists and their much needed money.

2 Income from tourism is usually greater than the income from the export of a few raw materials.

3 Creates domestic employment, e.g. hotels, entertainment and guides. It is labour intensive.

4 Encourages the production of souvenirs.

5 Creates a market for local farm produce.

6 Locals can use tourist facilities.

7 Overseas investment in airports, roads and hotels.

8 Profits can be used to improve local housing, schools, hospitals, electricity and water supplies.

9 Increased cultural links with foreign countries, and the preservation of local customs and heritage.

10 Reduces migration.

. . . Tourism raises the standard of living'

△ **Figure 15.33** The advantages and disadvantages of tourism for a developing country

▽ **Figure 15.34(a)** Luxury hotels along the coast at Salvador (Bahia), Brazil (inset photo, left)

▽ **Figure 15.34(b)** A favela as seen from a coastal luxury hotel in Salvador (inset photo, right) (Both photographs were taken from the same position, but looking in different directions.)

Tourism – benefits and costs

A conference held in 1985 concluded that 'International tourism is causing severe damage to the culture and economies of many developing countries and contributes little to their development'. Yet to many developing countries tourism appears as their only hope of escape from their vicious circle of poverty. Figures 15.33 and 15.34 are intended to help you to draw your own opinion.

Recreation and tourism

1 *National Parks (pages 112-113)*

Using pages 112-113 and the map opposite showing the Peak District National Park:

a) Name *two* towns within a short distance of the Peak District. (2)

b) List *three* different physical attractions referred to on the map. (3)

c) Giving map evidence, list *three* different types of summer activity which can take place in this National Park. (3)

d) Give two separate pieces of evidence to show that the Peak District also attracts visitors on cultural (historical) trips. (2)

e) (i) Give reasons why the Peak District National Park is likely to be very busy on a sunny Sunday in August. (4)
(ii) Why might some visitors be attracted to the Peak District in winter? (2)

f) Choose the correct word from each pair of words given in brackets: 'Most visitors to the Peak District National Park will go in (summer/winter). They will tend to go mainly (in the week/at weekends) and stay there for (a week/a day). Most will travel for less than (1 hour/3 hours).' (4)

g) *Castleton* is said to be a 'honeypot'.
(i) What is meant by the term 'honeypot'? (1)
(ii) Give three problems that may result from the increased numbers of visitors to a honeypot. (3)
(iii) Describe and explain three ways in which these problems may be solved by the National Park planners. (3)
(iv) Give three ways in which the pressure on a honeypot may be reduced. (3)
(v) From your general knowledge can you name any two famous buildings in Britain, and any two places of national beauty which have become honeypots? (1)

h) Visitors to a National Park may come into conflict with the local inhabitants. Suggest three conflicts which might occur between the visitors and *different* groups of residents in the park. (3)

i) For any National Park that you have studied:
(i) Explain why the use of its recreational activities has increased in the last 20 years. (4)
(ii) Describe two ways by which the authorities have tried to solve the problem of an increasing amount of traffic within the park. (4)

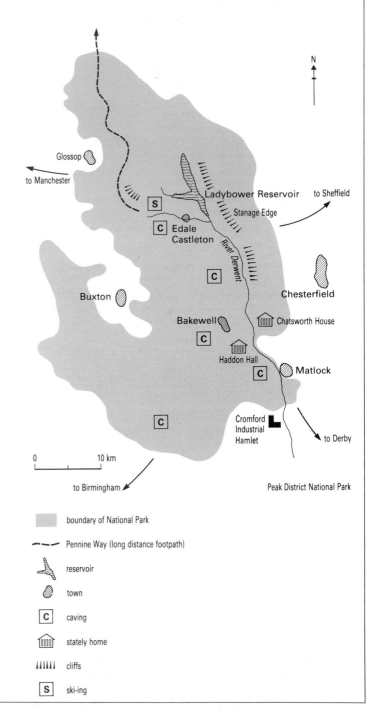

(shaded)	boundary of National Park
- - -	Pennine Way (long distance footpath)
	reservoir
	town
C	caving
	stately home
|||||	cliffs
S	ski-ing

---

2 *Using the information on page 116:*

a) Draw a simple sketch map to show the location of Plat. (3)

b) (i) Using the photo and land use map, name four *types* of holiday accommodation. (4)
(ii) For each type of accommodation, describe and give reasons for its location. (4)

c) Using all the information on page 116:
(i) Give four natural advantages of Plat that will attract tourists. (4)
(ii) What amenities have been added to encourage a family holiday at Plat? (3)

d) Using the land use map, describe and give reasons for the location of:
(i) Places of entertainment. (2)
(ii) Places to eat and drink. (2)

e) Why have so many complexes like this one in Yugoslavia been built in the last few years? (2)

f) How does the style of building differ from that of traditional houses in this part of Yugoslavia (see photo of Dubrovnik, Figure 8.20)? (2)

g) The holiday brochure says 'not suitable for the elderly or disabled'. Why is this so? (1)

3 *Using the landsketch on page 118:*

a) Divide the following list of activities into two groups – one headed summer activities and the other winter activities: rock climbing; swimming; ice-skating; walking; skiing; sailing and sitting outside admiring the views. (3)

b) All of the places labelled on the landsketch cater for tourists, but most visitors stay at Interlaken, Wengen and Brienz. Which of the three places would you choose if you were:
(i) a teenager   *(ii)* a disabled person   *(ii)* with two young children?
In each case give reasons for the resort that you chose, and say why you rejected the other two. (6)

c) Tourism has changed the way of life and the environment in the Swiss Alps. Using Figure 15.26 describe how:
(i) The way of life of the local inhabitants has been improved in terms of employment and services provided. (4)
(ii) The ways in which the environment and the traditional way of life of the people have been harmed by the growth of tourism. (4)

---

4 *(Page 121)*

a) Using the climate graph of Montego Bay:
(i) What is the maximum temperature?
(ii) What is the annual range in temperature?
(iii) Which month has both the lowest rainfall and the most hours of sunshine?
(iv) Which month has both the highest rainfall and the fewest hours of sunshine?
(v) Jamaica is likely to experience several hurricanes in autumn. How are hurricanes indicated in the climate graph? (5)

b) *(i)* From which continent do most visitors to Jamaica come?
(ii) Give two reasons why most visitors come from this continent.
(iii) Why do so few visitors to Jamaica come from Europe? (4)

c) *(i)* Give three reasons why Jamaica is receiving an increasing number of tourists from Europe. (3)
(ii) At which two airports do most visitors arrive? (2)
(iii) Kingston is the capital of Jamaica. Do most visitors stay in Kingston? (1)
(iv) Do most visitors to Jamaica stay in hotels or in resort cottages? Give a reason for your answer. (1)
(v) Name three physical attractions of the area around Montego Bay. (3)

d) It is proposed that a beach village be developed between Montego Bay and Negril.
(i) How may the building of this beach village both benefit and harm: the natural environment; the local economy; the local community? (6)
(ii) Who else may benefit from the building of the beach village? Give two reasons for your answer. (3)
(iii) What steps can the government of Jamaica take to try to ensure that its own people get the maximum benefit from tourism? (3)

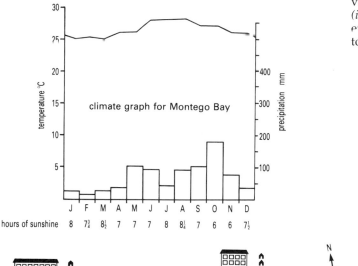

climate graph for Montego Bay

hours of sunshine   8   7¾   8½   7   7   7   8   8¼   7   6   6   7½

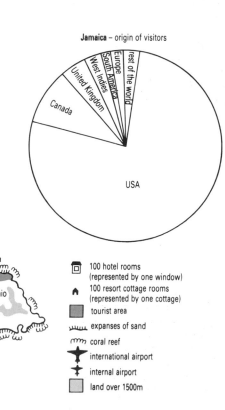

Jamaica – origin of visitors

100 hotel rooms (represented by one window)
100 resort cottage rooms (represented by one cottage)
tourist area
expanses of sand
coral reef
international airport
internal airport
land over 1500m

ENVIRONMENTAL LOSS
Acid rain

Acid rain was first noticed in Scandinavia in the 1950s when large numbers of fresh water fish died. Research showed that the water in which these fish had lived contained more than average amounts of acid. Later it was discovered that this extra acid had been carried by rain, hence the term 'acid rain'. The acid is formed in the air by coal-fired power stations which give out sulphur dioxide and nitrogen oxide (Figure 16.1). These are carried by prevailing winds across seas and national frontiers to be deposited directly on to the earth's surface (dry deposition) or converted into acids (sulphur and nitric acid) which then fall to the ground in the rain (wet deposition). Clean rainwater has a pH value of between 5 and 6 (pH7 is neutral). Today, over much of North West Europe, the pH readings are between 4 and 4.5 with the lowest ever being 2.4 (Figure 16.2). A falling pH is the sign of increasing acidity, and remember when pH falls by one unit it means that the level of acid has increased ten times.

Europe's pollution budget

Most European countries add acids to the air, but Britain is believed to contribute the most. However only about one-third of this pollution lands back on our own soil. Some falls into the North Sea but most is carried by the prevailing winds towards Scandinavia. Figure 16.2 shows how acidity has increased between 1960 and 1980, and how Scandinavia is one of the main sufferers from acid rain.

In September 1986 the British Government announced an increase in money to combat acid rain yet it still maintained that Britain had, in the previous ten years, reduced its sulphur emission by more than any other European country.

The effects of acid rain

These can be summarised as:

☐ Increased acidity of lakes where concentrations may kill the fish and plant life.

☐ Increased acidity of soils which reduces the number of crops that can be grown.

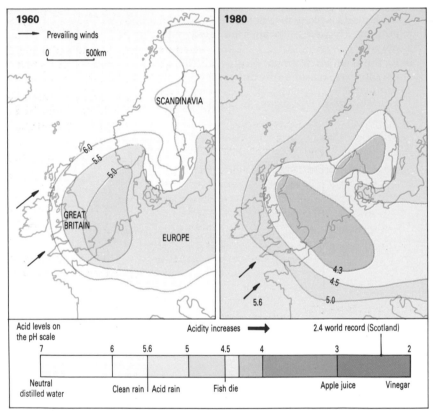

☐ Forests being destroyed as important nutrients (calcium and potassium) are washed away (leached). These are replaced by manganese and aluminium which are harmful to root growth.

☐ Water supplies are becoming more acidic and this could become a future health hazard.

☐ Buildings are also being eroded by chemical action due to acid rain. The Acropolis in Athens and Taj Mahal in India have both deteriorated rapidly in recent years, while St. Paul's Cathedral has lost over 2cm thickness of stone since it was built.

△ **Figure 16.1** Causes and effects of acid rain

△ **Figure 16.2** The increase in levels of acid rain in North West Europe, 1960–80

△ **Figure 16.3** Trees dying from acid rain – the Black Forest, West Germany (inset photo, top)

ENVIRONMENTAL LOSS
Disappearing wetlands

Wetlands are transition zones between land and sea where the soil is frequently waterlogged and the water table is at or near the surface:

This in-between country, neither sea nor lake, nor dry land, is a curious zone, sometimes inhospitable, often highly productive, always a haven for a special kind of flora and fauna. But the wetlands are fragile places, subject to mounting pressures which threaten their existence. (Geographical Magazine)

The Broads (Norfolk)

This is an area of 200km of navigable waterways, near to the mouth of the River Yare. It is the largest area of wetland left in Britain. The surrounding land is either unreclaimed marsh or drained marsh used as pastureland (Figure 16.4). Two attempts to have the area accepted as a National Park have failed.

Environmental problems:

☐ The water table has been lowered recently as modern pumps are more efficient than the traditional windmills. The land has 'sunk' below river levels and so has to be protected by floodbanks, many of which need urgent, expensive repairs.

☐ The water has become increasingly polluted by diesel oil from the motorboats, effluent from the tourists and fertiliser (nitrates and phosphorous) and sewage from the surrounding farms.

☐ Reeds are being cleared or are dying, leaving fewer habitats for birds, animals and insects. As more of the banks are exposed to waves formed by the passing boats, soil is washed into the channel and has to be removed by dredging.

☐ An increase in algae has reduced plant growth in the water causing a decrease in the number of fish.

☐ The now estimated 250 000 motorboats, carrying nearly half a million tourists a year, cause congestion and noise (Figure 16.5).

☐ Conflicts between users such as: preservers of wildlife versus dredging channels for motorboats and anglers versus motorboat users.

Proposals to protect the area:

☐ A barrier at the mouth of the River Yare to prevent tidal flooding.

☐ Speed limits imposed on motorboats.

☐ Increasing tolls on boats to discourage some users.

☐ Opening up the quieter southern Broads to relieve pressure on the busier northern ones.

△ **Figure 16.4** A non-tourist scene of the Norfolk Broads

△ **Figure 16.5** A tourist scene of the Norfolk Broads (inset photo)

▽ **Figure 16.6** The loss of the wetlands – how the Everglades (Florida) have changed between 1950 and 1986

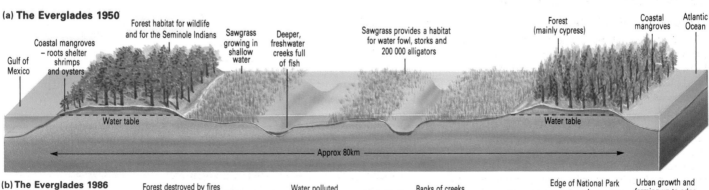

(a) The Everglades 1950

Gulf of Mexico

Coastal mangroves – roots shelter shrimps and oysters

Forest habitat for wildlife and for the Seminole Indians

Sawgrass growing in shallow water

Deeper, freshwater creeks full of fish

Sawgrass provides a habitat for water fowl, storks and 200 000 alligators

Forest (mainly cypress)

Coastal mangroves

Atlantic Ocean

Water table

Water table

Approx 80km

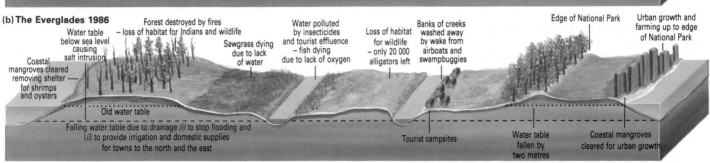

(b) The Everglades 1986

Coastal mangroves cleared removing shelter for shrimps and oysters

Water table below sea level causing salt intrusion

Forest destroyed by fires – loss of habitat for Indians and wildlife

Sawgrass dying due to lack of water

Water polluted by insecticides and tourist effluence – fish dying due to lack of oxygen

Loss of habitat for wildlife – only 20 000 alligators left

Banks of creeks washed away by wake from airboats and swampbuggies

Edge of National Park

Urban growth and farming up to edge of National Park

Old water table

Falling water table due to drainage (i) to stop flooding and (ii) to provide irrigation and domestic supplies for towns to the north and the east

Tourist campsites

Water table fallen by two metres

Coastal mangroves cleared for urban growth

ENVIRONMENTAL LOSS
Water pollution

Japan

In its attempts to industrialise, Japan initially paid little attention to the consequences this would have upon its environment. Water resources, in particular, have become severely polluted, causing serious health problems to both humans and water life.

Causes of water pollution

Farming Fertilisers and pesticides are washed through the soil by the heavy Japanese rainfall, and make their way into padi-fields, rivers, lakes and, eventually, the sea. Phosphates and nitrates encourage the growth of algae and other water plants which use up oxygen and leave insufficient for fish to live.

Domestic sewage Many rural areas are still too isolated to have mains sewerage, and so untreated waste may pollute water which is intended for either drinking purposes or for the padi-fields.

In the rapidly growing cities, the authorities have been unable to keep pace with the need for drains. As most cities are on the coast, untreated sewage is allowed to escape into the sea. The worst affected area is the inland sea (Figure 16.8). Here the tides are insufficient to carry the sewage away. As Figure 16.7 shows, sewage increases the amount of ammonia and nitrates in the water, and reduces oxygen and plant life.

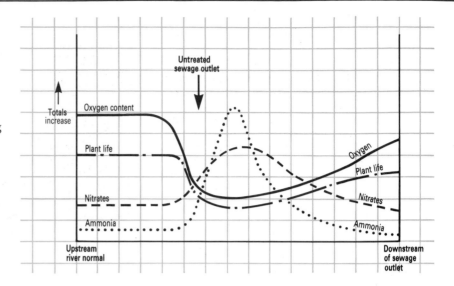

△ **Figure 16.7** The effects of untreated sewage entering a river

▽ **Figure 16.8** Water pollution in Japan

◁ **Figure 16.9** Polluted water in a Tokyo park

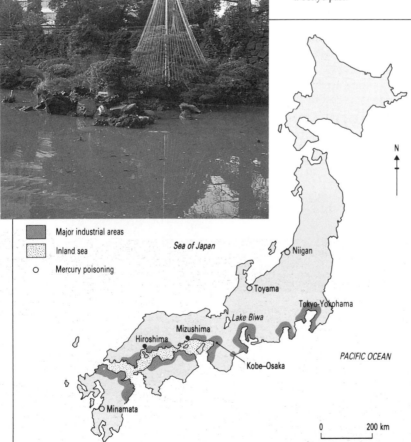

Major industrial areas
Inland sea
○ Mercury poisoning

Sea of Japan

Niigan
Toyama
Lake Biwa
Tokyo–Yokohama
Mizushima
Hiroshima
Kobe–Osaka
Minamata

PACIFIC OCEAN

N

0   200 km

Industry Industry also dumps its waste into water supplies. Water in inland lakes such as Lake Biwa (Figure 16.8) has become dull, lifeless and unsuitable for plant and animal life and for domestic consumption (although water from this lake is used by the inhabitants of Kobe-Osaka). The largest industries – steel, cars, engineering and chemicals – are all located on the coast, often on reclaimed land as at Hiroshima (page 59). They discharge their effluent directly into the sea. One consequence has been the rapid decline in the number of fish caught on what had previously been one of the world's major fishing grounds. During the 1950s mercury waste was released into Minamata Bay. It was converted by bacteria in the sea into a substance which was absorbed by the fish. The fish were later eaten by birds, cats and humans. The result was the deaths of many birds, cats and eventually, as the level of mercury accumulated in the body, of over 100 humans. Children were born with mental and physical defects (blindness, deformed limbs). In 1973 the government advised expectant mothers to avoid all sea foods and recommended the remainder of the population not to eat more than six prawns or 0.5kg of tuna fish a week.

Power stations Thermal power stations eject hot water into rivers and seas raising the local temperature beyond that tolerated by plants and fish, and reducing the oxygen content. Japan has over 25 nuclear power stations and although, as yet, there does not appear to have been the same radio-active leakages as at Sellafield in Cumbria, the threat is there.

Oil-tankers illegally wash their tanks at sea, and can also cause considerable environmental damage if they are involved in accidents. Japan's major disaster was in 1974 at Mizushima (Figure 16.8), though it was far less damaging than the effects of the Torrey Canyon off South West England in 1967 and the Amaco Cadiz off Brittany in 1978.

The future How long can the oceans continue to be a dumping ground for human waste? How much waste can the oceans absorb?

ENVIRONMENTAL LOSS
Soil erosion

Only 30% of the earth's surface is land, and only 11% of this is classed as prime agricultural land. It can take 100 to 400 years to produce 10mm of soil, and between 3000 and 12 000 years to produce a sufficient depth for farming. Yet, as Figure 16.10 shows, human development is ruining this essential ingredient; indeed it is estimated that by AD 2000 one-third of the area now ploughed will have been reduced to dust. Erosion is most rapid in areas where the land is misused and where climatic conditions are extreme. If the vegetation cover is removed it means no more humus is added, there are no roots to bind the soil together, and the surface is exposed to wind and rain. If the winds are strong and dry they will pick up the finer material. If rain falls as heavy thunderstorms in areas of steep slopes, the soil will be washed downwards. In both cases, the land will be reduced to bare rock or left with deep, unusable gullies.

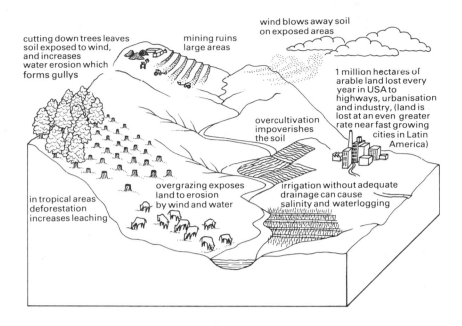

cutting down trees leaves soil exposed to wind, and increases water erosion which forms gullys

mining ruins large areas

wind blows away soil on exposed areas

1 million hectares of arable land lost every year in USA to highways, urbanisation and industry, (land is lost at an even greater rate near fast growing cities in Latin America)

overcultivation impoverishes the soil

in tropical areas deforestation increases leaching

overgrazing exposes land to erosion by wind and water

irrigation without adequate drainage can cause salinity and waterlogging

The dust-bowl, USA

The American Mid-West suffers from fluctuations in its annual amounts of precipitation (Figure 16.11). John Steinbeck's book, *The Grapes of Wrath*, gives a dramatic picture of the effect of a drought in the 1930s on the land and its people. The first chapter describes how the soil was blown away to form the dust-bowl. He describes how, by May, clouds had disappeared to allow the sun to beat down daily upon the corn (maize). By June, the vegetation turned pale through lack of moisture, and teams of horses drawing carts caused clouds of dust. With the passing of each day this dust seemed to rise higher into the sky and to take longer to settle. The rain clouds of mid-May came and went without giving rain, and were replaced by a wind which grew daily in strength. The topsoil was picked up and carried away. The sun became an increasingly dim red ring in a darkening sky. People put handkerchiefs around their noses and mouths and goggles over their eyes before going out, and unsuccessfully tried to stop the dust coming in through the doors and windows of their homes. Suddenly, one night, the wind dropped. The people waited for the morning:

They knew it would take a long time for the dust to settle out of the air. In the morning the dust hung like fog, and the sun was as red as ripe new blood. All day the dust sifted down from the sky, and the next day it sifted down. An even blanket covered the earth. It settled on the corn, piled up on the tops of the fence posts, piled up on the wires; it settled on roofs, blanketed the weeds and trees.   John Steinbeck, *The Grapes of Wrath*

Some of the dust was carried by the wind as far as Washington DC 2000km to the east, while in the worst affected states such as Oklahoma, many farms were left abandoned (Figure 16.12). Those farmers who remained were to suffer extreme poverty for many years.

△ **Figure 16.10** Some causes and consequences of soil erosion

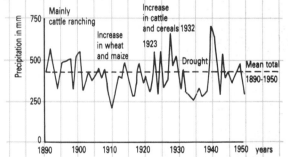

◁ **Figure 16.11** Variations in annual precipitation to the dust-bowl states (Springfield, Colorado) between 1890 and 1950

▽ **Figure 16.12** The dust-bowl – a farm scene following a dust storm in 1936

ENVIRONMENTAL LOSS
Deforestation

The rainforests – the Amazon

The forest has an evergreen appearance due to the continuous growing season. The tallest trees, called emergents, reach over 40 metres in height. Below them are three distinct layers. The highest is the main canopy (30m) which forms, from the air, a complete cover and limits the amount of light penetrating to the forest floor. Below the canopy are the under canopy (20m) and the shrub layer (5m). The straight, branchless trunks of the emergents are supported by huge buttress roots which, if growing near to the Amazon and its tributaries, may be submerged following the rainy season when the river rises by over 15m (Figure 16.13). Lianas, vine-like plants, use the giant trunks as a support to reach the sunlight. The leaves are broad and have drip tips to shed the heavy rainfall. The forest floor is covered by rapidly decaying leaves, but the undergrowth is only thick near to rivers and clearings where the sunlight can penetrate the otherwise unbroken canopy. The rainforests of Brazil account for one-third of the world's total of trees.

Why are the rainforests being cleared?

□ To help satisfy the needs of the developed world for an increasing amount of timber. Most clearances have taken place along the more accessible rivers and beside the new highways.

□ To build an increasing number of highways in an attempt to develop the area and to tap its natural resources.

□ To try to provide land for the many landless Brazilians, many of whom have been brought in from even poorer parts of Brazil (e.g. the drought stricken areas in the north-east). In places, 10km strips have been cleared alongside the highways for new settlements.

□ For large cattle ranches run by the multinationals who sell the beef for the developed countries to consume as hamburgers and frankfurters. Most ranches tend to be on the southern edges of the rainforest, but to create them large areas have been burnt (Figure 16.15).

□ To try to develop some of the region's natural wealth including iron ore, bauxite, copper, manganese and water power (Figure 16.14).

Rates of forest clearances

Estimates suggest that about one-fifth of the Amazon forest was cleared between 1960 and 1985. That meant that about 14 hectares (14 football pitches) were lost every minute. The most recent FAO report claims that clearances have in fact been less than first thought. However experts still believe that most of the rainforests in Central America, Africa and South East Asia will have gone by the year 2000, and in Brazil by AD 2020.

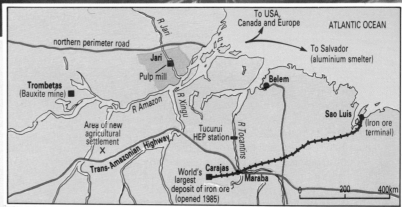

Consequences of the clearances

□ The loss of countless birds, insects, reptiles and animals which find their food and shelter in the forest, as well as numerous species of tree. A typical patch of rainforest, 10km square, may contain as many as 1500 species of flowering plant, 750 species of tree, 400 species of bird, 150 varieties of butterfly, 100 different reptiles and 60 types of amphibian. Many types have still to be identified and studied. How many may be valuable? Over half of our modern drugs have their origin in the rainforests. Recently one plant has been used to treat leukaemia in children, and deaths have fallen from 80% of total cases to 20%. Another plant, given to girls at puberty, prevents pregnancies for six to eight years – a useful form of family planning in areas with a high birth rate and rapid population growth.

□ In the hot, wet climate fallen leaves soon decompose and the nutrients released are taken up again by the vegetation. If trees are removed, humus is lost, the nutrient cycle is broken, and the nutrients are rapidly washed (leached) out of the soil leaving it infertile. Even the Indians have to move every three or four years to new clearances (shifting cultivation).

△ **Figure 16.13** The tropical rainforest near Manaus, Brazil. The buttress roots are concealed below the flooded tributary of the Amazon-Negro river.

△ **Figure 16.14** Some major projects which have led to parts of the Amazon rainforest being destroyed

▷ **Figure 16.15** Burning the tropical rainforest in Amazonas State, Brazil

▷ **Figure 16.16** A member of the Megkronotis tribe in his black war paint

□ Destruction of the traditional Indian ways of life and even the possibility of their extinction. When Europeans arrived in the Amazon there were an estimated 6 million Amerindians. Now there are only about 200 000 – a decrease of 96%. Many have been killed by Europeans, others have died by contracting western illnesses to which they had no immunity. Those remaining have been forced to live in reservations, or to become 'tourist attractions'. The Megkronotis Tribe (Figure 16.16) have been massacred by illegal settlers.

□ The tree canopy protects the soil from the heavy rain, and the tree roots help to bind the soil together and to retain moisture. Without the trees the rain soon washes away the soil. The results of soil erosion include an increase in the size and frequency of floods, and the deposition of silt in lakes and reservoirs.

□ Some of the cattle ranches and new settlements along the highways have already been abandoned as the soil has been leached and so yields have fallen.

□ Recent investigations suggest that between one-third and one half of the world's oxygen supply comes from trees in the rainforest, and that one-quarter of the world's fresh water is stored in the Amazon Basin. Both reserves would be lost if the Amazon was totally deforested.

□ Without trees there would be a decrease in evaporation. This in turn will mean less rainfall and increase, according to many experts, the chances of the Amazon becoming a desert (just as several areas of forest in Africa have become semi-desert).

□ Deforestation could lead to changes in the world's climate. The burning of trees releases carbon which turns into carbon dioxide in the atmosphere. Carbon dioxide traps heat (greenhouse effect) and so this could cause a rise in world temperatures (one suggestion is that Britain's temperatures could rise by up to 3°C). The consequences would include the melting of the polar ice caps which would cause a 30m rise in sea level (so flooding land on which, at present, 30% of the world's population lives). It would also cause the climate belts to shift (e.g. the Sahara would extend into the Mediterranean.) An opposing theory suggests the layer of carbon dioxide would limit incoming heat from the sun to give a new ice age.

How do Brazilians view the problem?

Brazilians do not appear to share the same concerns as westerners over the loss of the rainforests. Indeed, as one Indian guide said, 'Europeans have exploited us for years and now they expect us not to develop our resources.' Other views expressed included those of:

□ An Amerindian guide who was not a lover of what the white man had done to his forest, who said 'It is western propaganda. How can the forest be cleared? When the Amazon and its tributaries rise by 15m a year 60% of the trees stand in water. Why clear them when the land can be used for no other purpose?'

□ A geography lecturer at São Paulo University who expressed surprise at our concern, saying 'Deforestation is not regarded as a major problem in Brazil.'

□ Another geography lecturer who said 'It is an over-reaction by the western world. At present we are making various studies of the forest to see how we can organise its development on an economic basis. Development cannot be stopped, but it should be made to harmonise with the environment.'

In a two-hour flight over the rainforests to Manaus on the River Amazon, contrary to expectations, not one fire nor any signs of large-scale clearances were seen.

Has the western world over-reacted, especially over Brazil? Even *if* we have, then we must not become complacent.

Consequences

Deaths It is estimated that since 1850 there has been an average of 12 deaths a year in Norway (the higher figure of 25 a year in Switzerland is due to the extra number of skiers). To this can be added the loss of livestock.

Loss of buildings, even though many are built to withstand avalanches.

Breakdown of services as telephone wires and electricity pylons are pulled down.

Blocking of roads and railways and, in some cases, the temporary damming of rivers which can cause floods later.

Loss of forests and farmland when the avalanche is accompanied by rocks and boulders.

Norway

An avalanche is a sudden downhill movement of snow or rock which may, on its way, also pick up trees, stones, boulders and other debris. Usually everything in its path is destroyed. Between 1948 and 1960 Norway had 1500 recorded avalanches. But how many more occurred in isolated areas?

Conditions favouring avalanches

□ Heavy snowfalls compressing and adding weight to earlier falls.

□ Steep slopes of over 25 degrees where stability is reduced and where there are few trees growing.

□ A sudden rise in temperature, especially on south facing slopes, which will melt ice and snow previously frozen to the valley side.

□ Winds: either those which can cause rapid accumulation through drifting on the upper slopes, or the warm Föhn wind which raises temperatures in spring.

□ Heavy spring rainfall which adds weight to the existing snow.

Causes and movement of avalanches

Many avalanches are started by a series of vibrations which upset the finely balanced snow. The worst human catastrophe ever was in Peru in 1970 when an earthquake loosened masses of ice and snow on Mount Huascaran (Figure 17.5). On its downward path the avalanche picked up rocks and boulders, reached possible speeds of 480km per hour, and demolished all towns and villages in its path. The death toll was put at 20 000.

In Norway many avalanches are begun by small tremors – falling trees, the rumbling of trains and lorries and even the passing of skiers. At first only a small amount of snow will slip forward, but this soon 'snowballs' in amount and speed. Usually a cloud of powdery snow (powder avalanche) is pushed ahead of the main mass of snow (ground avalanche), often hiding the main mass, and travelling at speeds in excess of 200km per hour (Figure 17.1).

△ **Figure 17.1** An avalanche showing powdery snow in front of the main weight of snow (top left)

△ **Figure 17.2** Snow bridges in Norway – steel and wooden structures to slow down the movement of an avalanche

Prevention

Although Norway tries to record and locate its avalanches, it is impossible to predict where and when they will occur. Figures 17.2 and 17.3 illustrate several methods used in Norway to try to reduce the impact of avalanches.

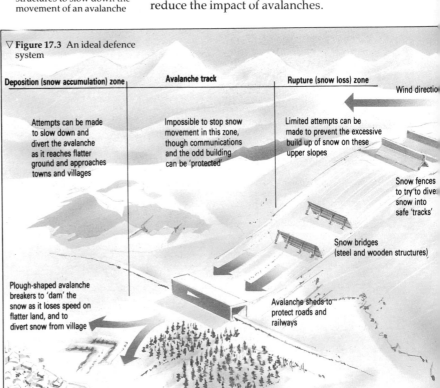

▽ **Figure 17.3** An ideal defence system

Deposition (snow accumulation) zone | Avalanche track | Rupture (snow loss) zone

Wind direction

Attempts can be made to slow down and divert the avalanche as it reaches flatter ground and approaches towns and villages

Impossible to stop snow movement in this zone, though communications and the odd building can be 'protected'

Limited attempts can be made to prevent the excessive build up of snow on these upper slopes

Snow fences to try to divert snow into safe 'tracks'

Snow bridges (steel and wooden structures)

Plough-shaped avalanche breakers to 'dam' the snow as it loses speed on flatter land, and to divert snow from village

Avalanche sheds to protect roads and railways

Trees can reduce damage by up to 50%

ENVIRONMENTAL HAZARDS
Earthquakes

Earthquakes occur where two areas of the earth's crust try to move in different directions. If friction between these two areas prevents movement then pressure will build up. This pressure is released by a sudden earth movement causing an earthquake. Earthquakes are measured on the Richter scale (Figure 17.4). Each level of magnitude is ten times greater than the one before. A recent earthquake in Carlisle registered about 4 on the Richter scale; one in Mexico City measured almost 8. This means that Mexico City's earthquake was 10 000 times stronger than Carlisle's ($10 \times 10 \times 10 \times 10 = 10\,000$) (see page 54).

Causes

The earth's crust can be divided into seven large plates and several smaller ones. Because of heat from within the earth, these plates move either towards, away from or sideways relative to other plates. It is at plate boundaries that volcanoes and mountain building zones occur, and where earthquakes are most frequent and dangerous. Although earthquakes occur at all three types of plate boundary, most occur either where:

1   Two plates try to slide past each other as on either side of the San Andreas fault in California. One such movement occurred in 1906 when San Francisco was badly damaged.

2   Two plates move together, such as the Juan de Fuca, Cocos and Nazca plates moving towards the North and South American plates (Figure 17.5). As one plate is forced downwards, it is slowly destroyed and the friction produces a series of earthquakes.

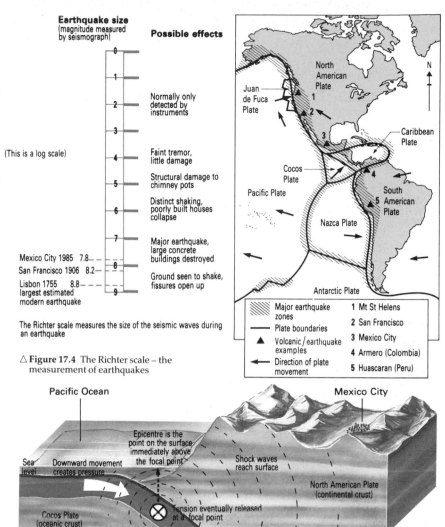

Earthquake size
(magnitude measured
by seismograph)

Possible effects

(This is a log scale)

0
1
2   Normally only detected by instruments
3
4   Faint tremor, little damage
5   Structural damage to chimney pots
6   Distinct shaking, poorly built houses collapse
7   Major earthquake, large concrete buildings destroyed
8   Ground seen to shake, fissures open up
9

Mexico City 1985   7.8
San Francisco 1906   8.2
Lisbon 1755   8.8
largest estimated
modern earthquake

The Richter scale measures the size of the seismic waves during an earthquake

△ **Figure 17.4** The Richter scale – the measurement of earthquakes

Major earthquake zones
Plate boundaries
▲ Volcanic / earthquake examples
← Direction of plate movement

1 Mt St Helens
2 San Francisco
3 Mexico City
4 Armero (Colombia)
5 Huascaran (Peru)

Pacific Ocean / Mexico City

Epicentre is the point on the surface immediately above the focal point

Shock waves reach surface

North American Plate (continental crust)

Sea level   Downward movement creates pressure

Tension eventually released at a focal point

Cocos Plate (oceanic crust)

△ **Figure 17.6** Causes of the Mexican earthquake

△ **Figure 17.5** The locations of five major catastrophes resulting from earth movements along the Pacific coasts of North and Latin America (top right)

Mexico City, 1985

Two weeks before this earthquake, two Mexican seismologists published a map showing that along the junction of the Cocos and North American plates (Figure 17.5) there was a 160km gap which had been free of small earthquakes for several years. It is possible that this lack of earthquake activity resulted in the build up of pressure that was suddenly released in 1985. Although the epicentre was just off the west coast, shock waves reached Mexico City. Unfortunately parts of the city had been built upon silt and peat that had accumulated when the site of the city was previously a shallow lake. The shock waves made Mexico City 'wobble like a jelly', and caused the collapse of many buildings.

Primary Effects

According to police figures, the quake had claimed 4596 lives by yesterday morning, with another 1500 people thought to be still trapped.

Four hundred buildings have been destroyed, 700 are severely damaged and 57 are on the verge of collapse. About 31,000 people are homeless.

At least three hospitals were among buildings either seriously damaged or destroyed with doctors and patients trapped under wreckage. Several churches had caved in only minutes before they would be filling for morning mass.

Secondary Effects

The confusion which dominated the first 24 hours of the earthquake, whose epicentre 250 miles south-west of Mexico City registered 7.8 on the Richter scale, continued yesterday. Fires caused by gas leaks added smoke to the normally polluted city air.

The three minutes of terror caused by the earthquake were followed by explosions as petrol stations blew up and fires were started by ruptured power and gas lines.

With rail, road, and telephone links cut or badly disrupted, contact with nearby villages was impossible.

Thirty fishing vessels, mostly Colombian, were also reported missing, while

reports from Spain listed 19 trawlers and four freighters as unaccounted for and feared sunk by waves which "boiled up" to heights reaching 20 metres.

Mexico City was struck by fresh tremors last night. Little extra damage was reported but the tremors hampered the rescue work by 50,000 troops, police and firemen already struggling with dwindling supplies of water and medicine against water, fear of disease and the cries of the trapped and injured. The threat of disease from contaminated water was increasing.

Meanwhile it was suggested that 1 million jobs were lost due to destroyed factories and shops.

◁ **Figure 17.7** Destruction in Mexico City, 1985. Ten days after the earthquake two babies were dug out of the collapsed maternity hospital still alive. But by then the official death toll had exceeded 5500 and the numbers injured had been put at 20 000.

ENVIRONMENTAL HAZARDS
Volcanic eruptions and mudflows

Mt St Helens

Figure 17.10 attempts to show the causes of the Mt St Helens eruption. The Juan de Fuca plate is moving eastwards, only to be forced downwards by the North American plate. This downward movement results in friction which causes earthquakes and an increase in temperature which in turn causes magma to rise to the surface. Over the years a series of volcanic eruptions have formed the Cascades mountain range, of which Mt St Helens is one peak.

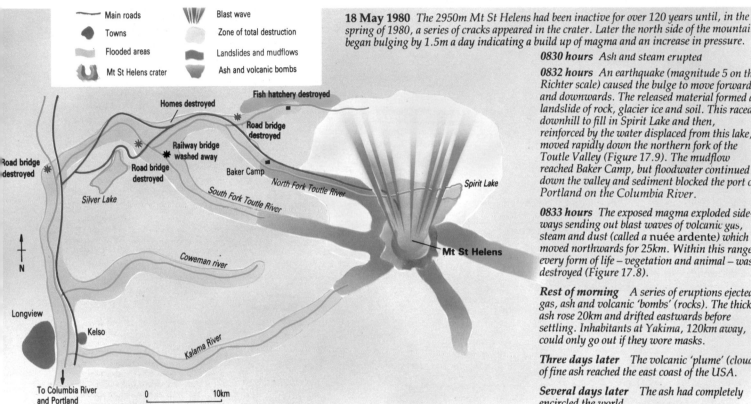

Legend:
- Main roads
- Towns
- Flooded areas
- Mt St Helens crater
- Blast wave
- Zone of total destruction
- Landslides and mudflows
- Ash and volcanic bombs

Map labels: Fish hatchery destroyed; Homes destroyed; Road bridge destroyed; Railway bridge washed away; Baker Camp; Road bridge destroyed; North Fork Toutle River; South Fork Toutle River; Silver Lake; Spirit Lake; Mt St Helens; Coweman river; Longview; Kelso; Kalama River; To Columbia River and Portland; Road bridge destroyed; 0 10km; N

18 May 1980 *The 2950m Mt St Helens had been inactive for over 120 years until, in the spring of 1980, a series of cracks appeared in the crater. Later the north side of the mountain began bulging by 1.5m a day indicating a build up of magma and an increase in pressure.*

0830 hours *Ash and steam erupted*

0832 hours *An earthquake (magnitude 5 on the Richter scale) caused the bulge to move forwards and downwards. The released material formed a landslide of rock, glacier ice and soil. This raced downhill to fill in Spirit Lake and then, reinforced by the water displaced from this lake, moved rapidly down the northern fork of the Toutle Valley (Figure 17.9). The mudflow reached Baker Camp, but floodwater continued down the valley and sediment blocked the port of Portland on the Columbia River.*

0833 hours *The exposed magma exploded side- ways sending out blast waves of volcanic gas, steam and dust (called a nuée ardente) which moved northwards for 25km. Within this range every form of life – vegetation and animal – was destroyed (Figure 17.8).*

Rest of morning *A series of eruptions ejected gas, ash and volcanic 'bombs' (rocks). The thicker ash rose 20km and drifted eastwards before settling. Inhabitants at Yakima, 120km away, could only go out if they wore masks.*

Three days later *The volcanic 'plume' (cloud) of fine ash reached the east coast of the USA.*

Several days later *The ash had completely encircled the world.*

Consequences of the eruption (Figure 17.9)

Mt St Helens itself had been reduced by 390m to 2560m. A crater (more like an amphitheatre in appearance) 3km long and 0.5km deep had been created on the north facing slope.

Human life Sixty-one deaths were reported, most caused by the release of poisonous gases accompanying the blast waves.

Settlements Several logging camps were destroyed – luckily, it being a Sunday, no one was working or living there.

Rivers and lakes Ash falling into rivers and lakes raised the water temperature while sediment and mud also choked channels. The combined effect was the death of all fish, including those in a hatchery, and the loss of 250km of former top class salmon and trout rivers. Spirit Lake was filled in, and sediment blocked all main rivers.

Communications Floodwaters washed away several road and railway bridges. Falling ash hindered the smooth running of car engines in three states.

Forestry Every tree in the 250km square forest lying within the 25km blast zone north of the volcano was totally flattened and destroyed. Trees carried down by rivers in flood caused a jam 60km away. Some 10 million trees had to be replanted.

Services Electricity supplies were interrupted and telephone wires cut.

Wildlife As with the trees, nothing survived within the blast zone.

Farming Estimates suggested 12% of the total crop was lost due to the effect of the dust. Fruit and alfalfa were hardest hit. Crops and livestock on valley floors were lost due to flooding.

△ **Figure 17.8** Aerial view of the crater of Mt St Helens following the eruption on 18th May 1980

△ **Figure 17.9** Destruction resulting from the Mt St Helens eruption

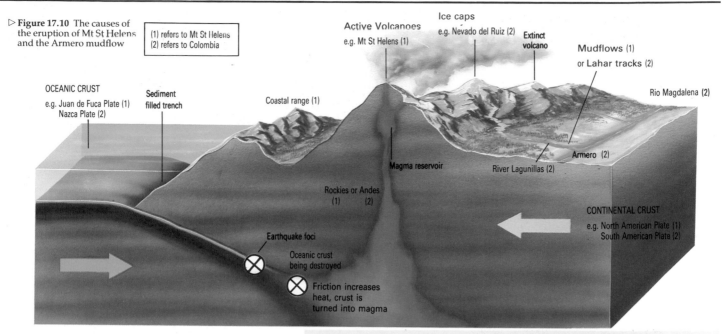

▷ **Figure 17.10** The causes of the eruption of Mt St Helens and the Armero mudflow

(1) refers to Mt St Helens
(2) refers to Colombia

OCEANIC CRUST
e.g. Juan de Fuca Plate (1)
Nazca Plate (2)

Sediment filled trench

Coastal range (1)

Active Volcanoes
e.g. Mt St Helens (1)

Ice caps
e.g. Nevado del Ruiz (2)

Extinct volcano

Mudflows (1)
or Lahar tracks (2)

Rio Magdalena (2)

Armero (2)

River Lagunillas (2)

Magma reservoir

Rockies or Andes (1) (2)

Earthquake foci

Oceanic crust being destroyed

Friction increases heat, crust is turned into magma

CONTINENTAL CRUST
e.g. North American Plate (1)
South American Plate (2)

Armero, Colombia

The mudflow which destroyed the town of Armero in November 1985 was the result of processes similar to those which triggered the Mt St Helens eruption and the earthquake which devastated Mexico City – oceanic crust was crushed as it moved eastwards beneath continental crust. The Andes range with its numerous volcanoes has been formed by the collision of the Nazca plate with the South American plate and Nevado de Ruiz is a volcano created as a result of this plate movement (Figure 17.10). Its snow-capped summit rises to 5200m and although this is small by Andes standards, it is high enough to support a glacier.

Nevado del Ruiz had not erupted since 1595 until, in November 1985, the volcano showed signs of activity by emitting gas and steam. As more magma moved upwards towards the crater, the whole peak must have become warmer. Evidence of this was the increased melting of the glacier causing a small mudflow, 20m in height, to travel 27km down the Lagunillas Valley. The warning went unheeded. Ice and snow continued to melt until, on 13 November, there was a volcanic eruption. Although this eruption was small in comparison with Mt St Helens, the lava, ash and hot rocks ejected were enough to melt the remaining snow and ice, and to release a tremendous volume of meltwater. Combined with melted snow, torrential rain (often associated with volcanic eruptions) and raging flood waters from the Lagunillas River, the ash from previous eruptions was turned into mud. The front of this wave of mud was probably 30m high and travelled at over 80km per hour. Some 50km from the summit the mudflow (or lahar to use its proper name) emerged on to more open ground upon which was situated the town of Armero. The time was 2300 hours and most of the 22 000 inhabitants had already gone to bed when the mudflow struck. The few survivors (the death toll was put at 21 000) claimed that the first onrush of muddy water was ice cold, but it became increasingly warm. By morning a layer of mud, up to 8m deep, covered Armero and the surrounding area (Figure 17.11).

◁ **Figure 17.11** Mudflow near Armero, Colombia, following the eruption of Nevada del Ruiz, November 1985. Nevada del Ruiz had twice previously caused major mudflows – in 1595, following three volcanic eruptions, and 1845, when an earthquake loosened a mass of glacier ice. The latter destroyed a village of 1000 inhabitants and deposited mud over the valley sides on which Armero was later to be built

▽ **Figure 17.12** Omayra Sanchez, aged 12, died after rescue attempts failed to release her from the mud, water and debris in which she had been trapped for two days

ENVIRONMENTAL HAZARDS
Hurricanes and tornadoes

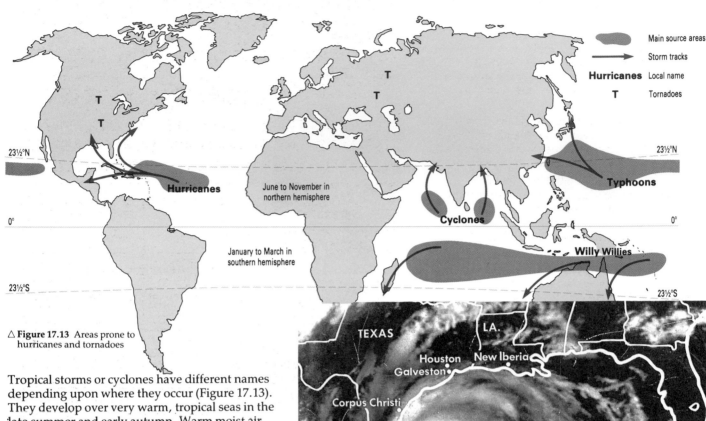

△ **Figure 17.13** Areas prone to hurricanes and tornadoes

Tropical storms or cyclones have different names depending upon where they occur (Figure 17.13). They develop over very warm, tropical seas in the late summer and early autumn. Warm moist air rises in a spiral to form a storm several hundred kilometres in diameter (Figure 17.14). Such storms follow fairly unpredictable and often erratic tracks rotating anticlockwise in the northern and clockwise in the southern hemispheres. Once the storm reaches the coastline it loses its source of energy (the warm ocean) and either dies out or, more frequently, is diverted parallel to the coast. This is one of nature's ways of transferring surplus energy from the tropics to temperate latitudes.

The weather in a hurricane

As the storm approaches, both temperature and pressure fall rapidly, and clouds and wind speed both increase. The wind tends to come in gusts accompanied by squally showers which get longer and heavier until they merge into a period of torrential rain. Wind speeds are usually over 160km per hour (Figure 17.15), and over 100mm of rain can fall in an hour. Thunder and lightning are associated with the thick, towering, cumulonimbus clouds. Atmospheric pressure is extremely low. Suddenly the centre of the storm – the 'eye' – passes. For perhaps two or three hours the skies clear, a watery sun may appear, temperatures rise and the wind drops to a calm. Then, just as suddenly as it stopped, the storm begins again with renewed force. Winds again exceed 160km per hour, blowing this time from the opposite direction, and the torrential rain recommences. Gradually the storm moves away (perhaps moving at 25km per hour) with pressure and temperatures rising as the rain and wind die away, and the clouds disperse.

△ **Figure 17.14** Hurricane Allen, one of the largest and most powerful storms ever to fill the Gulf of Mexico, registered 250km/hr

▽ **Figure 17.15** Hurricane Inez, with winds of over 160km/hr, caused flooding in coastal areas

Hurricane damage

Hurricane tracks are plotted by using satellite photographs, and warnings are given out over TV and radio.

☐ High winds can damage housing even in Florida where many residents have the money to erect reinforced buildings. In the less developed West Indian islands and countries of Central America whole villages may be devastated.

☐ The winds also damage crops which can ruin the economies of several islands and countries which rely upon agriculture. This is even more acute in areas of monoculture (the growing of only one crop) e.g. bananas in Nicaragua.

☐ The greatest loss of life, however, results from the high tides and stormwaves driven onshore. (One cyclone was responsible, in 1970, for the drowning of a quarter of a million people in Bangladesh (page 139)).

☐ A further source of flooding is from rivers swollen by the torrential rain. In 1974, in Honduras, 8000 people died as their flimsy homes were washed away by storm waters.

☐ The high winds and floods often cut off electricity and water supplies, and the unfortunate inhabitants have to face the threat of cholera from polluted water.

Using the hurricane warning poster (Figure 17.16):

1 List the precautions that people are advised to take when a warning is given.

2 Why might people in less developed countries either not hear the warning, or choose to ignore it?

3 Why are people advised to take care immediately after the storm has passed?

4 What damage may they find when they do return home?

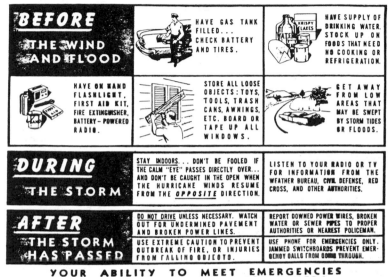

△ **Figure 17.16** Hurricane warning poster

△ **Figure 17.17** A tornado in Minnesota on the Great Plain of the USA

Tornadoes

These form a major hazard on the Great Plains of the USA in a belt from Texas in the south, northwards through Oklahoma and into the Prairies (the same area described as the dust-bowl on page 127). Unlike the hurricanes to the south, tornadoes form and blow overland, but like hurricanes they are also caused by rapidly rising warm air. Although the 'funnel' may only be a few hundred metres across, it rotates at speeds of up to 200km per hour, and contains, at ground level, a calm 'eye'. (Figure 17.17).

Any property in the path of the tornado is likely to be destroyed and, since 1930, over 9000 deaths have been reported in the United States.

Storm damage

During the night of 15 October 1987 an unpredicted storm with hurricane force winds reaching 175km per hour caused unprecedented damage in south-eastern England. The entire rail network of the region came to a halt as fallen trees blocked lines and power was cut off, a channel ferry was swept ashore, thousands of trees were uprooted and many areas were without electricity for several days. Nineteen people died as a result of the storm.

ENVIRONMENTAL HAZARDS
Drought

England and Wales 1976

In an average year, as a result of the rainfall distribution in Britain, there is a water surplus in the north and west, and a water deficit in the south and east (Figure 13.6). Reservoirs have therefore to be built in the upland areas of Central Wales, the Lake District and the Scottish Highlands so that water can be stored there and then transferred to the more populated and industrial areas of Britain. However 1976 was not an average year.

Climatic conditions 1975–1976

During the summer of 1975, the depressions which bring cloud and rain from the Atlantic were diverted to the north of Britain. The result was a hot, dry summer causing reservoirs and underground supplies of water to run low. The winter of 1975-76 remained mild and dry. Apart from a wet May in northern England the dry weather continued throughout the country until the last few days of August 1976. During June, July and August all of England and Wales received over 30% more than their expected amounts of sunshine, with some areas in eastern England getting almost 50% more. Water already in the soil and reservoirs was lost due to the high rates of evaporation and rainfall amounts were also correspondingly lower. Figure 17.18 shows that only the extreme north west of England received anywhere near its usual amount of rainfall.

Consequences of the drought

Figure 17.19 shows some of the difficulties resulting from the drought:

□ A ban on hosepipes for gardens and cars was imposed in some areas by June, and by August several parts of the country were affected by rationing. Parts of Devon could only obtain water through standpipes for two weeks in late August.

□ People were encouraged to use showers rather than baths, and even to share their bathwater. Suggestions were made to reduce the size of water tanks in toilets from two gallons to one.

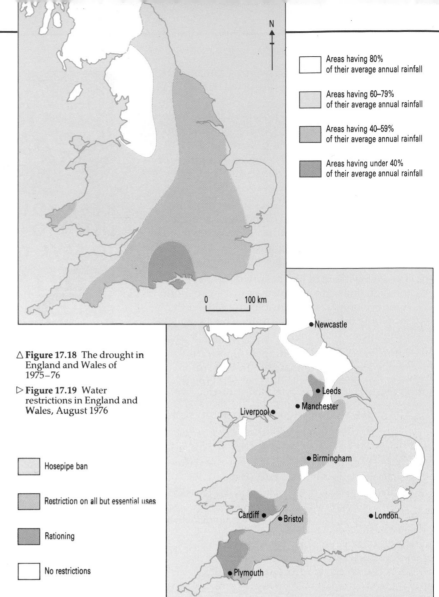

Areas having 80% of their average annual rainfall

Areas having 60–79% of their average annual rainfall

Areas having 40–59% of their average annual rainfall

Areas having under 40% of their average annual rainfall

0   100 km

△ **Figure 17.18** The drought in England and Wales of 1975–76

▷ **Figure 17.19** Water restrictions in England and Wales, August 1976

Hosepipe ban

Restriction on all but essential uses

Rationing

No restrictions

▽ **Figure 17.20** Haweswater Reservoir (Lake District) during the 1976 drought

□ As soils became drier in southern England, the clay shrank and cracked causing buildings to be damaged as their foundations moved.

□ Farmers were badly hit, as the grass turned brown and stopped growing, and crops wilted under the hot sun. Yields of all crops fell, while grass was insufficient for cattle, and the lack of hay meant winter fodder was in short supply.

□ Recreation and sport were affected. Cricket pitches and bowling greens could not be watered, while the drop in the level of lakes and reservoirs curtailed water-based activities.

□ In southern England much of the heather growing on the heathlands died due to lack of moisture. As the area became tinder dry, fires broke out and large areas were destroyed. In the north and west of England and in Wales coniferous woodland likewise became tinder dry. Visitors were asked to avoid these forests in the hope of reducing the fire risk.

□ Two reservoirs which fell to their lowest levels since they had been built were Haweswater in Cumbria (Figure 17.20) and Derwent in North Derbyshire. In both cases 'lost' villages which had been drowned as the reservoirs had filled were exposed again.

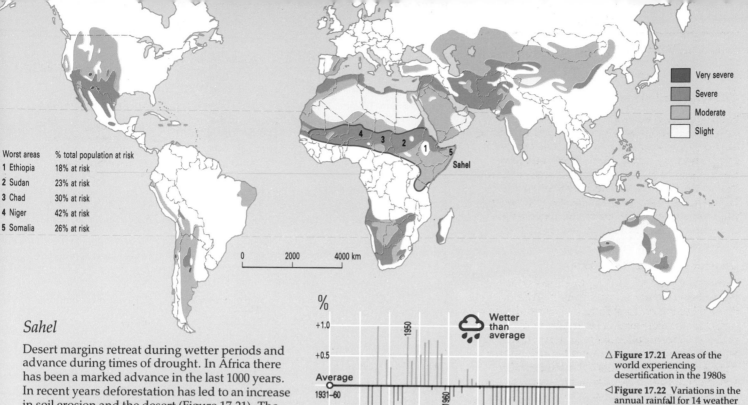

Worst areas	% total population at risk
1 Ethiopia	18% at risk
2 Sudan	23% at risk
3 Chad	30% at risk
4 Niger	42% at risk
5 Somalia	26% at risk

△ **Figure 17.21** Areas of the world experiencing desertification in the 1980s

◁ **Figure 17.22** Variations in the annual rainfall for 14 weather stations in the Sahel since 1931

Sahel

Desert margins retreat during wetter periods and advance during times of drought. In Africa there has been a marked advance in the last 1000 years. In recent years deforestation has led to an increase in soil erosion and the desert (Figure 17.21). The present drought which began in the Sahel in 1968 (Figure 17.22) now affects 150 million people in 24 countries. However it has not only been the lack of rain which has caused the present famine, but also the misuse of the land by its inhabitants.

Factors accelerating desertification in Ethiopia

Ethiopia's population had grown from 13 million in 1940 to 32 million in 1984. (The 2000 AD estimate is 50 million.) This recent annual population increase of 2.5% has outstripped the 1.7% annual increase in food production. As population has grown, so too has pressure on the land. This has forced some farmers to cultivate marginal areas which are more easily eroded.

Deforestation is a result of people needing wood for fires and for shelter. Village populations must walk further each year in their search for fuelwood (page 51).

Soil erosion follows the loss of trees. The now bare soil is exposed to the sun and so dries, cracks and becomes loose. It is then blown away by the wind in the dry season, or washed away by the rain in the wet season.

Overgrazing also encourages soil erosion. The nomads of the area measure their wealth in terms of the number of animals they own. Recently nomads have been confined to smaller areas, so increasing over-grazing with the loss of the natural grass cover.

Changed pattern of agriculture Farmers have been encouraged to grow a single cash crop for export instead of growing food for themselves. By growing the same crop each year (monoculture) nutrients in the soil are used up. Yields fall and there is no money to buy fertilisers.

Water tables have fallen due to irrigation schemes and the lack of replacement due to the drought. In parts the water table has fallen below the root level of trees and beyond the reach of wells.

Irrigation has also led to salts being raised to the surface, forming a crust which spoils farming.

Civil war Over half of Ethiopia's total annual expenditure is spent on arms – money which could be better spent developing agriculture. The war has disrupted food supplies which international agencies and Live Aid have tried to provide. War has also increased the number of refugees (page 29).

Drought The consequences of the misuse of the land increase as the rains fail. Just when it appeared that the area was recovering from the 1968-1973 drought, an even worse one began in 1977.

Consequences of the drought

1983 was the worst year known for lack of water and food. The result was widespread deaths among humans and their animals (Figure 17.23).

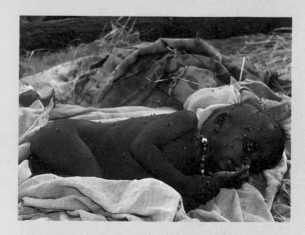

◁ **Figure 17.23** A child dying from the drought in Tigré, Ethiopia. The government supplied relief only to those areas which it controlled. For the rest of the Tigréans the choice was move or die. Every day another 3000 Tigréans set off on a walk of up to six weeks over mountains, through deserts with temperatures over 45°C, and without food or water, to reach refugee camps in the Sudan. Many died on the way through hunger, tiredness, malaria, and bombing by planes. A fifth of those left in Tigré were too weak to move. Most of those who reached the camps had little prospect of improvement in the future

ENVIRONMENTAL HAZARDS
Floods

Rivers

Rivers throughout the world provide an attraction for human settlement and economic development. They provide a water supply for domestic, industrial and agricultural use: a source of power, food and recreation, and a means of transport. However under extreme climatic conditions, possibly aided by human mismanagement, rivers can flood causing death and widespread damage.

△ **Figure 17.24** A hotel in Lynmouth is destroyed during the 1952 flood

▽ **Figure 17.25** Causes and consequences of the River Lyn flood, August 1952

Lynmouth 1952

One of the worst floods in living memory in Britain was that which devastated the North Devon town of Lynmouth in 1952 (Figure 17.24).

Study Figure 17.25:

1 What were some of the natural features of the area drained by the River Lyn which made Lynmouth vulnerable to a possible flood?

2 How had the development of Lynmouth increased the risk of damage from flooding?

3 What extreme conditions in 1952 resulted in the worst flood for over 200 years in Lynmouth?

4 What was the scale of damage to (*a*) human life (*b*) property (*c*) the economy of the town?

A flood the size of that which hit Lynmouth may only occur once in every 100 or more years.

   Suppose you have been put in charge of a scheme to prevent a repetition of flooding in Lynmouth. The following ten suggestions have been put to you. How appropriate do you think each one is? Give reasons for your answers.

1 Widen the river so that it can hold more water.

2 Straighten the river to reduce friction and carry excess water away more quickly.

3 Build wider arches to any bridges.

4 Plant trees on the valley sides to stop water reaching the river so quickly.

5 Install a flood warning system.

6 Build large flood banks alongside the river.

7 Divert the course of the river away from the town.

8 Move Lynmouth away from the mouth of the river.

9 Build a dam on the river to hold back any flood waters.

10 Do nothing and hope that the flood will not happen again for another 200 years.

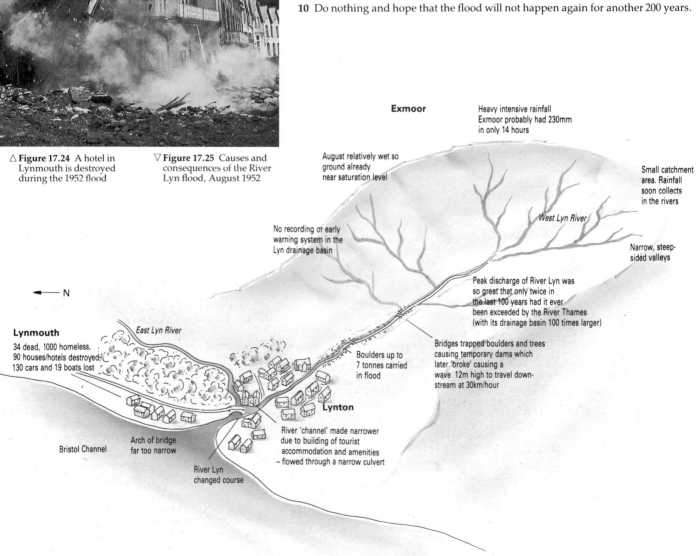

Exmoor

Heavy intensive rainfall
Exmoor probably had 230mm in only 14 hours

August relatively wet so ground already near saturation level

Small catchment area. Rainfall soon collects in the rivers

West Lyn River

No recording or early warning system in the Lyn drainage basin

Narrow, steep-sided valleys

Peak discharge of River Lyn was so great that only twice in the last 100 years had it ever been exceeded by the River Thames (with its drainage basin 100 times larger)

Bridges trapped boulders and trees causing temporary dams which later 'broke' causing a wave 12m high to travel downstream at 30km/hour

← N

East Lyn River

Lynmouth

34 dead, 1000 homeless, 90 houses/hotels destroyed, 130 cars and 19 boats lost

Boulders up to 7 tonnes carried in flood

Lynton

River 'channel' made narrower due to building of tourist accommodation and amenities – flowed through a narrow culvert

Bristol Channel

Arch of bridge far too narrow

River Lyn changed course

Coastal – Bangladesh

12 November 1970

A tropical cyclone or typhoon (page 134) moved northwards up the Bay of Bengal towards Bangladesh. Winds of over 200km per hour and an eight metre high tidal wave hit the densely populated Ganges Delta (Figure 17.26). In this, the worst disaster of its kind this century, 300 000 people died; one million were made homeless; 500 000 cows and oxen as well as farm equipment were lost; 65% of the fishing fleet was destroyed and 80% of the rice crop was ruined.

Why Bangladesh is prone to coastal floods

Silt brought down by the River Ganges has formed a large delta. As the silt has built upwards it has created many flat islands which have divided the river into numerous muddy distributaries. Although these islands are marshy, they are ideal for rice growing and so attract large numbers of poor farmers. Estimates suggest that 30 million people are crammed into this small part of the world.

Typhoons (usually in autumn) funnel up the Bay of Bengal. The force of the wind drives water northwards. As the Bay of Bengal becomes narrower and the sea shallower (due to the silt from the Ganges and Brahmaputra Rivers) water builds up to form a storm surge (Figure 17.27).

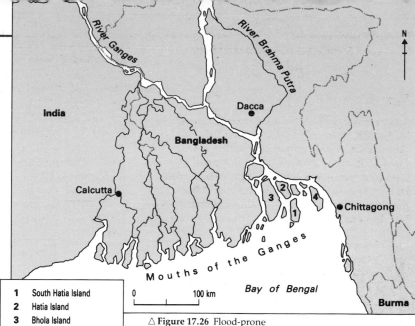

1 South Hatia Island
2 Hatia Island
3 Bhola Island
4 Sandwip Island

–·–·– National frontiers

△ **Figure 17.26** Flood-prone areas at the head of the Bay of Bengal

▽ **Figure 17.27** Development of storm surges in the Bay of Bengal

▽ **Figure 17.28** Bangladesh schoolboys carry bottled water to a helicopter for shipment to areas affected by a massive storm

High winds and tides combine to produce a storm surge topped by waves reaching 8m in height

Low pressure (typhoon) over Bay of Bengal gives winds gusting up to 180kph

Top of surge

4m

4m

Normal high tide level

Low-lying coastal area with little protection from flooding Intensively farmed

Funnel-shaped bay getting shallower towards coast

This surge may be 4m in height but can be topped by waves which might reach another 4m. The wall of water sweeps over the flat, defenceless islands in the delta carrying away all buildings and life in its path. Local inhabitants, without telephones, radios or TVs, cannot be warned in advance, though even those who are informed rarely heed the warning.

May 1985

Three days after the tropical cyclone hit the coastal islands of Bangladesh, countless bodies are floating in the Bay of Bengal. Hundreds of survivors on bamboo rafts and floating roof tops, stalked by sharks and crocodiles, are awaiting rescue. The Red Cross suggested that the tidal wave, 9m in height and extending 150km inland, may have claimed the lives of 40 000 people. An official source in Hatia claimed that 6000 people, many in their sleep, were washed out to sea and the only survivors were those who climbed to the top of palm trees and clung on despite the 180km per hour winds. No links have yet been made with the more remote islands. Already there is the threat of typhoid and cholera, as fresh water has been contaminated (Figure 17.28). Famine could result as the rice crop has been lost, and it will take the monsoon rains to wash the salt out of the soil. The people of Bangladesh, already amongst the world's poorest, will be even more destitute.

Tsunamis

These are series of very large waves which result from a submarine earthquake or volcanic eruption. The tremors may cause waves on the surface. These waves can travel at great speeds (800km per hour) with a height of under 1m in open water. However on approaching a shelving coastline they can reach a height of 10m. In 1960 an eruption off the coast of Chile led to the drowning of 61 people in Hawaii, 10 000kms away and only 15 hours later.

The largest tsunami in recent times led to the deaths of 36 000 people following the eruption of Krakatoa in 1883. Most tsunamis occur in the Pacific Ocean where there is now an elaborate early warning system.

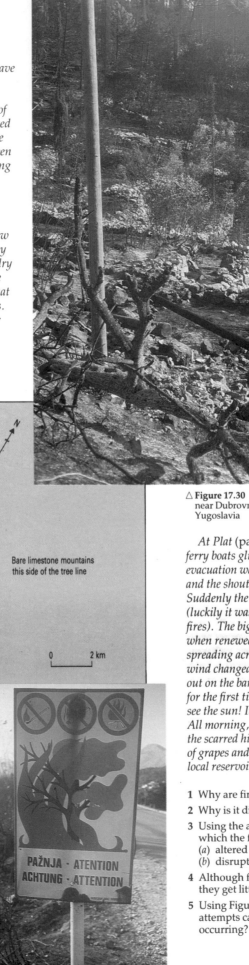

ENVIRONMENTAL HAZARDS
Forest and bush fires

Yugoslavia (August 1985)

The fires which had cut off Cavtat by land seemed to have been brought under control (Figure 17.29).

However at 1000 hours the next morning, flames, fanned by the rising wind, reappeared from the ashes of the previous day. By midday the dense smoke had closed Dubrovnik airport and, later, flames licked around the runway. Traffic on the busy Adriatic Highway had been brought to a halt, but this hindered the tankers bringing water to fight the flames. By evening the strong wind had shifted to the south, and the airport was safe. However the flames now rapidly spread northwards. Each time it looked as if the tireless firefighters had controlled the flames, sparks could be seen starting new fires. Thirty metre tall cypresses were swallowed up by flames twice their size, and the undergrowth, tinder dry after three months of drought and temperatures in the 30s (°C), was quickly consumed. Goodness knows what happened to the wildlife – animals, insects and snakes. Just before midnight the wires leading from the power station were severed and Cavtat was plunged into darkness.

△ **Figure 17.30** Fire damage near Dubrovnik Airport, Yugoslavia

At Plat (page 116) tourists noticed several small ferry boats gliding into the small harbour in case evacuation was necessary. By now the roar of the flames and the shouts of the firefighters could be heard. Suddenly the flames enveloped a small isolated house (luckily it was built of stone as a protection against these fires). The big battle to save Plat came at 0400 hours when renewed efforts were made to stop the fire spreading across the Adriatic Highway. Suddenly the wind changed to the west and the flames beat themselves out on the bare limestone mountains. Dawn came – but for the first time in ten days there, the tourists could not see the sun! It was hidden behind a pall of black smoke. All morning, ash settled on Plat. The tourists could see the scarred hillsides (Figure 17.30) and the ruined crops of grapes and olives. There was no water all day as the local reservoir had been drained.

1 Why are fires most likely to occur in summer?
2 Why is it difficult to control these fires?
3 Using the above passage, list six different ways in which the forest fire had:
   (a) altered the natural environment and/or
   (b) disrupted normal everyday life.
4 Although forest fires can cause much damage, why do they get little attention in the media?
5 Using Figure 17.31 and your own knowledge, what attempts can be made to try to prevent future fires occurring?

To Dubrovnik 9km
Mlini
Tree line
Plat
ADRIATIC SEA
Power station
Bare limestone mountains this side of the tree line
Pylons from dam in mountains
Cavtat
0   2 km
Dubrovnik airport

—— Adriatic Highway
------ Link roads
▨ Vegetation destroyed
▨ Vegetation untouched

△ **Figure 17.29** The extent of the damage caused by a forest fire in Yugoslavia

▷ **Figure 17.31** Fire warnings in four languages, alongside the Adriatic Highway near Dubrovnik Airport, Yugoslavia

PAŽNJA · ATENTION
ACHTUNG · ATTENTION

ENVIRONMENT HAZARDS
Arctic areas

Permafrost and blizzards

All the hazards referred to in this chapter can occur without warning, and they can vary in their frequency and size. Their real danger lies in the fact that they cannot be predicted, and so precautions are insufficient to limit the damage.

Arctic areas are different. It can be assumed that each year winters will be extremely cold, that blizzards will occur and that the extent of the permafrost (permanently frozen ground) will only alter slightly over a long period of time. As a result it is easier to try to live with these problems. But mismanagement can, as with other hazards, cause problems. Blizzards are strong, bitterly cold winds accompanied by the fall or transport of dry powdery snow. These can now be predicted fairly accurately and precautions, such as grounding all aircraft, can be taken.

The distribution of permafrost in the northern hemisphere is shown in Figure 17.32. Continuous permafrost means that all of the ground in the area is frozen throughout the year. Discontinuous permafrost occurs further south, and refers to areas where local conditions may prevent the ground being frozen all year, e.g. near to lakes and rivers. (Notice the influence the sea has on permafrost areas.) When Arctic areas began to be developed for their economic wealth, new problems faced the engineers. The problems of laying the Alaskan pipeline have been described on page 57, but the building of houses also created difficulties. Figure 17.33 tries to show how houses

have subsided and services have been interrupted as the permafrost began to melt. This melting was partly due to the heat from the buildings, but was mainly because the buildings protected the ground from the extreme cold. Figure 17.33 also shows some of the new methods of house building adopted to try to overcome these problems.

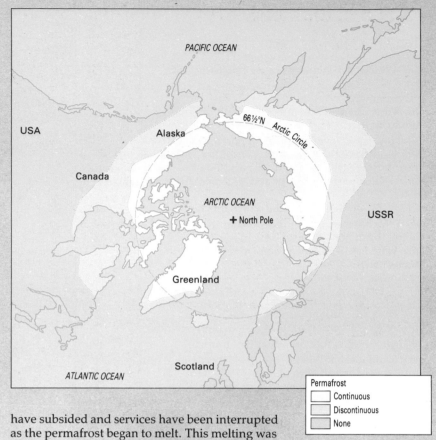

Permafrost	
	Continuous
	Discontinuous
	None

△ **Figure 17.32** Distribution of permafrost in the Arctic

▽ **Figure 17.33** Houses in the Arctic – old and new

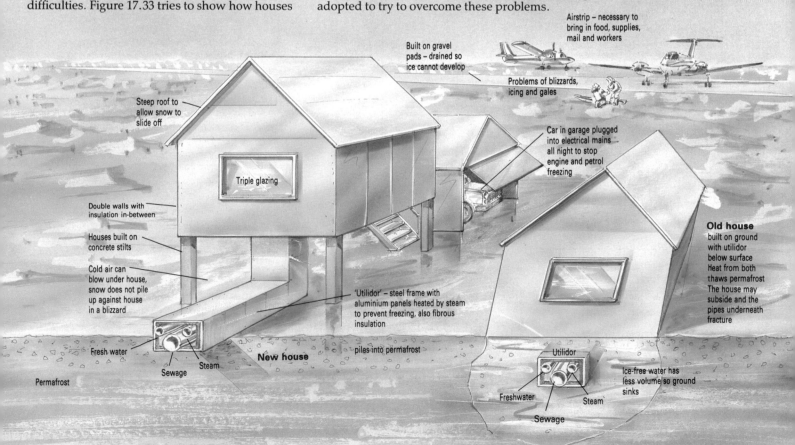

Environmental loss and hazards

1 *(Page 124)*

a) (i) What are the two main causes of acid rain?
(ii) Which two chemicals cause rain to be acid? (4)

b) (i) Give three ways in which acid rain affects the natural environment.
(ii) How can acid rain affect the 'built' (human) environment? (4)

c) (i) How is the level of acidity in rain measured?
(ii) How have the levels and distribution of acid rain in Europe increased between 1960 and 1980?
(iii) Which parts of Europe suffered most from acid rain in 1980?
(iv) Why are these areas the worst affected? (6)

d) (i) Why have several European countries accused Britain of being the major 'exporter' of acid rain?
(ii) Why has Britain been slow to respond to these accusations? (4)

2 *(Page 125)*

a) (i) What do you understand by the term 'wetland'?
(ii) Why are wetlands under threat?
(iii) Why is it important to conserve our wetlands? (3)

b) Why do the Norfolk Broads attract tourists? (2)

c) Why might the following groups object to large numbers of tourists visiting the Broads?
(i) Farmers (ii) Villagers (iii) Bird watchers (3)

d) Why might the following groups welcome tourists to the area?
(i) Teenagers (ii) Shopkeepers (iii) Marina owners (3)

e) How might future damage to the environment of the Broads be limited? (3)

3 *Using the diagram below and page 127:*

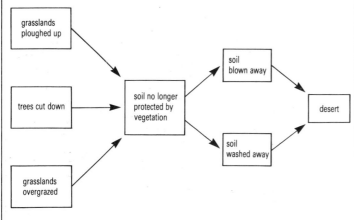

a) (i) What is meant by overgrazing?
(ii) Why are trees cut down?
(iii) Why is it necessary to plough up grasslands? (3)

b) Why does the removal of vegetation increase the risk of soil erosion? (2)

c) Under what climatic conditions will the soil be blown away/washed away? (2)

4 *(Pages 128–129)*

a) (i) List four features of the vegetation of the tropical rainforest. (4)
(ii) How is the tropical rainforest adapted to the hot, wet climate? (2)

b) (i) Give four reasons why the rainforest in the Amazon Basin is being cleared. (4)
(ii) How fast are these clearances taking place? (1)

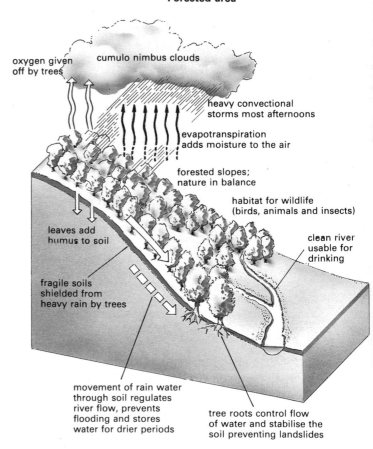

Forested area

- oxygen given off by trees
- cumulo nimbus clouds
- heavy convectional storms most afternoons
- evapotranspiration adds moisture to the air
- forested slopes; nature in balance
- habitat for wildlife (birds, animals and insects)
- clean river usable for drinking
- leaves add humus to soil
- fragile soils shielded from heavy rain by trees
- movement of rain water through soil regulates river flow, prevents flooding and stores water for drier periods
- tree roots control flow of water and stabilise the soil preventing landslides

5 *Earthquakes (page 131)*

a) (i) What is an earthquake?
(ii) How are earthquakes measured?
(iii) Why is an earthquake of 7.0 on the Richter scale 100 times more severe than one which measures 5.0? (3)

b) (i) On which two types of plate boundary are earthquakes most likely to occur? (2)
(ii) Give reasons for your answer. (2)

c) Mexico City 1985:
(i) Why is this area likely to experience serious earthquakes? (2)
(ii) Describe the 'primary effects' of the earthquake. (3)
(iii) Describe the 'secondary effects' of the earthquake. (3)
(iv) How might Mexico City be rebuilt to minimise the effects of any future earthquake? (2)

c) How does the forest help to protect the following?
   (i) The soil   (ii) Water supplies   (iii) Local wildlife   (6)
d) Describe how the removal of trees will affect:
   (i) Soils   (ii) Water supplies   (iii) The Indians
   (iv) Animals and birds   (v) The climate
   (vi) Oxygen supplies.   (12)

Deforested area

ranching
mainly for poor quality
meat for hamburgers
and frankfurters

fewer trees mean less
evapotranspiration
and less oxygen
returned to air

heavy rainfall (both in amount
and intensity) washes away the
unprotected surface soil

ntation
ps

mining

highways

lack of trees
creates a
fuel shortage
and no humus

timber
loss of wildlife and
many species of tree
destruction of Indian
way of life

heavy rainfall
causes leaching,
ruining the soil

rapid surface run off
causes gulley erosion
and flooding

no roots to hold soil
together – results
in landslides

muddy water
undrinkable

silt blocks rivers
and fills reservoirs

6 *(Page 132)*

a) (i) Why did Mt St Helens erupt in 1980?   (2)
   (ii) How did the shape of the mountain alter between 8.30
   and 8.33 on the morning of 18 May 1980?   (2)
   (iii) In which direction was the wind blowing at the time of
   the eruption? Give a reason for your answer.   (2)
b) (i) What were the effects of the blast wave?   (2)
   (ii) Describe three other effects of the eruption on the area
   within a 50km radius of the volcano.   (3)
   (iii) What were the major causes of human death as a result
   of the eruption?   (2)
c) Despite warnings of threatened hazards many people refuse
   to move. In the case of Mt St Helens name two groups who
   may have refused to move, and in each case give a reason
   why.   (2)
d) Why would rescue work prove to be difficult following the
   eruption?   (2)

7 *(Page 136)*

a) (i) Which parts of England and Wales usually get most
   rainfall?   (1)
   (ii) Which parts received most of their usual amount of rain
   in the summers of 1975-76?   (1)
   (iii) Which parts of Britain suffered most from the
   drought?   (1)
   (iv) Name three cities which experienced water rationing.   (1)
b) What problems did the drought of 1975-76 create for each of
   the following groups of people: farmers; sports enthusiasts;
   industrialists; forestry workers; householders?   (5)
c) Name two groups of people who benefited from the
   drought.   (2)

8 *(Pages 134 and 139)*

The coastal areas of Bangladesh suffer frequently from two
natural hazards – tropical cyclones and flooding.

a) (i) What is a tropical cyclone?
   (ii) Why do these occur in the Bay of Bengal?   (2)
b) (i) Give two reasons why the coast of Bangladesh is
   vulnerable to coastal floods.   (2)
   (ii) Why do so many people live in this flood-prone area?   (2)
   (iii) Why is it difficult to warn people about the imminent
   threat of a flood? Why do relatively few people heed the
   warning?   (2)
c) (i) Why are the waves which hit the coast so high?   (2)
   (ii) What are the primary (immediate) problems resulting
   from flooding?   (2)
   (iii) What are the secondary (longer term) problems caused
   by flooding?   (2)
d) (i) What is a tsunami?   (1)
   (ii) Why do most of these occur in the Pacific Ocean?   (2)

9 *(Chapter 17)*

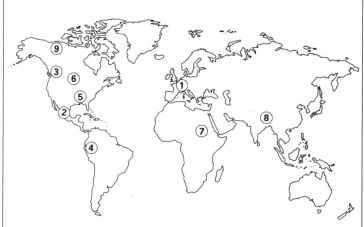

a) The world map above shows nine areas which may
   experience natural hazards. Match up these nine areas with
   the nine hazards listed below:
   avalanches; blizzards; drought; earthquakes; floods;
   hurricanes; mudflows; tornadoes and volcanic eruptions.   (9)
b) Choose any *one* natural hazard. Describe what steps you
   would take:
   (i) To limit the effect of the hazard.
   (ii) To organise relief work following the hazard.   (4)

Index